BIODIVERSITY, BIOTECHNOLOGY AND ENVIRONMENTAL CONSERVATION

ENV BOOKS SERIES

BIODIVERSITY, BIOTECHNOLOGY AND ENVIRONMENTAL CONSERVATION

Editors

Dr. Pawan Kumar 'Bharti'

Vice President (Executive)
Society for Environment, Health, Awareness of Nutrition & Toxicology (SEHAT)
1775, Sohan Ganj, Near Clock Tower
Delhi-7, (India)
E-mail: gurupawanbharti@rediffmail.com

Mr. Govinda Bhandari

President,
Progressive Sustainable Developers (PSD-Nepal)
Kathmandu, Nepal

Associate Editor

Dr. Pankaj Sharma

Himachal Pradesh State Biodiversity Board
Himachal Pradesh State Council for Science, Technology & Environment
B-34, SDA Complex, Kasumpti
Shimla-171 009 (Himachal Pradesh)
(India)

DPH

DISCOVERY PUBLISHING HOUSE PVT. LTD.
NEW DELHI-110 002

Published by:
Tilak Wasan
DISCOVERY PUBLISHING HOUSE PVT. LTD.
4383/4B, Ansari Road, Darya Ganj
New Delhi-110 002 (India)
Phone : +91-11-23279245, 43596064-65
Fax : +91-11-23253475
E-mail : discoverypublishinghouse@gmail.com
sales@discoverypublishinggroup.com
web : www.discoverypublishinggroup.com

***First Edition:* 2015**

ISBN: 978-93-5056-750-0

Biodiversity, Biotechnology and Environmental Conservation

Printed at:
Infinity Imaging Systems
Delhi

ENV Books Series, India

Calls lengthy and error free chapters for further volumes of books on various environmental issues. (Send your manuscripts to envbooks@gmail.com)

Founding Editor (Editor-in-Chief)

Dr. Pawan Kumar 'Bharti'

Society for Environment, Health, Awareness of Nutrition & Toxicology (SEHAT-India)
1775, Sohanganj, Near Clock Tower, Delhi-7, India
E-mail:*gurupawanbharti@rediffmail.com*

Other Titles by Editor-in-Chief:

1. **Advances in Biotechnology and Ecological Sciences (2013)**
   Bharti, P.K., Chauhan, A. and Ray, J. (eds.)
   (ISBN: 978-93-5056-358-8).
2. **Advances in Agriculture and Ecology (2013)**
   Bharti, P.K.; Chauhan, A. and Ezeaku Peter Ikemefuna (eds.)
   (ISBN: 978-93-5056-362-5).
3. **Agriculture and Environmental Biotechnology (2014)**
   Bharti, P.K. and Chauhan, A. (eds.)
   (ISBN: 978-93-5056-479-0).
4. **Agriculture Ecology and Environment (2014)**
   Bharti, P.K. and Olubukola O. Babalola (eds.)
   (ISBN: 978-93-5056-480-6).
5. **Agro-forestry and Climate Change (2014)**
   Bharti, Pawan K. and Singh, Narayan (eds.)
   (ISBN: 978-93-5056-514-8).
6. **Aquaculture and Fisheries Environment (2014)**
   Gupta, S.K. and Pawan K. Bharti (eds.)
   (ISBN: 978-93-5056-408-0).
7. **Aquatic Biodiversity and Pollution (2013)**
   Bharti, P.K.; Chauhan, A. and Kaoud, H.A.H. (eds.)
   (ISBN: 978-93-5056-359-5).

8. **Aquatic Ecology and Biotechnology (2014)**
Bharti, P.K. and Zaki, M.S.A. (eds.)
(ISBN: 978-93-5056-451-6).

9. **Aquatic Environment and Toxicology (2013)**
Bharti, Pawan K. (ed.)
(ISBN: 978-93-5056-236-9).

10. **Biodiversity of Aquatic Ecosystem: *Significance, Threat and Conservation* (2013)**
Bharti, P.K. and Kaoud, H.A.H. (eds.)
(ISBN: 978-93-5056-297-0).

11. **Clean Technologies and Environmental Protection (2015)**
Chauhan, A.; Sharma, S. and Bharti, P.K. (eds.)
(ISBN: 978-93-5056-731-9).

12. **Climate Change and Agriculture (2012)**
Bharti, P.K. and Chauhan, Avnish (eds.)
(ISBN: 978-93-5056-148-5).

13. **Climate Change and Biodiversity (2013)**
Bharti, P.K. and Chauhan, Avnish (eds.)
(ISBN: 978-93-5056-360-1).

14. **Conservation and Cultivation of Medicinal Plants (2015)**
Bharti, P.K. and Singh Narayan (eds.)
(ISBN: 978-93-5056-740-1).

15. **Eco-toxicology and Eco-technology (2013)**
Bharti, P.K. and Zaki, M. (eds.)
(ISBN: 978-93-5056-313-7).

16. **Environmental Biotechnology and Application (2013)**
Bharti, P.K. and Chauhan, Avnish (eds.)
(ISBN: 978-93-5056-262-8).

17. **Environmental Conservation and Biotechnology (2014)**
Chauhan, A. and P.K. Bharti (eds.)
(ISBN: 978-93-5056-512-4).

18. **Environmental Health and Problems (2013)**
Bharti, P.K. and Gajananda, Kh. (eds.)
(ISBN: 978-93-5056-263-5).

19. **Environmental Pollution and Biodiversity (2012)**
Bharti, P.K.; Chauhan, Avnish and Kumar, P. (eds.)
(ISBN: 978-93-5056-149-2).

20. **Fisheries and Toxicology (2014)**
Zaki, M.S.A.; Bharti, P.K. and Chauhan, A. (eds.)
(ISBN: 978-93-5056-452-3).

21. **Fish Habitat and Aquaculture (2015)**
Bharti, P.K.; Gupta Kr. Sanjay (eds.)
(ISBN: 978-93-5056-744-9).

22. **Freshwater Ecosystem and Xenobiotics (2013)**
Bharti, P.K.; Zaki, M. and Chauhan, A. (eds.)
(ISBN: 978-93-5056-299-4).

23. **Limnology and Aquatic Science (2015)**
Sharma, S. and Bharti, P.K. (eds.)
(ISBN: 978-93-5056-735-7).

24. **Medicinal Plants:** ***Distribution, Utilization and Significance*** **(2015)**
Sharma, P.; Bharti, P.K. and Narayan Singh (eds.)
(ISBN: 978-93-5056-734-0).

25. **Microbial Applications and Environment (2014)**
Bharti, Pawan K. (ed.)
(ISBN: 978-93-5056-515-5).

26. **Microbial Ecology and Habitat (2014)**
Bharti, Pawan K. (ed.)
(ISBN: 978-93-5056-514-8).

27. **Natural Ecosystem and Climate Change (2015)**
Bharti, P.K., and Kh. Gajananda (ed.)
(ISBN: 978-93-5056-745-6).

28. **Prakriti me Aushadhi (*in Hindi*) (2012)**
Singh, J.R.; Bharti, P.K. and Bharti, B.
(ISBN: 978-93-5056-200-0).

29. **Seed Technology, Plant Growth and Cropping System (2015)**
Tyagi, P.K. and Bharti, P.K. (eds.)
(ISBN: 978-93-5056-738-8).

30. **Soil Contamination and Conservation (2015)**
Ezeaku, P.I. and Bharti, P.K. (eds.)
(ISBN: 978-93-5056-737-1).

31. **Soil Quality and Contamination (2013)**
Bharti, P.K. and Chauhan, Avnish (eds.)
(ISBN: 978-93-5056-361-8).

32. **Waste Disposal and Management (2015)**
Bharti, P.K.; Tabassum, B. and Bajaj, P. (eds.)
(ISBN: 978-93-5056-729-6).

33. **Water Resources and Agriculture (2014)**
Bharti, P.K. and Ezeaku Peter Ikemefuna (eds.)
(ISBN: 978-93-5056-481-3).

Preface

Biodiversity is the term used to describe the variety of life found on Earth and all of the natural processes. This includes ecosystem, genetic and cultural diversity, and the connections between these and all species. 'Biological diversity' means the variability among living organisms from all sources including, *inter alia*, terrestrial, marine and other aquatic ecosystems and the ecological complexes of which they are a part; this includes diversity within species, between species and of ecosystems.

In literature, conservation of biodiversity is linked to protection of wildlands. In current usage, wildlands are defined as relatively large areas that can also be habitat for small groups of humans who are living primarily in relatively traditional lifestyles and are primarily sustaining themselves with local hunting, gathering native plants, or small scale gardening. Some scientists have noted a strong correlation between indicators of high species diversity and diversity of small scale human communities.

Scientists and historians are documenting the biological effects of accelerating human activities on the Earth that lead to species extinction. The negative effects of human activities are summarized by the acronym HIPPO: Habitat destruction, invasive exotic species introduced into ecosystems by humans, pollution, human population growth and resultant increase in consumption, and over-harvesting.

Biotechnology is the use of living systems and organisms to develop or make useful products, or "any technological application that uses biological systems, living organisms or derivatives thereof, to make or modify products or processes for specific use (UNCBD). Depending on the tools and applications, it often overlaps with the related fields of bioengineering and biomedical engineering. For thousands of years, humankind has used biotechnology in agriculture, food production, and medicine. The term itself is largely believed to have been coined in 1919 by Hungarian engineer Károly

Ereky. In the late 20th and early 21st century, biotechnology has expanded to include new and diverse sciences such as genomics, recombinant gene technologies, applied immunology, and development of pharmaceutical therapies and diagnostic tests.

Conservation of environment simply implies the sustainable use as well as management of natural resources which include wildlife, water, air, and earth deposits. There are renewable and non-renewable natural resources. Conservation of natural resources generally focuses on the needs & interests of human beings, for instance the biological, economic, cultural and recreational values. Conservationists have the view that development is necessary for a better future, but only when the changes occur in ways that are not wasteful.

This book updates the subject matter, illustrations and problems to incorporate new concepts and issues related to biodiversity, biotechnology and environmental conservation.

Thanks are due to contributors from different institutions and publisher for their interest in this book. We hope this book will provide a multi-disciplinary forum to explore emerging areas in the field of biological diversity, biotechnology, environmental conservation, environmental science and pollution.

–Editors

(envbooks@gmail.com)

Contents

Pages: 1-4
BIODIVERSITY, BIOTECHNOLOGY AND ENVIRONMENTAL CONSERVATION
Edited by: Dr. Pawan Kumar 'Bharti'; Mr. Govinda Bhandari
ISBN: 978-93-5056-750-0
Edition: 2015
Published by: Discovery Publishing House Pvt. Ltd., New Delhi (India)

CHAPTER 1

Introduction to Biodiversity

Govinda Bhandari

Biodiversity is the measure of number, variety and variability of living organisms. It includes diversity within species, between species, and among ecosystems. It includes all organisms, from microscopic bacteria to more complex plants and animals.

The regions of both sides of equator especially Himalayan regions are rich in biodiversity. Majority of the plants are of medicinal importance. Many plants and animals that are found in the environment possess medicinal values. For e.g. Neem that is available in Terai region is known as antiseptic plant, Yarsagumba that is available in Mountain region is helpful for the treatment of digestive disease. Similarly, horns of Rhinocerous and Bina of musk deer also have medicinal importance. Further, research helps to identify some other medicinal plants in Nepal.

During the last century, loss of biodiversity has been increasingly observed. Some studies show that about one of the eight known plant species is threatened with extinction. Some estimates put the loss at up to 140,000 species per year. Most of the species extinctions are due to human activities,

Progressive Sustainable Developers (PSD-Nepal), Kathmandu, Nepal.

in particular destruction of plants and animals habitat. Greater rates of extinction are being driven by human consumption of organic resources, especially related to tropical forest destruction. Factors contributing to loss of biodiversity are: overpopulation, deforestation, pollution and global warming and climate change, driven by human activity.

Biodiversity means the existence of organisms and species of living beings per square unit. It indicates the system and structure of living beings in nature. It includes diversity within a species and among species, and comparative diversity among ecosystems. The term biological diversity was coined by W.G Rosen in 1985 and defined it as "totality of genes, species, and ecosystems of a region". Biodiversity can be studied at three levels (Bhandari and Malla, 2008);

GENETIC DIVERSITY

It is the diversity of genes with in a species. There is a genetic variability among the populations and the individuals of the same species. It is the variability among the population and the individuals of the same species.

SPECIES DIVERSITY

It is the diversity among species in an ecosystem.

ECOSYSTEM DIVERSITY

It is the diversity at a higher level of organization, the ecosystem; variety of ecosystems on earth. It is not distributed evenly on earth. It is consistently richer in the tropics. As one approaches Polar Regions one finds fewer species. Flora and fauna vary depending on climate, altitude, soils and the presence of other species.

Every species today in the earth:

1. Contains genetic information that represents thousands to millions of years of adaptation to the earth's changing environmental conditions
2. Is the raw materials for future adaptations (Miller, 2004)

The importance of biodiversity can be explained through their use in the human activities. Some of the activities related to the human life are settlement, lifestyles, social functions and economic aspects. It means the biodiversity is the main source that helps to meet the need of people (Bhandari, 2013).

The importance of the biodiversity is presented below:

- Agricultural crops like rice, maize, wheat, barley, vegetable and fruit etc are the most valuable sources of biodiversity.
- Animals are the source of milk, meat, labour, raw materials etc. Fish is another source of food for people. Birds are the beauty of nature. Horses, ass and camel are the means of transport. Dogs are pet animals that take care of house. Their intelligence is used for investigation. Some of the medicines are also made from animal products.

- Biodiversity is the source for the production of the domestic resources. The domestic resources are fire-wood, edible plants, fish, fruits, constructional materials, medicinal plants and herbs etc.
- Plants that are either in the forest or in the agricultural land are useful to human beings. They are the source of raw materials, fruits, flowers, timber etc.
- Vegetation is the basic ground that protects the land. In land there are innumerable plants that are contributing to soil conservation. The vegetation and plants conserve moisture. Their roots contribute to keep together the particles of soil. This conserves soil and protects from the soil erosion.

Biodiversity is one of the main sources through which people get their basic necessities. They are food, clothes, medicines, recreation etc. Biodiversity is the source for most of the raw materials needed for the industries. Thus it helps to improve the lifestyles of the people.

Biodiversity is a main part of ecosystem. The physical and biological aspects are the components of the ecosystem. A number of species either of plant or animal kingdom are the part of the biological aspects. These aspects are contributing to the natural function of the ecosystem. They contribute to the regulation of the cycles of carbon, nitrogen, oxygen and other gases. This process maintains the atmosphere in balance.

The biodiversity is a major field of study for natural and biological scientists. It is equally important to the social scientists too. Various research studies can be done in the areas of biodiversity. These studies promote the development of human being, animals and plants, social development and economic development.

MEASURING BIODIVERSITY

Many methods of estimating biodiversity have been proposed. However, the following are the major mathematical indices used at different geographical scales (Sharma, 2001).

1. Alpha diversity

   It refers to number of species in a single community. This comes closest to the popular concept of species richness and can be used to compare the number of species in different ecosystem types.

2. Beta diversity

   It refers to the degree to which species composition changes along an environmental gradient. Beta diversity is very high, for example, if the species composition of lichen communities changes at successively higher elevations on a mountain slope, but are low if the same species occupy the whole mountainside.

3. Gamma diversity

   It applies to larger geographicscales and defined as "the rate at which additional species are encountered as geographical replacements within a habitat type in different localities.

REFERENCES

Bhandari, G. and Malla, B., 2008. Overview of Global Environmental Issues. *Environmental Education*. National Institute of Natural Sciences, Nepal. 1st Edition, pp. 129-130.

Bhandari, G., 2013. Global Environmental Issues. *Environmental Science: Basics and Concepts*. Lambert Academic Publishing, Germany. pp. 312-313.

Miller, JT., 2004. Ecosystems: Components, Energy Flow, and Matter Cycling. *Living in the Environment*, Jack Carey, US. 13th Edition, p. 76.

Sharma, PD., 2001. Conservation Biology. *Ecology and Environment*. Rastogi Publications, India. pp. 623-645.

Pages: 5-30

BIODIVERSITY, BIOTECHNOLOGY AND ENVIRONMENTAL CONSERVATION

Edited by: Dr. Pawan Kumar 'Bharti'; Mr. Govinda Bhandari

ISBN: 978-93-5056-750-0

Edition: 2015

Published by: Discovery Publishing House Pvt. Ltd., New Delhi (India)

CHAPTER 2

Spatial Patterns of Terrestrial Biodiversity *An Overview*

Rajesh Kumar Sharma[1*] and Pankaj Sharma[2]

ABSTRACT

Nowadays, biodiversity is among the most developmental trends in the field of Ecological Science. It is the biodiversity on which human depend for food, fibers and shelters. The biodiversity loss could diminish the ability of natural ecosystems to provide essential services such as clean water and removal of pollutants from the biosphere, etc. Biodiversity pattern varied with increasing altitudes and latitudes and vice-versa. Variations in biodiversity are recognized at different scales i.e. global, regional and local. A center of biodiversity defined as an area of high species richness, which may or may not be a great significance regionally or globally. Usage of center of diversity concept in this context should not discourage, as the detection of local center of richness is essential for the elucidation of regional and global patterns.

1 G.B. Pant Institute of Himalayan Environment and Development, Himachal Unit, Mohal-Kullu - 175 126, Himachal Pradesh, (India).

2 Himachal Pradesh State Biodiversity Board, Himachal Pradesh State Council for Science, Technology & Environment, B-34, SDA Complex, Kasumpti, Shimla - 171 009, Himachal Pradesh, (India).

Among the major drivers of biodiversity change are landuse changes, have the largest impact followed by climate changes, nitrogen depositions, biotic exchanges and elevated CO_2 concentrations. Many human activities such as agricultural practices, hydroelectric schemes, mining and cultivation of illegal narcotics causes biodiversity loss directly but the factors that have lead to the expanding of ecological niche of humans are directed responsible for the loss of biodiversity in terrestrial ecosystems.

Key words: Biodiversity; Centre of biodiversity; Drivers; Anthropogenic impacts; Significance; Variations.

INTRODUCTION

Lovejoy (1980) coined the term 'biological diversity' to describe the total number of species in a given habitat (Swingland, 2001). Norse & Mc Manus (1980), who first time defined biodiversity to include the two related concept of genetic diversity and ecological diversity of a community (Heywood & Watson, 1995). Biodiversity, an abridged form of "biological diversity" was coined by Walter G. Rosen in 1985 (Wilson & Peter, 1988). Frequently used definition of bio-diversity is "totality of genes, species and ecosystems of a region" (WRI, IUCN & UNEP, 1992). Biodiversity acknowledges life forms, ecosystems processes and the hierarchy at genetic, taxon and ecosystem levels (Mc Neely et al., 1990). Di castri et al. (1992) has given an operational definition, which treats biodiversity as the interaction among the genetic, species and ecological diversity in a given place and at a given time. Recently, Sarkar & Margules (2002) discussed the depth meaning of biodiversity and suggested 'complementarity and biodiversity surrogates as pragmatic measures to be used as the guiding principle to undertake conservation planning and prioritization processes. Biodiversity is not uniformly distributed throughout the earth therefore biologists were interested in patterns of species richness since the European began their natural history exploration (Ricklefs, 2004). Since then much work have been done on the spatial pattern of biodiversity but still principles underline spatial patterns of biodiversity not well understood (Allen et al., 2002). However, analysis of current species distribution patterns could be a very powerful approach for estimating the levels of threat for many regions and taxa (Wilson et al., 2004) and can identify the areas of special conservation interest. Rehbek (2005) emphasized on differentiation between local and global approaches to spatial data analysis. Minimum level of biodiversity is required for the proper functioning of an ecosystem, below which the ecosystem may collapse (McCann, 2000). Ecosystem functioning refers to collection of the ecological process such as primary production, decomposition, nutrient cycling and their interactions. Four hypotheses were proposed to explain the relationships between the diversity and ecosystem functions.

1. **Diversity-stability hypothesis** (Elton, 1958): This hypothesis predicts that there is a linear relationship between species diversity and ecosystem functions in which the rate of ecosystem processes increases with number of the species.
2. **Rivet hypothesis** (Ehrlich & Ehrlich, 1981): This hypothesis predicts a positive and non linear relationship and also assumes that all species are equally important i.e. deletions of species gradually weaken the system and beyond some threshold numbers, may cause the ecosystem to collapse.
3. **Redundancy hypothesis** (Walker, 1992): This hypothesis considers that certain species have the ability to expand their 'Jobs' in ecosystems in order to compensate with associated species that go to extinct. These species may be separated based on functional groups.
4. **Idiosyncratic hypothesis** (Lawton, 1994): Addresses the possibility of a null or intermediate relationship between the species diversity and ecosystem functions, the identity and the order of deletion of species will affect the ecosystem function.

Studied are not sufficient to support each of four hypotheses, but conclusion remains equivocal. At this stage it could be assumed that the losses in biodiversity are mostly depend upon the order in which the species lost.

Biodiversity has attracted world attention because of the growing awareness of human towards its uncountable benefits and biodiversity loss, on other. Therefore, this article aimed to document all the information about its socio-economic importance, spatial patterns along altitudes, latitudes, and also emphasizes changes in biodiversity at local, regional and global scales. This review paper would also explain major drivers and human impacts that could cause significant changes in the future biodiversity.

ECONOMIC IMPORTANCE OF TERRESTRIAL BIODIVERSITY

Biodiversity offers several direct and indirect socio-economic benefits to the humankind (Ehrlich & Ehrlich, 1992). There are two important functions, first on which the stability of climate, water values regime, soil fertility, quality of air and over all health of biosphere depends and second is the natural resources on which human races are depend for food, clothes, medicine, building material, shelter, medicine, raw materials for industrial goods (Khoshoo, 1994; Dobson, 1995) and biofuel (Groom et al. 2008).

Biodiversity is also responsible for essential ecological services such as productivity, maintenance of gaseous composition of atmosphere, preservation of soil fertility, cycling of minerals, control of pest outbreaks, maintenance of genetic library, etc (Fisher & Turner, 2008).

Biodiversity, a vast genetic library, where the number of genes ranging from about 1000 in bacteria, to 400,000 or more in many flowering plants and a few animals (Hinegardner, 1976). It also provides unfolds future benefits (Ehrlich & Ehrlich, 1992). It is reported that biodiversity have incalculable value for the human health, although only 1100 of the world's 365,000 species of plants have the medicinal properties are known (Dobson, 1995). Thus all the socio-economic activities related to human are directly derived from environmental and biological resources. Costanza et al. (1997) have estimated the current economic value of 17 ecological services for 16 biomes, and extrapolated this for entire biosphere in the range of US $ 16-54 trillions (10^{12}) per year (Table 2.1).

Table 2.1: Ecosystem Services and Functions (Costanza et. al 1997)

No.	Ecosystem Services	Ecosystem Functions	Examples
1.	Gas regulation	Regulation of atmospheric chemical composition.	CO_2/O_2 balance, O_3 for UVB protection, and SO_4 levels.
2.	Climate regulation	Regulation of global temperature, and other Biologically medicated climatic processes at global or local level.	Greenhouse gas regulation, DMS production affecting cloud formation.
3.	Disturbance regulation	Capacitance, damping and integrity of Ecosystem response to environmental fluctuations.	Storm protection, flood control, drought recovery and other aspects of habitat response to environmental variability mainly controlled by vegetation structure.
4.	Water regulation	Regulation of hydrological flows.	Provisioning water for agricultural (such as irrigation) or industrial (such as milling) processes or transportation.
5.	Water supply	Storage and retention of water.	Provisioning of water by watersheds, reservoirs and aquifers.
6.	Erosion control and sediment retention.	Retenction of Soil within an Ecosystem.	Prevention of loss of soil by wind, runoff or other removal processes, storage of stilt in lakes and wetlands.
7.	Soil formation	Soil formation processes.	Weathering of rock and the accumulation of Organic Material.
8.	Nutrient cycling	Storage, internal cycling, processing and acquisition of nutrients.	Nitrogen fixation, N, P and other elemental or nutrient cycles.
9.	Water treatment	Recovery of mobile nutrient and removal or breakdown of xeric nutrients and compounds.	Water treatment, pollution control, detoxification.
10.	Pollination	Movement of floral gametes.	Provisioning of pollinators for the reproduction of plant populations.
11.	Biological control	Trophic-dynamic regulation of populations.	Keystone predator control of prey species, reduction of herbivory by top predators.

(Table Contd...)

12.	Refugia	Habitat for resident and transient populations.	Nurseries, habitat for migratory species, regional habitat for locally harvested species, over wintering grounds.
13.	Food production	That portion of gross primary production extractable as food.	Production of fish, game, crops, nuts, fruits by hunting, gathering, subsistence farming or fishing.
14.	Raw materials	That portion of gross primary portion of extractable as raw materials.	The production of Timber, Fuel or Fodder.
15.	Genetic resources	Sources of unique Biological material and products.	Medicine products of materials science, gence for resistance to plant pathogens and crop pests. Ornamental species (pests and horticultural varieties of plants).
16.	Recreation	Provide opportunities for recreational activities.	Eco-tourism, support fishing, and other outdoor recreational activities.
17.	Cultural	Providing opportunities for non-commercial uses.	Aesthetic, artistic, educational, spiritual, and/or scientific value of Ecosystems.

Included are Ecosystem goods with Ecosystem services (N*ature Vol, 387 MAY 1997*).

Earlier studies have indicated that the composition and quality of biodiversity play a prominent role in controlling ecosystem functions and its stability. Higher diversity allows more availability of resources for increasing net primary productivity and prevents nutrient loss. Relating the biodiversity with ecosystem functioning is one of the most intractable problems for the ecologists. There are two schools of thought on this issue. According to one school, there is a clear causative relationship between diversity and ecosystem functioning (Ives & Carpenter, 2007) while according to other school, ecosystem properties are not necessarily driven by species diversity per se (Huston et al., 2000), rather the main drivers of the ecosystems properties are key functional attributes or traits of the dominants species, present and the composition of functional types.

PATTERNS OF BIODIVERSITY

Various patterns of biodiversity along the altitudes and the latitudes have been reported earlier (Daniels, 1992; Latham & Ricklefs, 1993; Ryvarden, 1993). Tree species richness has been shown to increase with decrease in latitudes (Latham & Ricklefs, 1993). The effect of latitudes on species richness varies from one group of the plants to other and from one region to other. For example, temperate forests of the Eastern Central Asia, Eastern North Asia and Europe have overall tree species in the ratio of 6:2:1. Though, these three regions have similar latitudinal spreads. The number of plant species recorded in African continent (low latitude region) is 10 times higher than that of the Europe (high latitude region) but there is nominal difference in the number of polypore fungi recorded in above two continents (Ryvarden, 1993). It is also reported that the richness of terrestrial organisms decreases with increase in altitude (Stevens, 1992). Examples include bird species in New Guinea (Kikkawa & Williams, 1971) and on Eastern slope of Andes in Peru (Terborgh, 1977), woody plant species in forest (Gentry, 1988), amphibian in Western Ghats of India (Daniels, 1992). Humped pattern of diversity on elevation gradients with lower diversity near foot and summit and higher at the mid-slope is known in particular groups in some geographical areas. For example, a wide range of taxa including flowering plants on the Western slope of Andes in Northern Chile (Arroyo *et al.*, 1988), birds in the Mediterranean climate zone of California (Cody, 1975), and large moths in Northern Sulawesi (Holloway & Stork, 1991). In Chile, vertebrate's diversity increases with altitude from pacific coastal desert up to the high Andean Plateau, indicating the influence of local environmental conditions on diversity-altitude relationships (Pearson & Ralph, 1978). Several factors paralleled with altitude might impinge directly the processes that influencing the diversity on elevation gradients. For example, land area decreases with increasing elevation. In addition, several environmental factors such as moisture, rainfall, light intensity, wind speed, ultra-violet radiation and temperature co-vary positively with elevation and influence the pattern of biodiversity.

A trend of increasing biodiversity has been found with decreasing latitude (Fischer, 1960; Stevens, 1992). Many groups of organisms can occur in a given area of the tropics than in similar sized area at higher latitudes. This pattern is mostly reported for trees (Latham & Ricklefs, 1993), mammals (Simpson, 1964), reptiles and amphibians (Kiester, 1971), insects (Stork, 1988) and ecoregions (Kier *et al.*, 2005). It is very difficult for any one to suggest that latitude per se drives biodiversity gradients but many studies indicate that several factors such as temperature, total precipitation and seasonal variations in precipitation and ecosystem energy fluxes, etc., might influence biodiversity at various scales and co-vary with latitude e.g. total land area decreases with increase in latitude (Terborgh, 1973; Osman and Whitlatch, 1978; Rosenberg & Abramsky, 1993). In some major groups, however the distribution of biodiversity exhibits no strong relationship with latitude, but it has been found that the biodiversity even increases to a maximum in temperate zones, for example, only slightly more species of polypore fungi have been recorded in the entire continent of Africa (330) in contrast to a plant species ratio of about 10:1 (Ryvarden, 1993). This broad trend is differentiated in all parts of the earth by mountainous regions which are characterized by generally higher species richness than the surrounding lowland areas when referring to chosen standard area of 10,000 km^2. Interestingly, not all tropical regions are necessarily richer in plant species than subtropical or temperate ones. Biodiversity differences among continents and hemispheres can sometime be easily explained with reference to corresponding differences in factors such as climate and landscape heterogeneity. Greater climate equitability in Southern America compared to West coast of North America allowing the retention of more older tertiary groups is cited as potential factor contributing to hemisphere differences in plant diversity in rainforest floras (Arroyo *et al.*, 1995) and bird diversity at species, genus and family levels (Jaksic & Feinsinger, 1991). Mangroove species, genera and families are several times more diverse in Indo-West Pacific region than the Atlantic-Caribbean and East Pacific regions (Ricklefs & Latham, 1993). For terrestrial environments, generally biodiversity increases towards the tropics in many large taxa, soil-dwelling organisms provide better knowledge of latitudinal and altitudinal biodiversity.

Centre of Diversity

In its simplest definition this is mainly an area of high levels of diversity or those having unique assemblage of species such as endemic species. Species diversity is produce through isolation allowing genetic differentiation between populations and exchange of population between semi-isolated areas allowing newly allopatrically formed species into sympatry. This species richness may be also through gaining of species by migration from out side or from production of new species through natural selection. Species loss could be due to extinction, unpredictable drastic changes in physical condition, stochastic events and biological factor including competition, predation, pathogen and dispersal agents. Centres of diversity for some groups do not necessarily correspond with those of other groups because each taxonomic group has specific needs and peculiarities and its own evolutionary history (Kuper et al., 2004).

Within a country, a centre of diversity will often represent an area of high species richness that may or may not be of great significance regionally or globally. Although the area for centre of diversity is rich in species but the number of species present, may or may not be accurately known. But the site selected for the centre of biodiversity must have the first two or all of the following criteria:

- The area is known to contain a large number of endemic species.
- The site contains an important gene pool of plants or animals that have valuable advantages to humans or potentially useful animal to humans.
- The site contains a large number of habitat types.
- The site contains a significant proportion of species adapted to special edaphic conditions.
- The site is threatened or under imminent threat of large-scale devastation.

According to Williams & Humphries (1994), centre of diversity may be recognized at three scales.

Local Pattern of Biodiversity

Within a particular habitat type, variation in species diversity is reflected by factors such as history of land use or natural disturbance. Frequently, areas protected from natural cycles, such as those associated with fire, will experience a decline in diversity owing to the loss of species typical of early succession stages (Connell, 1978). Diversity may be locally sensitive to natural disturbances, creating difference between windward and leeward sides of mountain (Smith, 1972) and between sites with different slopes or exposure to wave action (Lewis, 1964). The value of centres of diversity concept could be greatly strengthened by ranking and functional roles of species concerned and assessing their phylogenetic status. For example, the relative diversity content of temperate rainforest of Southern South America with many monotypic, endemic genera and family and a wide spectrum of woody life forms could turn out to be much higher than of adjacent more Speciose area of Mediterranean climate area to it north in Chile (Arroyo et al., 1995). Greater biodiversity at local scale decreases the chance of successful establishment of the invaders (Kennedy *et al.,* 2002). The various theories regarding the biodiversity distribution at local scale are listed in Table 2.2.

Table 2.2: List of Theories with their General Descriptions and Principal Assumptions

Theory	General Description	Principal Assumption
(a) Exploitative Competition		
Resource partitioning	Species differ sufficiently in there ability to exploit different limiting resources such that competitive exclusion does not occur.	Trade-offs exist in species abilities to compete for two or more limiting resources.
Spatial heterogeneity	The environment is composed of number distinct microhabitats in each of which one species competitively excludes all others.	There are at least as many different microhabitats as plant species.
Neighbourhood effects	Intraspecific spatial aggregation of species serves to increase the relative strength of iontra-rather than interspecific competition and thus facilitates coexistence	Plant spatial distributions are typically intrspecifically clumped and some time interspecifically segregated.
Temporal heterogeneity	Temporal variation in 'favorable' periods ensure that different species will be the dominant competitors at different times.	Communities are composed of long lived and highly fecund fugitives species.

(Table Contd...)

(b) Pre-emptive Competition		
Regeneration Niches	Species differ sufficiently ion their regeneration requirements so that competitive exclusion does not occur.	The environment is composed of numerous distinct macro sites.
Disturbance	Species richness should be greatest at intermediate level of disturbance since dominance is prevented and the pool of potential colonists is relatively large.	Habitat productivity is inversely proportional to the degree of disturbance.
Lottery models	Seeds colonize vacant micro sites at random, resultant adults are competitively superior for the microsite and sufficiently long lived and fecund to ensure further colonisation.	Species are long-lived and highly fecund probability of colonisation is a simple function of seed production.
Patch-dynamics	The dispersal ability of the inferior competitor sufficiently great for its rate of successful colonisation to be higher than its rate of extinction from micro sites.	Trade-offs exist between competitive ability and dispersal.

The studies on sal (*Shorea robusta*) communities of Gorakhpur forest also tend to support the intermediate disturbance hypothesis (Pandey & Shukla, 1999).

Intermediate Disturbance Hypothesis

According to this hypothesis (Connell, 1978), disturbance caused by physical conditions, predators or other factors, opens space for colonization and initiates cycle of succession by pioneer species. In frequently disturbed area, species do not exist because they do not have any opportunity to recover, however, in rarely disturbed area, species diversity is frequently low because competitive exclusion resulting in local extinctions. It has been shown that the highest level of species diversity is maintained at intermediate level of disturbance. The light to moderate grazing disturbances increase species diversity as well as net production in tropical grasslands but exclusion of grazing reduces (Pandey & Singh, 1992a & b).

Equilibrium versus Non-equilibrium

Equilibrium theories suggests that under natural circumstances, species addition or loss are balanced, displacement of species from the equilibrium results in changes in speciation or extinction rate tend to restore the systems to its equilibrium state. Non-equilibrium theory suggests that diversity is not at equilibrium and that number of species decreases or increases depending on how the environment influences the species production, exchange and extinction at any particular time. Drastic reduction in biodiversity during mass extinction followed by slower recovery and the gradual global increase in the diversity of many taxa such as flowering plants and bony fish illustrate non-equilibrium process (Knoll, 1986; Sepkoksi, 1992). At the local scale, diversity represents the balance between local extinction and movement of individual between habitats. Human activities tend to exacerbate some of this natural cause to remove species. Regionally, the rate of human mediated removal of species by extinction is probably often in excess of the natural evolutionary capacity response although there is much variation from one region to another region (Arroyo *et al.,* 1992). Local removal clearly exceeds natural rate of migration and reestablishment. Under non equilibrium theories, slow rate of species production maintain biodiversity within large region depend primarily on preventing extinction. There will be often a good chance that species loss locally can be recaptured while total extinction of species affects both regional and local diversity.

Spatial Heterogeneity Hypothesis

According to this hypothesis, more complex the physical environment, more complex and diverse will be the plant and animal communities. Pianka (1966) distinguish two sub categories of this hypothesis one on a macro and the other on a micro scale. Simpson (1964) has shown that highest diversity of mammals in United States occur in mountain areas of topographical relief. These areas contain many different habitats and hence more species are found there. Mountainous areas also experience more topographic isolation of populations and so may promote speciation (Krebs, 1985). Mac Arthur (1965) has argued that there may be more land bird species in tropics because of an increase in the number of species per habitat as well as increase in the number of habitats per unit area. Micro-spatial heterogeneity, on the other hand, operates on a more local scale and the size of environmental elements corresponds roughly to size of the organisms inhabiting the region (Pianka 1966). Elements of the environmental complex in this class might be soil particles size, rock and the complexity of the vegetation. Habitat with a more complex or variegated structure contains more species than do simpler habitats. Thus within any group or taxa, there are generally fewer species in a rock desert than in the adjacent grassland, fewer in the grassland than in adjacent savanna and, fewer in savanna than in Tropical rain forest (Diamond, 1988). Mac Arthur & Mac Arthur (1961) measured bird species diversity on a series of sites and attempted to relate this to foliage height diversity. Foliage height diversity is a measure of stratification and foliage height diversity is good predictor of bird species diversity. Findings of Davis et al. (2005) support the hypothesis in grassland experiment detecting negative correlation between native and exotic species at small spatial scale and positive relationship at large spatial scale.

Temporal Heterogeneity Hypothesis

Pianka (1966) has argued that the longer growing season of tropical regions allow the component species to partition the environment temporally as well as spatially, there by permitting the coexistence of more species. Temporal partitioning of environmental resources is also shown in mixed grass prairies (Singh *et al.*, 1983). Different in the photosynthetic adaptation of plants to the cool and moist (C_3) and to the warm and dry (C_4) conditions permit temporal separation of species into warm and cool season guilds. The seasonal expression of plant diversity varies with time. The mid season experiencing maximum diversity as the recruitment of the community is completed and the resource tends to be more equitability shared among the species at that time.

Neighbourhood Effect Theory

Spatial distributions patterns of plants are typically intra-specifically clumped and sometimes segregated. Intra-specific aggregation is likely to result in higher intensity of intra rather than site-specific competition enabling species to coexist (Pacala, 1986; Kreft and Jets, 2007). Species diversity enhances invasion resistance (Kennedy *et al.*, 2002) and productivity also alters scale of diversity-invasibility relationship (Davies et al. 2007).

Neutral or Lottery Models

Neutral or lottery models rule out any significant role of niche segregation or competitive coexistence in supporting diversity. Fugitive species adapted to large scale production or long disposal mechanisms could survive with superior competitor by continually colonizing unoccupied space (Tilman, 1994).

Patch Dynamics

This model was proposed by Levin (1974) based on an assumption that trade off exists between competitive ability and dispersal capacity. The high dispersal ability compensates for the risk of extinction form micro sites as a result of interior competitive ability. This theory has some analogy with the explanation provided by Grime (1973) for disturbance as a factor influencing community structure. Species richness is likely to be greatest at an intermediate level of disturbance regime.

Regeneration Niches Models

According to this model the environment is composed of numerous distinct microsites (Grubb, 1977). Species differ sufficiently in their regeneration requirements so that competitive exclusion does not occur.

Regional Pattern of Biodiversity

Centres of diversity are related with particular habitat types, typically the most productive or structurally complex. For example, the subtropical

Pantanal marshes of Paraquary River in South America support the enormous diversity of mammals. These marshes are seasonally flooded and a complex mosaic of xerophytes and mesophytes vegetations occurs there because the prevailing soil is sandy. Although none of the mammalian species is endemic to the Pantanal, the entire xeric and mesic vegetation of terrestrial and aquatic habitats result in a rich mammalian fauna, which are also richer than typical tropical areas (Alho & Larcher, 1991). In some cases regional centers of high species richness have been shown to contain large number of closely related species. For example, Fynbos habitat of Cape Floristic region of Southern America has 526 species of Erica (Cowling, 1992), some of which have probably proliferated recently owing to special conditions (Fire) that promote occasional isolation of sub populations in their life history (Cowling & Holmes, 1992, Freeman et al., 2007). Cycling, creation and rejoining of forest Refugia within Australia are similarly related in Speciose genera of birds (Keast, 1961; Cracraft, 1985) and 600 species of Eucalyptus (Groves, 1994).

Myers (1988) introduced the term 'Hotspots' for geographical regions particularly rich in endemic, rare, and threatened species found in relatively small areas but facing significant threats of habitat loss. According to Myers et al. (2000) to qualify an area as 'Hotspot', it must contains at least 0.5% or 1500 of the world's 300,000 plant species and should have lost 70% or more of its original primary habitats. According to Mittermeir et al. (2004) 34 hotspots covered 15.7% of the earth's land surface. These hotspots hold at least 15000 plant species as endemic i.e. 50% of the world's total. The total number of terrestrial vertebrates endemic to hotspot is 11980 i.e. 42% of all terrestrial vertebrates species. These hotspots remain under tremendous human pressure. Cincotta et al, (2000) estimated that in 1995 nearly 20% of the world population was living in hotspots and population growth rate of the world (1.3 % yr^{-1}) or that of developing countries (1.6 % yr^{-1}) which is substantially lower than population growth rate in hotspots (1.8 % yr^{-1}) observed in 1995 – 2000. Hotspots have a higher population density as compared to the global average. Myers et al, (2000) recognized nine as leading hotspots while eight as 'Hottest hotspots' based on analysis of five key factors: number of endemic plant and animal species, endemic species area ratio, and the habitat loss. The hottest hotspots are Madagascar, the Philippines, Sunderland, Brazil's Atlantic forest, the Caribbean, Indoburma, Western Ghat /Srilankka and Eastern arc and coastal forest of Tanzania /Kenya. Nayer (1996) has recognized 40 hotspots of Indian flora. Eastern Himalaya and Western Ghats of India contain 5332 endemic species of plants, mammals, reptiles, amphibians, and butterflies (WCMC 1993).

All global centers with a species density of more than 3,000 species per 10,000 km^2 were considered Diversity Zones (Barthlott et al., 2005). This classification results in 20 global centers characterized by high to highest values of species richness. Five centers fall into the highest category of more than 5,000 species per 10,000 km^2 i.e., Costa Rica-Chocó, Tropical Eastern Andes, Atlantic Brazil, Northern Borneo, and New Guinea. Interestingly, all five centers with maximum species richness represent mountainous regions in the humid tropics (Barthlott et al., 2005).

Global Pattern of Biodiversity

The hierarchy of factor made the possibility of accommodation of a large number of species on the earth. The occurrence of the large number of species on the earth is the result of separation and somewhat parallel diversification of earth into five continents. The biodiversity at global scale is discussed as under sections:

Forest Ecosystem

Humans are affecting biodiversity in tropical system primarily through forest destruction, largely for conversion to pastures, croplands and plantations (Ruger et al., 2008). Current rates of loss of habitat and associated species loss are higher in tropical regions than elsewhere in the world (Janzen, 1986; Whitemore & Sayer, 1992). Large plantations of single species of conifer and hardwood combined with more frequent harvesting exert a major impact on ecosystem functioning and biodiversity in temperate forest. In the last half century, air pollution has changed the properties of the atmosphere and precipitation of this has resulted in the removal of some species, alterations in nutrient cycling and the creation of ecosystem more susceptible to outbreaks of insects and diseases. Loss of some keystone species and the introduction of others further destabilized temperate forest ecosystem. Properties of boreal ecosystem can change rapidly with changes in species composition, whether because of natural succession (Wien & E-I Bayoumi, 1983; Paster & Mladlenoff, 1992; Payette, 1992), herbivory (Pastor et al., 1993), human induced changes through climate warming (Pastor & Post, 1998) or water logging (Mladenoff *et al.*, 1993; Haila, 1994). The loss of few species, therefore have significance consequences for ecosystem functioning but the direction of change depends great extent on the functional group of which the species belongs.

Grassland Ecosystems

On a worldwide basis the response of grasslands to the major human use domestic livestock grazing has been variable (Michunas & Lauenroth, 1993). In some area where the negative vegetation is well adopted as the result of evolution, changes in biodiversity have been very small (Milchunas *et al.*, 1998). In other area changes are very large. In some cases especially in tropical and subtropical grasslands, large changes have been evolved a shift from grass dominated vegetation to one dominated by woody plants (Van Vegten, 1983; Archer 1989). In other cases the large changes have involved invasion of exotic plants, which have profoundly after the ecosystems conversion of grasslands to cropland or seeded pastures also had a major influence on biodiversity and ecosystem functioning. In many cases these converted grasslands have become net sources of carbon and nutrients accelerating global changes. This major transpiration of grasslands and their effect on biodiversity modify the water, carbon and nutrient cycles to the extent that significantly contributes in altering the earth's life supporting systems.

Arctic and Alpine Ecosystem

Arctic and Alpine ecosystems are cold-dominated ecosystem lacking trees. This ecosystem occupies approximately 8% of the terrestrial surface of the globe (5% Arctic and 3% Alpine) but support about only 4% of the global flora (1500 Arctic species, 10,000 Alpine species) and fauna. Species diversity of plants and animals in Arctic and Alpine regions decline with increasing altitude and latitude, but genetic diversity within species appears unrelated to climatic changes. Within both regions species diversity of plants and animals is concentrated in areas of high vertical relief, lacking a well developed organic matter. The vast expenses of heat covered landscape in the Arctic and in level terrain in Alpine region have a very few species (generally < 10 vascular plant species sq. m), with widespread geographic distribution but under threat due to climate change (Pickering et al., 2008). Landscape diversity strongly influences terrestrials-aquatics exchanges particularly in permafrost-dominated Arctic terrain/ where water and nutrient flow laterally among ecosystems (Kling, 1995).

Arctic and Alpine ecosystems are particularly exposed to anthropogenic activities because there are few species in most widespread vegetation to loss or gain, even one or two species has a large proportional impact on biodiversity. Furthermore landscape biodiversity is easily altered by anthropogenic activities due to its sensitivity to disturbance of steep alpine slopes and the sensitivity of Arctic soils to permafrost degradation. Resulting ecosystem changes affect local inhabitants, primarily by reducing the productivity of animal species reindeer, marine mammals fishes on which they depends. In alpine and down slope ecosystems these changes influences runoff, land slide danger and quality of drinking water. Other effects of human induced changes on Arctic and alpine ecosystems are indirectly, resulting from potential positive feed back of CO_2 and CH_4 emission which causes climate warming because human impacts on Arctic and Alpine region originate primarily outside these regions. Generally they are decoupled and irresponsible to, the effects they cause.

Savanna Ecosystems

Savanna are "tropical ecosystem ...forming a continuum of physiogramic types ranging from closed woodlands with a heliophytic grasses under story through open savanna woodlands to treeless edaphic grassland" (Huntley & Walker, 1982). In all there are grasses with the C_4 photosynthetic pathway dominates the herbaceous layer while the woody components at the moist ends of moisture gradient comprise fire tolerant trees and shrubs. Savanna ecosystem constitutes the largest simple type of terrestrial biomes. Savannas develop in soil of generally low fertility under regimes of seasonal rainfall and are submitted to recurrent disturbances through herbivory and fire (Sarmianto, 1984). These environmental constraints largely determine structure and productive capacity of these ecosystems (Walker, 1987). Population reduction due to disturbance and spatial patchiness, contributes to the maintenance of species and functional group diversity (Huston, 1979). Lowering perturbation frequently result in a large accumulation of litter loading to a reduction in a diversity of grass layer (Tilman, 1993). However the diversity of tree layer increases in the absence of protuberances due to survival of fire or grazing sensitive species (San Jose & Farinas, 1991). Human has profoundly modified savanna ecosystem throughout history. Mostly modification are related to over population and mismanagement of natural resources, reduction in landscape, community and species diversity, have effected ecosystem functioning as expressed by habitat deterioration and diminished capacity of savanna. The ecological consequences relevant for continued use of their environments are erosion, pollution of water sources, reduction in soil fertility and diminishing carrying capacity of herbivores. Therefore, the restoration of ecosystem through the recovery of biodiversity is an essential step in the planning of sustainable use of savannas.

MAJOR DRIVERS OF BIODIVERSITY CHANGE

Changes in biodiversity for the year 2100 are now based on scenarios of changes in atmospheric carbon dioxide, climate vegetation and land use and, the known sensitivity of biodiversity to these changes. Sala *et al,* (2000) prepared a list of important drivers of biodiversity changes in terrestrial ecosystems. Land use changes probably will have the largest effect followed by climate change, nitrogen deposition, biotic exchange and elevated CO_2 concentration (Table 2.3). Mediterranean climate and grassland ecosystems likely will experience the greatest proportional changes in biodiversity because of the substantial influence of all drivers of biodiversity change. Northern temperate ecosystems are estimated to experience the least biodiversity changes because major landuse changes have already occurred. Plausible changes in biodiversity in other biomes depend upon interaction among the cases of biodiversity. These interactions represent one of the largest uncertainties in projection of future biodiversity changes (Table 2.3). Most land use change will continue to forests of South America and that the least landuse changes will occur in Arctic and Alpine where human population density probably will remain low and Northern temperate forests where reforestation is expected to exceed deforestation also causing small negative effects on biodiversity. The extent of habitat modification is projected to be modest in desert and boreal forestlands, intermediate in savanna, grassland and Mediterranean ecosystems. Atmospheric CO_2 mixed globally within a biomass i.e. same CO_2 presence in all biomass. Nitrogen deposition is largest in Northern temperate zone near cities, smallest in biomes such as Arctic and southern temperate forest, which are generally distant from the source of pollution. Other biomes are intermediate with the regional variation in deposition generally associated with cities or industrial point sources. Climate will expect warm most dramatically in Arctic and Boreal zones, least in tropics and show intermediate levels changes in other biomes.

Table 2.3: Expected changes for the year 2100 in five major drivers of bio-diversity changes (Lands use, atmospheric composition CO_2, Nitrogen deposition, climate, and biotic exchanges) for principal terrestrial biomes of the Earth (Arctic Tundra, Alpine tundra, Boreal forest, Grasslands, Savannas, Mediterranean ecosystems, Deserts, Northern temperate forests, Southern temperate forests and tropical forests) (Sala et al. 2000).

	Arctic	Alpine	Boreal	Grass-land	Savanna	Med.	Desert	N temp.	S temp.	Tropic
Land use	1.0	1.0	2.0	3.0	3.0	3.0	2.0	1.0	4.0	5.0
Climate	5.0	3.0	4.0	2.0	2.0	2.0	2.0	2.0	2.0	1.0
Nitrogen deposition	1.0	3.0	3.0	3.0	2.0	3.0	2.0	5.0	1.0	2.0
Biotic exchange	1.0	1.0	2.0	3.0	3.0	5.0	3.0	3.0	2.0	2.0
Atmospheric CO_2	2.5	2.5	2.5	2.5	2.5	2.5	2.5	2.5	2.5	2.5

The impact of a unit change in each driver on biodiversity of major biomes has shown in Table 2.4. Landuse changes are the most severe driver of biodiversity changes (Sala, 1995, Rodríguez, E.R. 2007). For example, conversion of temperate grassland into cropland and tropical forest into grassland results in local extinction of most plant species and the associated animal whose habitat is largely determined by plant species composition. Below ground organisms are also affected most severely by landuse (Anderson, 1995). The increase in atmospheric CO_2 is expected to have the largest impact on biodiversity in those biomes where plant growth is most limited by water availability and where there is a mixture of C_3 and C_4 species exist because of known difference on the effect of CO_2 on water use efficiency (Mooney *et al.*, 1991). The maximum impact of elevated CO_2 has been found in grassland and savanna which are water limited biomes, mixture of contrasting plant functional types. The smallest impact factors are recorded for arctic, alpine, boreal forest, tropical forest.

Table 2.4: Impacts of the driver changes on the different type of biome biodiversity: In this exercise, a unit change of the driver was defined for land use as conversion of 50% of land area to agriculture, for CO_2 as a 2.5-fold increase is elevated CO_2 as projected by 2100, for Nitrogen deposition as 20 Kg ha^{-1} $year^{-1}$ for climate as a 4^{0}C change or 30% change in precipitation, and for biotic exchange as the arrival of 200 new plant or animal species by 2100. Estimates very low (1) to high (5) and result from existing global scenarios of the physical environment and knowledge from expert in each biomes (Sala et al. 2000)

	Arctic	Alpine	Boreal	Grass-land	Savanna	Med	Desert	N temp.	S temp.	Tropic
Land use	5.0	5.0	5.0	5.0	5.0	5.0	5.0	5.0	5.0	5.0
Climate	4.0	4.0	3.5	3.0	3.0	3.0	4.0	2.0	2.0	3.0
Nitrogen deposition	3.0	3.0	3.0	2.0	2.0	2.0	1.0	3.0	3.0	1.0
Biotic exchange	1.0	1.0	1.0	2.0	2.0	3.0	2.0	1.5	3.0	1.5
Atmospheric CO_2	1.0	1.0	1.0	3.0	3.0	2.0	2.0	1.5	1.5	1.0

Increased nitrogen deposition should have the largest impact on biodiversity in those biomes which are most nitrogen limited primarily by giving a competitive advantage to plant species with high maximum growth rates which then exclude the slower growing species (Tilman, 1993). Consequently it is assigned that the largest impact factor to temperate forest, boreal forest, arctic and alpine. Biodiversity, in desert and tropical forest may respond least to nitrogen deposition because plant growth is strongly limited by phosphorous and water respectively (Vitousek, 1997). When the data are averaged across biomes, the landuse change is the driver that is expected to have the largest global impacts on biodiversity by the year 2100 mostly because of its devastating effects on habitat availability and consequent species extinctions. Climate change will be the second most important driver of biodiversity change. Change in atmosphere CO_2, biotic exchange and nitrogen deposition also will have substantial effects on future biodiversity with the relative importance being regionally variable. Variability about the impacts of different drivers among biomes is highest for landuse change sensitivity to all biomes. In contrast, atmospheric CO_2 showed the smallest variability of the three drivers because CO_2 is well mixed in the atmosphere and ranges of ecological responses are quite narrow. The other drivers have intermediate variability. There are few large differences among the biomes in the cause of future changes in biodiversity. Biomes such as tropical and southern temperate forest show large change in land use with relatively small effect due to other drivers. Arctic ecosystems are also influenced largely by a single factor climate change. In contrast, most drivers substantially affect Mediterranean ecosystems, Savannas and grasslands. Finally, all the drivers contributed in biodiversity changes in biomes such as Northern temperate forest and desert.

IMPACTS OF HUMAN ACTIVITIES ON BIODIVERSITY

The 'Global Biodiversity Strategy' (WRI, IUCN, UNEP, 1992) identified both direct and indirect impacts that affect current level of bio-diversity, nearly all of which have significant human components. The indirect impacts include habitat loss and fragmentation, invasion by introduced species, the over exploitation of living resources, pollution, domestication and selection, global climate change, local and industrial agriculture and forestry. The environment have been used/misused by human beings to raise its dominance through biotic impoverishment. The factors that are responsible to expand the ecological niche of human are indirectly causes the loss of biodiversity. The current evidence of the impacts of anthropogenic activities on biodiversity is presented in Table 2.5. These impacts invariably involve a complex interplay of biological, social, historical, economic and political factors (Grainger, 1992). Lamprey (1975) showed linkage among the various factors affecting desertification in northern Kenya and threats to the 54% of European birds (Tucker & Heath, 1994) and tropical shoebird (Yasué et al. 2008) which are experiencing substantial population decline.

Many studies showed that the extirpation of species are not explainable from knowledge of ecological attributes or particular anthropogenic impacts but are probably due to the cumulative effects of multiple impacts (Moyal & Leidy, 1992; Frissell 1993; Angermeir, 1995). Additional researches are required to improve the understanding of such multiple and possibly synergistic or non-linear influence of factors on biodiversity. Further, study is also required on the relationship between the data and other ecological components, including subsurface and surface water, riparian zones, watersheds, landscapes and human influences on biodiversity (Karr, 1991; Angermeier & Williams, 1994; Angermeier & Karr, 1994). The driving forces of human induced changes will vary with the type involved, and forces that drive some changes may lessen others (Mayer & Turner, 1992). For example rising of agricultural practices may provide an incentive for clearing forests while also providing an incentive to adopt soil conservation measures. Second the same kind of land cover change can have the different sources in different areas with deforestation in some area, primarily for timber extraction, in other for shifting cultivation and another for establishment of plantations. In the dynamics of underlying causes, no agreements yet exist on the land at which adequate explanation is achieved. For example some may consider that deforestation by agricultural expansions is driven by population growth, while others would contend that agricultural expansion helps to cause population growth.

Table 2.5: Responses of mammals to human Interference Modified after (Happold, 1995)

Group (Example)	Responses	Species Characteristics	Reason for Responses
A. Population decrease (elephants, Rhinos, large/medium artiodactyls and carnivorous, most primates)	Negative	Large size, low reproduction rate compete directly with humans/stock for resources.	High value to humans' high trophy value cause damage high momentum value competition for land hosts for resources.
B. Population remain static (Many medium sized mammals many orders.	Neutral	Variable size, moderate reproduction rate, limited competition with humans/stocks for resources.	Low value human limited values for tropics low monitory value limited competitions for land not known as hosts for diseases.
C. Population decreases (certain small rodents, shrews, bars, other small species).	Positive	Usually small size usually higher reproductive rate, limited competitions with humans fcr resources or good at exploiting human resources.	No value or limited value to humans difficult to hunt.

Population growth needs to be explained in the term of the social, political and the economic conditions that promote it. Ehrlich & Ehrlich (1990) have attempted to provide single comprehensive approach to the question of driving forces using the equation I=PAT where I represents environmental impacts, as the product of P (Population), A (Affluence) and T (Technology). These human impacts are the product of the number of people, the level at which they consume and the characters of material and energy flow in the production and consumption. Mayer & Turner (1992) have pointed out that this formula suffers from the handicap of mismatch between its categories of driving forces and the categories customarily used in social sciences. Neither 'Affluence' nor 'Technology' is associated with a substantial body of social science theory. Natural world mean that the genetic diversity of many species is being reduced because the total size of the populations are decreasing and they are often being splitting into small and widely separated into subgroups which cannot interbreed. Other might argued that this is the one of process of speciation, with human serving as a new isolation mechanism.

CONCLUSION

Since, spatial heterogeneity is important for overall population survival and can determine the persistence of interacting species (Levin, 1974). From this review paper, it can be said that there is a need of more researches regarding the patterns of terrestrial biodiversity at local, regional and global scale. Observations of pattern and processes at one scale or in one system may not be generalized to other scale or system. To elucidate the clear patterns of diversity we will need to know more about biological processes of variation, ecological specialization and role of geographical heterogeneity. The major drivers of biodiversity changes such as land use, and nitrogen deposition are limiting factors for the biodiversity distributions at local scale. The anthropogenic impacts also have the significant effects on the biodiversity loss. Therefore, there is also need of in-depth knowledge on biodiversity patterns that would also be helpful in its conservation and management as well as provide better economic benefits to the people living around rich biodiversity patches.

REFERENCES

Alho, C. & Larcher, T. (1991) Mammalian Conservation in the Pantanal of Brazil. *Latin American Memmalogy : History, Biodiversity, and Conservation* (ed. by M.A. Mares, and D.J. Schmidly), pp. 280-294. University of Oklahoma Press, Norman, Oklahoma.

Allen, A.P., Brown, J.H. & Gillooly, J.F. (2002) Global Biodiversity, Biochemical Kinetics and the Energetic Equivalence Rule. *Science,* 297, 1545-1548.

Andersen, A.N. (1995) Measuring more of Biodiversity: Genus Richness as a Surrogate for Species Richness in Australian Ant Faunas. *Biological Conservation,* 73, 39-43.

Angermeier, P.L (1995) Ecological Attributes of Extinction-Prone Species: Loss of Fresh Water Fishes of Verginia. *Conservation Biology,* 9, 43-158.

Angermeier, P.L. & Karr, J.R. (1994) Biological Integrity vs. Biological Diversity as Policy Directors: Protecting Biotic Resources. *Bioscience,* 44, 690-697.

Angermeier, P.L. & Williams J.E. (1994) Conservation of Imperiled Species and Reauthorization of the Endangered Species Act of 1973. *Fisheries,* 19, 26-29.

Archer, S. (1989) Have Southern Texas Savannas been Converted to Woodland in Recent History? *The American Naturalist,* 134, 545-561.

Arroyo, M.T.K., Squeo, F. Armesto, J. & Villagran C. (1988) Effect of Aridity on Plant Diversity in Northern Chile Andes. *Annals of Missouri Botanical Garden* 75, 55-78.

Arroyo, M.T.K., Sarukhan, J. & Raven, P.H. (1992) Biodiversity. An Agenda of Science for Environment in to the 21st Century. (ed. by J.C.I., Dooge, G.T., Goodman, J.W.M., La Rivier, J., Mention-Lefevre, T. O' Riordan and F. Prederse), pp. 205-219 Cambridge University Press, Cambridge.

Arroyo, M.T.K., Riveros, M., Penaloza, A., Cavieres, L., & Faggi, A.M. (1995) Phytogeographic Relationship and Regional Richness Pattern of the Cool Temperature Rain Forest Flora of South America. *Forest and Riverine System of the West Cost of North and South America* (ed. by R. Lawford, P. Alaback, and E.R. Fuentes), Springer-Verlay, Hei delberg.

Barthlott, W., Mutke, J., Rafiqpoor, M.D. Kier, G. & Kreft, H. (2005) Global Centers of Vascular Plant Diversity. *Nova Acta Leopoldina,* 92(342), 61-83.

Barthlott, W., Hostert, A., Kier, G., Kuper, W., Kreft, H., Mutke, J., Rafiqpoor, M.D. & Sommer, J.H. (2007) Geographical Pattern of Vascular Plant Diversity at Continental to Global Scales. *Erdkunde,* 61(4), 305-315.

Cincotta, R.P., Wisnewski, J. & Engelman, R. (2000). Human Population in the Biodiversity Hotspots. *Nature,* 404, 990-992.

Cody, M.L. (1975) Towards a Theory of Continental Species Diversities: Birds Distributions Overs Medterranean Habitat Gradients. *Ecology and Evolutions of Communities* (ed. by M.L. Cody and J.M. Diamond), pp. 214-257. Harvard University Press Cambridge, Massachusetts.

Connell, J.H. (1978) Diversity in Tropical Rain Forests and Coral Reefs. *Science,* 199, 1302-9.

Costanza, R., Rd Arge R., R de Grott, S., Farber, M., grasso, B., Hannon, K., Limburg, S., Naeem, R.V.O., Neill, J., Paruelo, R.G., Raskin, P., Van den Bett, M. (1997) The Value of the World's Ecosystem Services and Natural Capital. *Nature,* 387, 253-260.

Cowling, R.M. (1992). *Ecology of Fynbos, Nutrient, Fire and Diversity,* Oxford University Press, Cape Town.

Cowling, R.M. & Holems, P.M. (1992) Endemision and Speciation in Low Land Flora from the Cape Floristic Region. *Biological Journal of the Linnean Society,* 47, 367-383.

Cracraft, J. (1985) Historical Biogeography and Patterns of Differentiation within the South American Avifauna: Areas of Endemism. *Ornithological Monograph,* 36, 49-84.

Daniels, R.J.R. (1992) Geographical Distribution Pattern of Amphibians in Western Ghats, India. *Journal of Biogeography,* 19, 521-529.

Davies, K.F., Chesson, P., Harrison, S., Inouye, B.D., Melbourne, B.A. & Rice, K. J. (2005) Spatial Heterogeneity Explains the Scale Dependence of the Native–exotic Diversity Relationship. *Ecology,* 86, 1602-1610.

Davies, K.F., Harrison, S., Safford, H.D. & Viers, J.H. (2007). Productivity Alters the Scale Dependence of the Diversity-invasibility Relationship. *Ecology,* 88(8), 1940-1947.

Di Castri, F., Vernhes, J. R & Younis. T. (1992) The Network Approach for Understanding Biodiversity. *Biology International,* 25, 3-9.

Diamond, J. (1988) Factors Controlling Species Diversity: Overview and Synthesis. *Annals of the Missouri Botanical Garden*, 75, 117-129.

Dobson, A. (1995) Biodiversity and Human Health. *Trends in Ecology and Evolution*, 10, 390-391.

Ehrlich, P.R. & Ehrlich, A.H. (1981) *Extinction: the Causes and Consequences of the Disappearance of Species*. Random House, New York.

Ehrlich, P.R. & Ehrlich, A. H. (1990) *The Population Explosion*, Simon & Schuster, New York.

Ehrlich, P.R. & Ehrlich, A. H. (1992) The Value of Biodiversity. *Ambio*, 21, 219-226.

Elton, C.S. (1958) *The Ecology of Invasions by Animals and Plants*. Methuen, London and Wiley, New York.

Fischer A.G. (1960) Latitudinal Variations in Organic Diversity. *Evolution*, 14, 64-81.

Fisher, B. & Turner, R.K. (2008) Ecosystem Services: Classification for Valuation. *Biological Conservation*, 141(5), 1167-1169.

Freeman, J.P., Stohlgren, T.J., Hunter, M.E., Omi, P.N., Martinson, E.J., Chong, G.W. & Browns, C.S. (2007) Rapid Assessment of Postfire Plant Invasions in Coniferous Forests of the Western United States. *Ecological Applications*, 17(6), 1656-1665.

Frissel, C.A. (1993) Topology of Extinction and Endangerment of Native Fishes the Pacific North-West and California. *Conservation Biology*, 7, 342-354.

Gentry, A.H. (1988). Changes in Plant Community Diversity and Floristic Composition on Environmental and Geographical Gradients. *Annals of the Missouri Botanical Garden*, 75 (1), 134.

Grainger, A. (1992) *Controlling Tropical Deforestation*. Earthscan, London.

Grime, J. P. (1973) Competitive Exclusion in Herbaceous Vegetation. *Nature*, 242, 344-347.

Groom, M.J., Gray, E.M. & Townsend, P.A. (2008) Biofuels and Biodiversity: Principles for Creating Better Policies for Biofuel Production. *Conservation Biology*, 22(3), 602-609.

Groves, R.H. (1994) *Australian Vegetation*. 2nd Edition, Cambridge University Press, Melbourne.

Grubb, P.J. (1977) The Maintenance of Species Richness in Plant Communities; the Important of the Regeneration Niche. *Biological reviews*, 52, 107-114.

Haila, Y. (1994) Preserving Ecological Diversity in Boreal Forest, Ecological Background, Research, and Management. *Annals Zoological Fennici*, 31, 203-217.

Happold, D.C.D. (1995) The Interactions Between Humans and Mammals in Africa in Relation to Conservation: A Review, *Biodiversity and conservation*, 4, 395-414.

Heywood, V.H. & Watson. R.T. (1995) Global Biodiversity Assessment. Cambridge University Press, UK.

Hinegardner R. (1976) Evolution of Genome Size. *Molecular Evolution* (ed. by F.J. Ayala), pp. 179-199. Massachustter, Sinauer.

Holloway, J.D., & Stork, N.E. (1991) The Dimension of Biodiversity, the Use of Invertebrates as Indicators of Human Impact. *The Biodiversity Microorganisms and Invertebrates. Its Role in Sustainable Agricultural* (ed. by D.I. Hawksworth), pp. 37-62. CAB International, Wallingford.

Huntley, B.J. & Walker, B.H. (1982) *Ecology of Tropical Savannahs*, Springer-Verlag, Berlin.

Huston, M. (1979) A General Hypothesis of Species Diversity. *American Naturalist*, 113, 81-101.

Huston, M.A., L.W., Aarssen, M.P., Austin, B.S., Cade, J.D., Fridley, E., Garnier, J.P., Grime, Hodgson,J., Lauenroth,W.K., Thompson, K., Vandermeer, J.H. & Wardle, D.A. (2000) No Consistent Effect of Plant Diversity on Productivity. *Science*, 289, 1255a-1255a.

Ives A.R. & Carpenter S.R. (2007) Stability and Diversity of Ecosystems. *Science,* 317, 58-62.

Jaksic, F.M. & Feinsinger, P. (1991) Bird Assemblages in the Temperate Forests of North and South America: A Comparison of Diversity, Dynamics, Guild Structure, and Resource Use. *Revista Chilena de Historia Natural,* 64, 491-510.

Janzen, D.H. (1986) The Future of Tropical Biology. *Annual Review of Ecology and Systematic,* 17, 305-24.

Karr, J.R. (1991) Biological Integrity: A Long-neglected Aspect of Water Resources Management's. *Ecological Applications,* 1, 66-84.

Keast, A. (1961) Bird Speciation on the Australian Continent. *Bulletin of the Museum of Comparative Zoology,* Harvard College, 123, 305-495.

Kennedy, T.A., Naeem, S., Howe, K.M., J.M.H., Tilman, D. & Reich, P. (2002) Biodiversity as a Barrier to Ecological Invasion. *Nature,* 417, 636-638.

Khoshoo, T.N. (1994) India's Biodiversity: Tasks Ahead. *Current Science* 67(8), 577-582.

Kier, G., Mutkel, J., Dinerstein, E., Ricketts, T.H., Kuper, W., Kreft, H. & Barthlott, W. (2005) Global Patterns of Plant Diversity and Floristic Knowledge. *Journal of Biogeography,* 32, 1-10.

Kiester, A.R. (1971) Species Density of North American Amphibians and Reptiles. *Systematic Zoology,* 20, 127-137.

Kikkawa, J. & Williams, W. T. (1971) Altitudinal Distribution of Land Birds in New Guinea. *Search,* 2, 64-65.

Kling, G. (1995) Land-water Interactions: The Influence of Terrestrial Diversity on Aquatic Ecosystem. Arctic and Alpine Biodiversity: Patterns, Causes and Ecosystem Consequence. (eds. by F.S. Champing and G. Korner), pp. 295-308. Springer-Verlog, Berlin.

Knoll, A.H. (1986) Patterns of Change in Plant Communities Through Geological Time. *Community Ecology* (ed. by J. Diamond and T.J. Case), pp. 126-144. Harper and Row, New York.

Krebs, C. J. (1985) *Ecology: The Experimental Analysis of Distribution and Abundance,* 3rd Edition. Harper Collins, New York.

Kreft, H. & Jetz, W. (2007) Global Patterns and Determinants of Vascular Plant Diversity. *Proceedings of National Acadamy of Science,* 104(14), 5925-5930.

Kuper, W., Sommer, J.H., Lovett, J.C., Mutke, J. Linder, H.P., Beentje, H.J., van Rompaey, R., Chatelain, C., Sosef, M. & Barthlott, W. (2004) Africa's Hotspots of Biodiversity Redefined. *Annals of the Missouri Botanical Garden,* 91, 525-535.

Lamprey, H.F. (1975) Report on the Desert Encroachment Reconnaissance in Northern Sudan, 21 October to 10 November, 1975. UNESCO/UNEP. pp. 16.

Lawton, J.H. (1994) What do Species do in Ecosystems? *Oikos,* 71, 367-374.

Latham, R.E. & Ricklefs, R.E. (1993) A Global Pattern of the Species Richness in most Forest, Energy Diversity Theory does not Account for Variation in Species Richness *Oikos,* 67, 325-333.

Levin, S.A. (1974) Dispersion and Population Interactions. *American Naturalist,* 108, 207-28.

Lewis, J.R. (1964) *The Ecology of Rocky Shores*. English University Press, London, pp. 323.

Lovejoy, T.E. (1980). Conservation Biology: An Evolutionary-ecological Perspective. (ed. by M.E. Soule and B.A. Wilcox) Vol IX. Sinauer Associates, Sunderland, Mass.

MacArthur, R.H. & MacArthur, J. (1961) On Bird Species Diversity. *Ecology,* 42, 594-598.

MacArthur, R.H. (1965) Patterns of Species Diversity. *Biological Review,* 40, 510-533.

McCann, K.S. (2000). The Diversity-stability Debate. *Nature,* 405, 228-233.

McNeely, J.A. Miller, K.R., Reid, W., Mittermeier, R. & Werner, T. (1990) *Conserving the World's Biological Diversity*. IUCN, WRI, World Bank, WWF-US, C.I. Washington, DC.

Meyer, W.B. & Turner, B.L. (1992) Human Population Growth and Global Land Use/ Cover Change. *Annual Review of Ecology and Systematic,* 23, 39-61.

Michunas, D.G. & Lauenroth, W.K. (1993) Quantitative Effects of Grazing on Vegetation and Soils Over a Global Range of Environments. *Ecological Monographs,* 63, 327-366.

Milchunas, D.G., Lauenroth, W.K. & Burke. I.C. (1998) Livestock Grazing: Animal and Plant Biodiverstiy of Shortgrass Steppe and the Relationship to Ecosystem Function. *Oikos,* 83, 65-74.

Mittermeier, R.A., Gil, P.R., Hoffmann, M., Pilgrim, J., Brooks, T., Mittermeier, C.G. Lamoreux, J. and Da Fonseca, G.A.B (2004) *Hotspots Revisited: Earth's Biologically Richest and Most Endangered Terrestrial Ecoregions* Conservation International, Virginia.

Mladenoff, D.J., White, M.A., Pastor, J. & Crow. T.R. (1993). Comparing Spatial Pattern in Unaltered Old-growth and Disturbed Forest Landscapes. *Ecological Application,* 3, 294-306.

Mooney, H.A., Drake, B.G., Luxmoov, R.J., Oechel, W.C. & Pitelka, L.F. (1991). Predicting Ecosystem Responses to Elevated CO_2 Concentrations. *Bioscience,* 41, 96-104.

Moyal, P.B. & Leidy R.A. (1992). Loss of Bio-diversity in Aquatic Ecosystems: Evidence from Fish Faunas. *Conservation Biology: The Theory and Practice of Nature Conservation, Preservation and Management.* (ed. by P.L. Fiedler and S.K., Jane), pp. 127-169. Chapman and Hall, New York.

Myers, N. (1988).Threatened Biota: 'Hotspots' in Tropical Forests. *Environmentalist,* 8, 187-208.

Myers, N., Mittermeier, R.A., Mittermeier, C.G., Da Fonseca, G.A.B. & Kent, J. (2000) Biodiversity Hotspots for Conservation Priorities. *Nature,* 403, 853-858.

Nayar, M.P. (1996) *Hotspots of Endemic Plants in India, Nepal and Bhutan*. Tropical Botanic Garden and Research Institute, Thiruvananthapuram, India.

Norse, E.A. & McManus, R.E. (1980) Ecology and Living Resources Biological Diversity. *In: Environmental Quality 1980.* The Eleventh Annual Report of the Council on Environment Quality, 31-80. CEQ Washington, DC, USA.

Osman, R.W. & Whitlatch, R.B. (1978) Patterns of Species Diversity: Fact or Artifact? *Paleobiology,* 4, 41-54.

Pandey, C.B. & Singh, J.S. (1992a) Influence of Rainfall and Grazing on Herbage Dynamics in a Seasonally Dry Tropical Savanna. *Vegetatio,* 102, 107-124.

Pandey, C.B. & Singh, J.S. (1992b) Influence of Rainfall and Grazing on Below Ground Bio-mass Dynamics in Dry Tropical Savanna. *Canadian Journal of Botany,* 70, 1885-1890.

Pandey S.K. & Shukla R.P. (1999) Plant Diversity and Community Patterns Along the Disturbance Gradient in Plantation Forests of Sal (*Shorea robusta* Gaertn.). *Current Science,* 77, 814-818.

Pastor, J. & Post, W.M. (1988) Response of Northern Forest to CO_2 Induced Climate Change. *Nature,* 334, 55-58.

Pastor, J. & Mladenoff. D.J. 1992. The Southern Boreal-northern Hardwood Forest Border. *A Systems Analysis of the Global Boreal Forest.* (ed. by H.H. Shugart, R. Leemans, and G.B. Bonan), pp. 216-240. Cambridge University Press, Cambridge, UK.

Pastor, J. Dewey, B., Naiman, R.J., McInnes, P.F. & Cohen, Y. (1993) Moose Browsing and Soil Fertility in the Boreal Forests of Isle Royale National Park. *Ecology,* 74, 467-480.

Payette S. (1992) Fire as a Controlling Process in the North American Boreal Forest. *A System for Analysis of the Global Boreal Forest.* (ed. by H.H. Shugant, R. Leemans, and G.B., Bonan), pp. 144-169. Cambridge, UK.

Pearson, O.P. & Ralph, C.P. (1978) The Diversity and Abundance of Vertebrates Along an Altitudinal Gradient in Peru. *Memorias del Museo de Historia Natural (Lima, Peru),* 18, 1-97.

Pianka, E.R. (1966) Convexity, Desert Lizards, and Spatial Heterogeneity. *Ecology,* 47, 1055-1059.

Pickering, C., Hill, W. & Green, K. (2008) Vascular Plant Diversity and Climate Change in the Alpine Zone of the Snowy Mountains, Australia. *Biodiversity and Conservation,* 17(7), 1627-1644.

Rehbek, C. (2005) The Role of Spatial Scale and the Perception of Large Scale Species Richness Patterns. *Ecology Letter.* 8, 224-239.

Ricklefs, R.E (2004) A Comprehensive Framework for Global Pattern in Biodiversity. *Ecology Letter,* 7, 1-15.

Ricklefs, R.E & Latham, R.E. (1993) Global Patterns of Diversity in Mangroves Floras. *Species Diversity: Historical and Geographical Perspectives.* (ed. by R.E Ricklef and D. Schluter), pp. 215-229. University of Chicago Press, Chicago.

Rodríguez-Estrella, R. (2007) Land Use Changes Affect Distributional Patterns of Desert Birds in the Baja California Peninsula, Mexico. *Diversity and Distribution,* 13(6), 877-889.

Rosenzwing M.L. & Abramsky, Z. (1993) How are Diversity and Productivity Related? *Species Diversity in Ecological Communities: Historical and Geographical Respectives.* (ed. by R.E. Rickets and D. Schluter), pp. 52-65. University of Chicago Press, Chicago.

Ruger, N., Williams-Linera, G., Kissling, W.D. & Huth, A. (2008) Long-term Impacts of Fuelwood Extraction on a Tropical Montane Cloud Forest. *Ecosystems,* 11(6), 868-881.

Ryvarden, L. (1993) Tropical Polypores. *Aspect of Tropical Mycology.* (ed. by S., Isaac, J.C., Franklard, R. Watling, and A.J.S. Whalley), pp.149-170. Cambridge University press, Cambridge.

Sala, O.E. (1995) Global Bio-diversity Assessment. *Section 5,* (ed. by H.A. Mooney, J. Lubchenco, R. Drizo, O.E. Sala), Cambridge University Press, Cambridge.

Sala, O.E., Chapin III, F.S., Armesto, J.J., Berlow, R., Bloomfield, J., Dirzo, R., Huber-Sanwald, E., Huenneke, L.F., Jackson, R.B., Kinzig, A., Leemans, R., Lodge, D., Mooney, H.A., Oesterheld, M., Poff, N.L., Sykes, M.T., Walker, B.H., Walker, M., & Wall, DH.. (2000) Global Biodiversity Scenarios for the Year 2100. *Science,* 287, 1770-1774.

San Jose, J.J. & Farinas, M. (1991) Temporal Changes in the Structure of a *Trachypogon* Savannah Protected for 25 Years. *Acta Oecologica,* 12, 237-247.

Sarmiento, G. (1984) *The Ecology of Neotropical Savannahs,* Harvard University Press, Cambridge, Mass.

Sepkoski, J.I. 1992. Phylogenetic and Ecological Patterns, the Phanerozoic History of Marine Biodiversity. *Systematic, Ecology and the Biodiversity Crisis.* (ed. by N. Eldredge), pp. 77-100. Columbia University Press, New York.

Smith, A.P. (1972) Buttressing of Tropical Trees: A Descriptive Model and New Hypotheses. *American Naturalist,* 106, 32-46.

Simpson, G.G. (1964) Species Density of North American Recent Mammals. *Systematic Zoology,* 13, 57-73.

Singh, J.S., Lauenroth, W.K. & Milchunas, D.G. (1983) Geography of Grassland Ecosystems. *Progress in Physical* Geography, 7, 46-80.

Sarkar, S. & Margules, C.R. (2002) Operationalizing Biodiversity for Conservation Planning. *Journal of Biosciences,* 27(S2), 299-308.

Stevens, G.C. (1992) The Elevation Gradient in Altitudinal Range: An Extension of Rapport's Latitudinal Rule to Altitude. *American Naturalist,* 140, 693-911.

Stork, N.E. (1988) Insect Diversity: Facts, Fiction and Speculation. *Biological Journal of the Linnean Society,* 35, 321-337.

Swingland, I.R. (2001) Definitions of Biodiversity. *Encyclopedia of Biodiversity I.* (ed. by S. A. Levin), pp. 377-391. Academic Press, San Diego, California.

Terborgh, J. (1973) On the Notion of Favorableness in Plant Ecology. *American Naturalist,* 107, 481-501.

Terborgh, J. (1977). Bird Species Diversity on an Andean Elevation Gradient. *Ecology,* 50, 1007-1019.

Tilman. D. (1993). Species Richness of Experimental Productivity Gradients: How Important is Colonization Limitation? *Ecology,* 74, 2179-2191.

Tilman, D. (1994). Competition and Biodiversity in Spatially Structured. *Habitat Ecology,* 75, 2-16.

Tucker, G.M. & Heath, M.F. (1994) *Birds in Europe: Their Conservation Status* Cambridge Bird Life International, U.K.

Van Vegten, J.A. (1983) Thornbush Invasion in a Savanna Ecosystem in Eastern Botswana. *Vegetatio*. 56, 3-7.

Vitousek, P.M., Aber, J.D., Howarth, R.W., Likens, G.E., Matson, P.A., Schindler, D.W., Schlesinger, W.H. & Tilman, D.G. (1997) Human Alteration of the Global Nitrogen Cycle: Sources and Consequences. *Ecological Applications,* 7, 737-750.

Walker, B.H. (1987) *Determinants of Tropical Savannas.* IRL Press, Oxford.

Walker, B.H (1992) Biodiversity and Ecological Redundancy. *Conservation Biology,* 6, 18-23.

Wein, R.W., & El-Bayoumi, M.A., (1983) Limitation to Predictability of Plant Succession in Northern Ecosystems. *Resources and Dynamics of the Boreal Zone* (ed. by Wein, R.W., Rieve, R.R., Methven, T.R.) pp. 214-225, ACUNS, Ottawa.

Whitemore, T.C. & Sayer, J.A. (1992) *Tropical Deforestation and Species Extinction*. Chapman and Hall, London.

Williams, P.H. & Humphries C.J. (1994) Biodiversity, Taxonomic Relatedness, and Endemism in Conservation. *Systematic and Conservative Evolution*. (ed. by P.L. Forey, C.J., Humphries and R.I., Vane-Wright), pp. 260-287 Clarendom Press, Oxford.

Wilson, E.O. & Peter, F.M. (1988) *Biodiversity*. National Academy Press, Washington, DC.

Wilson, R.J., Thomas, C.D., Fox, R., Roy, D.B. & Kunin, W.E. (2004) Spatial Patterns in Species Distributions Reveal Biodiversity Change. *Nature,* 432, 393-396.

WCMC (1993) *IUCN List of Threatened Animals* (ed. by B. Groombridge), WCMC, Cambaridge.

WRI, IUCN & UNEP. (1992) *Global Biodiversity Strategy: Guidelines for Action to Save, Study and Use Earth's Biotic Wealth, Sustainability and Equitably*. World Resources Institute Publications, Baltimore.

Yasué, M., Dearden, P. & Moore, A. (2008) An Approach to Assess the Potential Impacts of Human Disturbance on Wintering Tropical Shorebirds. *Oryx,* 42(3), 415-423.

Pages: 31-40

BIODIVERSITY, BIOTECHNOLOGY AND ENVIRONMENTAL CONSERVATION

Edited by: Dr. Pawan Kumar 'Bharti'; Mr. Govinda Bhandari

ISBN: 978-93-5056-750-0

Edition: 2015

Published by: Discovery Publishing House Pvt. Ltd., New Delhi (India)

CHAPTER 3

Diversity of Lichens in the Valley of Flowers National Park, India

Hem Chander

ABSTRACT

This chapter presents the first records of 128 species of lichens belonging to 43 genera namely *Aspicilia, Buellia, Bulbothrix, Caloplaca, Candelaria, Canomaculina, Canoparmelia, Chrysothrix, Cladonia, Collema, Dermatocarpon, Diploschistes, Dirinaria, Evernia, Everniastrum, Flavoparmelia, Flavopunctelia, Graphis, Heterodermia, Hypotrachyna, Lasallia, Lecanora, Leptogium, Lobaria, Parmelia, Parmotrema, Peltigera, Pertusaria, Phaeophyscia, Physcia, Porpidia, Punctelia, Pyxine, Ramalina, Rhizocarpon, Rhizoplaca, Rimelia, Staurothele, Stereocaulon, Sticta, Umbilicaria, Usnea, Xanthoparmelia* and *Xanthoria* of 20 families of lichens from the Valley of Flowers National Park.

Key words: Natural World Heritage Site, Western Himalaya, Nanda Devi Biosphere Reserve, morpho-chemotaxonomy, flora.

INTRODUCTION

The review of literature (Wadhwa et al. 1987; Kala 1998, 1999, 2004; Kala et al. 1998; Awasthi, 2007) reveals that no studies on lichen flora have

Wildlife Institute of India, Dehradun - 248 001, Uttarakhand, (India)

been conducted in this park and efforts were made during the present study for exploring the lichen diversity of this area.

The valley of flowers was incidentally explored by British Mountaineers Frank S. Smythe and R.L. Holdsworth during their expedition for ascent to Mount Kamet in 1931 (Smythe 1938). The Valley of Flowers established as National Park by Government of India in 1982 is a Natural World Heritage site inscribed by UNESCO in 2005 under criteria vii (to contain superlative natural phenomena or areas of exceptional natural beauty and aesthetic importance) and criteria x (to contain the most important and significant natural habitats for *in-situ* conservation of biological diversity, including those containing threatened species of outstanding universal value from the point of view of science or conservation). This national park spreads over an area of 87.5 Km^2, of which 63.58 Km^2 is under perpetual snow, 18.63 Km^2 is under alpine meadow and 5.29 Km^2 is under sub-alpine forest (Kala 1999). The park is under core zone of Nanda Devi Biosphere Reserve and situated between 30°41′ -30°48′ N latitude & 79°33′-79°46′E longitude in North Western Himalaya with an altitude range of 3,200m – 6,675m providing a great diversity of landscape and microhabitats. It is bounded by Gauri Parvat (6,500m) and Rataban (6,126m) in the East, Kunthkhal (4,430m) in the West, Saptshring (5,038m) in the South and Nilgiri Parvat (6,479m) in the North. River Pushpawati originates from the left bank of Tipra glacier and flows down through the park to drains into river Alaknanda which is a tributary of river Ganges. The climate of the park is moist temperate and alpine type annually with short period of cool summers and long period of severe winters.

This park accounts for 13 species of mammals including snow leopard (*Panthera uncia*), blue sheep (*Pseudois nayaur*), himalayan musk deer (*Moschus chrysogaster*), asiatic black bear (*Selenarctos thibetanus*), serow (*Namorhaedus sumatrensis*), himalayan tahr (*Hemitragus jemlahicus*) and forty one species of birds. The flora of the park account for 521 species of vascular plants including 499 Angiosperms, 4 Gymnosperms and 18 Pteridophytes (Kala et al. 1998; Kala 2004). The characteristic tree species in the park are maple (Acer cappadocicum), walnut (*Juglans regia*), hazelnut (*Corylus jacquemontii*), spruce (*Picea smithiana*), blue pine (*Pinus wallichiana*), birch (*Betula utilis*), rhododendron (*Rhododendron arboretum*), fir (*Abies pindrow*), chestnut (*Aesculus indica*) and oak (*Quercus semecarpifolia*).

METHODOLOGY AND MATERIALS

The specimens were collected from various habitats and substrates during the months September-October in 2009-2013. A total of 194 specimens of lichens were collected from nine study sites of the park namely Pairra (c 3200m), Nagtal (c 3300m), Baminidhaur (c 3450m), Semar (c 3500m), Bistoli (c 3500m), Kundaliyasain (c 3500m), Drunager (c 3550m), Sewachand (c 3600m) and Tiprakharak (c 3700m). The field data such as texture, size, colour, macroscopic features and form have been recorded in the field book during the excursions (Mueller et al. 2004). A hand lens (20 X), knife, hammer, chisel and a saw were the tools used while collecting the specimens. The collected specimens were placed in paper packets of suitable size and a paper slip containing the field data such as collection number, details of collection site, host/substrate, altitude in meters, the date of collection & name of the legator was placed in each paper packet. The fragile specimens were wrapped in cotton and/or placed in card boxes of suitable size. The fresh specimens were observed for morphological investigations and sun dried at the camping site. The detailed investigations of the specimens were carried out in Mycology and Plant Pathology laboratory at Department of Botany, Panjab University, Chandigarh, India.

Microscopic observations were recorded by using Olympus light microscope and Motic digital microscope. All the measurements were taken in 5% KOH solution. The specimens were photographed by Sony cybershot digital camera in the field/laboratory. The chemicals used for the chemical spot tests of lichens included (White & James 1985): 10% Potassium hydroxide (K), 10% aq. Calcium hypochlorite (C) and Stainer's stable solution of p-phenylenediamine (P) composing of p-phenylenediamine (1 g), Sodium sulphite (10 g) and Liquid detergent neutral solution in 100 ml of distilled water (0.5 ml). The specimens were placed in ultraviolet (UV) chamber at 350 nm to observe their fluorescence properties. The specimens have been preserved & maintained in PAN (Herbarium, Department of Botany, Panjab University, Chandigarh, India.

LICHEN DIVERSITY IN THE VALLEY OF FLOWERS NATIONAL PARK

The morpho-chemotaxonomic investigations of 194 specimens collected from nine study sites of the park have accounted for 128 species of lichens belonging to 43 genera of 20 families of lichens (Table 3.1). The site wise account of lichen species is as follows:

Pairra (c 3200m): It is sub alpine area dominated by birch (*Betula utilis*). The slope varies from 10-70° with 10-40% boulders (Kala et al. 1998). A total of sixty species of lichens have been recorded from this site during the present study.

Nagtal (3300m): It is sub alpine area comprising of scattered birch-rhododendron community, high density of birch saplings, gentle to moderate slopes and relatively unstable slopes (Kala et al. 1998). A total of thirteen species of lichens have been recorded from this site during the present study.

Baminidhaur (3450m): It is alpine area consisting of a moraine with huge boulders (Kala et al. 1998). A total of sixteen species of lichens have been recorded from this site during the present study.

Table 3.1: Lichens of the Valley of Flowers National Park

Family/Genus	Species	Substratum*	Study Sites**	Collections Examined (PAN No.)
1	2	3	4	5
Candelariaceae				
Candelaria	*C. concolor*	C	1	28389
Chrysothricaceae				
Chrysothrix	*C. candelaris*	C	2, 5, 7, 8, 9	28671, 28672, 28750, 28751, 28752
	C. chlorina	S	1	28501
Cladoniaceae				
Cladonia	*C. ceratophylla*	T	4	28804
	C. chlorophaea	T	3	28648
	C. coniocraea	T	1	28557
	C. glauca	T	2	28797
	C. pyxidata	T	9	28649
	C. uncialis	T	3, 5, 6, 7	28800, 28801, 28802, 28803
Collemataceaer				
Collema	*C. coccophorum*	T	2, 5, 6, 9	28678, 28679, 28680, 28725
	C. polycarpon	C	1	28661
Leptogium	*L. asiaticum*	C	1, 4	28728, 28729
	L. burgessii	T	9	28695
	L. subtile	C	7	28731
Graphidaceae				
Graphis	*G. arecae*	C	1	28561
Hymeneliaceae				
Aspicilia	*A. calcarea*	S	9	28906
Lecanoraceae				
Lecanora	*L. amorpha*	C	6	28884
	L. muralis	S	1	28559
	L. praeradiosa	C, T	2, 4, 8, 9	28888, 28889, 28890, 28891
Rhizoplaca	*R. chrysoleuca*	S	1	28451
	R. peltata	S	5	28901

(Table Contd...)

1	2	3	4	5
Lobariaceae				
Lobaria	*L. kurokawae*	C	1	28681
	L. meridionalis	C	2, 6	28663, 28664
	L. pseudopulmonaria	C	2, 4	28710, 28711
Sticta	*S. nylanderiana*	C	3	28765
Parmeliaceae				
Bulbothrix	*B. tabacina*	C	2	28792
Canomaculina	*C. subsumpta*	S	1	28511
	C. subtinctoria	C	4, 9	28855, 28856
Canoparmelia	*C. cinerascens*	C	1	28434
	C. crozalsiana	C	1	28658
	C. eruptens	C	1	28433
	C. texana	S	1	28398
Evernia	*E. divaricata*	C	1, 3, 4, 5, 7, 8, 9	28846, 28847, 28848, 28849, 28850, 28851, 28852
	E. prunastri	C	5	28842
Everniastrum	*E. billingsii*	C	1, 2, 6, 7, 9	28735, 28736, 28737, 28738, 28739
	E. cirrhatum	C	1	28544
	E. nepalense	C	1	28437
Flavoparmelia	*F. caperata*	C	2, 6, 7, 9	28683, 28684, 28706, 28707
Flavopunctelia	*F. soredica*	C	7	28704
Hypotrachyna	*H. brevirhiza*	C	1	28693
	H. flexilis	C	1	28377
	H. revolute	C	1	28350
Parmelia	*P. adaugescens*	C	3	28789
	P. marmariza	C	7	28794
Parmotrema	*P. austrosinense*	C	6	28654
	P. crinitum	C	1	28411
	P. cristiferum	C	5, 9	28868, 28869
	P. dilatatum	C	3	28861
	P. margaritatum	C	6	28755
	P. praesorediosum	C	1	28796

(Table Contd...)

1	2	3	4	5
	P. pseudocrinitum	C	1	28399
	P. pseudotinctorum	C	6	28859
	P. rava	C	7	28871
	P. saccatilobum	C	3	28864
	P. stuppeum	C	4	28865
	P. tinctorum	C	6	28795
Punctelia	*P. borreri*	C	9	28701
	P. neutralis	C, S	3, 5	28533, 28534
	P. rudecta	C	1, 6	28698, 28699
	P. subrudecta	C	1	28712
Rimelia	*R. reticulata*	C	1	28337
Usnea	*U. aciculifera*	C	1	28830
	U. austroindica	C	1	28546
	U. baileyi	C	2	28832
	U. fragilis	C	1	28441
	U. galbinifera	C	1	28545
	U.himalayana	C	7	28834
	U. longissima	C	2, 3, 5, 7, 8, 9	28812, 28813, 28814, 28815, 28821, 28822
	U. nepalensis	C	4, 6, 8	28826, 28827, 28828
	U. orientalis	C	7	28819
	U. perplexans	C	1	28549
	U. rigidula	C	8	28835
	U. robusta	C	1	28831
	U. rubicunda	C, S	4, 5, 6, 7, 8, 9	28835, 28836, 28837, 28838, 28839, 28840
	U. subsordida	C	1	28816
Xanthoparmelia	*X. tinctina*	S	1	28902
Peltigeraceae				
Peltigera	*P. canina*	T	3	28666
	P. horizontalis	T	1	28412
	P. polydactyla	T	1	28449
	P. praetextata	T, S	4, 7	28722, 28723

(Table Contd...)

1	2	3	4	5
Pertusariaceae				
Pertusaria	*P. leucosora*	S	2	28673
	P. pallidula	C	6, 7	28774, 28775
Physciaceae				
Buellia	*B. hemispherica*	S	1	28892
	B. indica	S	5	28885
Dirinaria	*D. applanata*	S	5	28903
Heterodermia	*H. angustiloba*	T, S	6, 8, 9	28782, 28783, 28784, 28785
	H. diademata	T	9	28659
	H. dissecta	S	4	28787
	H. isidiophora	S	6	28786
	H. leucomela	S	3, 8, 9	28717, 28718, 28719
	H. rubescens	S	9	28778
	H. speciosa	S	1	28445
Phaeophyscia	*P. ciliata*	S	1	28489
	P. hispidula	T, S	1, 2, 4, 6, 7	28744, 28745, 28746, 28747, 28748
	P. orbicularis	S	1	28388
	P. pyrrhophora	S	4	28772
Physcia	*P. abuensis*	C	1	28524
	P. caesia	S	1	28517
	P. clementei	C	1	28386
	P. crispula	C	1	28523
	P. dilatata	C	6	28896
	P. dubia	C	1	28510
	P. semipinnata	C	1	28352
	P. stellaris	C	7	28874
Pyxine	*P. berteriana*	C	3, 6, 7	28877, 28878, 28879
Porpidiaceae				
Porpidia	*P. albocaerulescens*	S	1	28904
Ramalinaceae				
Ramalina	*R. angulosa*	C	1	28335

(Table Contd...)

1	2	3	4	5
	R. pollinaria	C	1	28540
	R. roesleri	C	1	28373
	R. sinensis	C	1	28715
	R. subpussila	C	1	28448
Rhizocarpaceae				
Rhizocarpon	*R. confervoides*	S	4	28899
	R. geographicum	S	8	28893
	R. lindsayanum	S	1	28894
Stereocaulaceae				
Stereocaulon	*S. coniophyllum*	S	3	28685
	S. myriocarpum	S	1	28468
	S. piluliferum	S	9	28733
Teloschistaceae				
Caloplaca	*C. flavorubescens*	S	1	28556
Xanthoria	*X. candelaria*	C	6	28905
	X. elegans	S	1	28454
	X. parietina	S	3	28886
Thelotremataceae				
Diploschistes	*D. actinostomus*	S	1	29128
	D. scruposus	S	9	28897
Umbilicariaceae				
Lasallia	*L. pertusa*	S	3, 5, 8, 9	28647, 28658, 28659, 28660
Umbilicaria	*U. polyrhiza*	C	7	28790
	U. thamnodes	S	9	28762
Verrucariaceae				
Dermatocarpon	*D. miniatum*	S	1, 3, 5, 6, 7	28533, 28533, 28533, 28533, 28533, 28533
Staurothele	*S. clopima*	S	6	28642

* C = Corticolous, T = Terricolous, S = saxicolous

** 1 = Pairra, 2 = Nagtal, 3 = Baminidhaur, 4 = Semar, 5 = Bistoli, 6 = Kundaliyasain, 7 = Drunager, 8 = Sewachand, 9 = Tiprakharak

Semar (3500m): It is scrub meadows area with a flat table land dominated by *Cortia depressa* and carpet of various forbs. The area is boggy as one of the small streams flows through it (Kala et al. 1998). A total of fourteen species of lichens have been recorded from this site during the present study.

Bistoli (3500m): It is scrub meadows area with flat and less boulder area forming the central meadow. The eastern flank of this table land is bounded by a deep gorge which runs in North-South direction (Kala et al. 1998). A total of fourteen species of lichens have been recorded from this site during the present study.

Kundaliyasain (3500m): It is is scrub meadows area with a stable and flat area with deep soil located below Bistoli. This area along with Bistoli, Semar and Baminidhaur forms the central part of the park (Kala et al. 1998). A total of twenty two species of lichens have been recorded from this site during the present study.

Drunager (3550m): It is scrub meadows area with buttressed boulder area in the valley fanning out from the northern slope. The upper portion of the site is saucer shaped (Kala et al. 1998). A total of twenty species of lichens have been recorded from this site during the present study.

Sewachand (3600m): It is scrub meadows area full of boulders deposited by glacial outwash with very little soil. The regular inflow of boulders and silt causes instability. The river bed is about 500m long and 200m wide (Kala et al. 1998). A total of ten species of lichens have been recorded from this site during the present study.

Tiprakharak (3700m): It is scrub meadows area located close to the terminal moraine nearly 6 Km from Baminidhaur flanked by stunted birch forest. This site is unstable due to frequent avalanches (Kala et al. 1998). A total of twenty two species of lichens have been recorded from this site during the present study.

DISSCUSSION

The dominant family of lichens in the park is Parmeliaceae with fifty one species belonging to fourteen genera followed by Physciaceae with twenty three species belonging to six genera.

Majority of the lichen species are corticolous (76 species) followed by saxicolous lichens (37 species) and terricolous lichens (12 species). *Lecanora praeradiosa* is corticolous & terricolous, two lichen species namely *Punctelia neutralis, Usnea rubicunda* are corticolous & saxicolous and three lichen species namely *Peltigera praetextata, Heterodermia angustiloba, Pheophyscia hispidula* are terricolous & saxicolous. Out of the 79 corticolous lichen species, 22 have been recorded on angiospermous bark whereas 13 have been recorded on gymnospermous bark and the other 44 have been recorded on angiospermous & gymnospermous bark.

Majority of the lichenized fungi grow in foliose form (73 species) in NDBR followed by fruticose (35 species), crustose (16 species), leprose (2 species) and squamulose (2 species) growth forms.

REFERENCES

Awasthi DD (2007) A Compendium of the Macrolichens from India, Nepal and Sri Lanka. Bishen Singh Mahendra Pal Singh, Dehra Dun, India.

Kala CP (1998) Ecology and Conservation of Alpine Meadows in the Valley of Flowers National Park, Garhwal Himalaya. Ph.D. Thesis, Forest Research Institute, Dehradun, India.

Kala CP (1999) Phenology of Alpine Plants in the Valley of Flowers National Park and Hemkund, Western Himalaya. The Indian Forester 125(6): 581-590.

Kala CP (2004) The Valley of Flowers – Myth and Reality. International Book Distributors, Dehradun, India

Kala CP, Rawat GS, Uniyal VK. (1998) Ecology and Conservation of the Valley of Flowers National Park, Garhwal Himalaya. Wildlife Institute of India, Dehradun, India.

Mueller GM, Gerald FB, Mercedes SF (2004) Biodiversity of Fungi – Inventory and Monitoring Methods. Elsevier Academic Press, Burlington, MA 01803, USA pp. 128-158.

Smythe FS (1938) The Valley of Flowers. London.

Wadhwa BM, Rao RR, Hajra PK (1987) Botany of the Valley of Flowers National Park and its Environs. *Bull Bot Sur India* 29(1-4): 129-175.

White FJ, James PW (1985). A New Guide to the Microchemical Techniques for the Identification of Lichen Substances. *Bull Brit Lich Soc* 57 (Suppl.): 1-41.

Pages: 41-77

BIODIVERSITY, BIOTECHNOLOGY AND ENVIRONMENTAL CONSERVATION

Edited by: Dr. Pawan Kumar 'Bharti'; Mr. Govinda Bhandari

ISBN: 978-93-5056-750-0

Edition: 2015

Published by: Discovery Publishing House Pvt. Ltd., New Delhi (India)

CHAPTER 4

Floristic Diversity Along an Altitudinal Gradient in the Central Part of Himachal Pradesh, North West Himalaya

Sakshi Bhandari Rana[1*]; Man S. Rana[2] and S.S. Samant[3]

ABSTRACT

In the present chapter 620 species of vascular plants i.e., Angiosperms (113 families, 332 genera and 548 species), Gymnosperms (02 families, 05 genera and 06 species) and Pteridophytes (16 families, 26 genera and 66 species) were recorded from Chailchowk-Rohanda-Kamrunag Area (CRKA). The species have been analysed for altitudinal distribution, habitat preference, nativity and endemism. The altitudinal zone 1801-2800m was the richest in terms of maximum number of species (i.e., 512 spp.), native (237 spp.), near endemic (131 spp.) and endemic (02 spp.) species.292 species were native to the Himalayan Region, remaining species were non-natives. 02 species were endemic and 137 species near endemic to the Indian Himalayan Region.

1 Department of Botany, Government College, Kullu.

2 Department of Botany, Jawahar Lal Nehru Government College, Haripur, Kullu, HP, (India).

3 G.B. Pant Institute of Himalayan Environment and Development, Himachal Unit, Mohal - Kullu, HP, (India).

A total of 455 species were quantified in CRKA, of which 50.6% species were native to the Himalaya. 0.43% was endemic and 23.5% were near endemic to the IHR. This study can form the baseline data for developing the conservation policy for Chailchowk-Rohanda-Kamrunag Area (CRKA) of Mandi district.

Key words: Floristic Diversity, Altitudinal Gradient, Nativity, Endemism, Conservation, Himachal Pradesh

INTRODUCTION

Biogeographical variation in the floristic diversity is critical to the understanding and conservation of overall biological diversity and hence, its evaluation and/or assessment become all the more important in the Himlayan hotspot of biodiversity. The Himalayashows the largest altitudinal gradients in the world, from 60m amsl at the gangetic plains to some of the world's largest mountain peaks above 8000m (Pant, 2003). The distribution of plants is determined by various climatic variables like rainfall, temperature, soil conditions, moisture, nutrients, historic events, palaeoclimatic changes, interaction with fauna, competition between tree species for crown and root space as well as human influence (Veenendaal *et al.*, 1996). Among these, altitudinal gradient is well known to be one of the decisive factors shaping the spatial patterns of species diversity (Lieberman *et al.*, 1996, Lomolino, 2001). Moreover, a large environmentalvariation within a small geographical area makes altitudinal gradients ideal for investigating several ecological and biogeographical hypotheses (Korner, 1998).

At global scale, the majority of studies based on altitudinal gradient have focused on species richness (Lieberman *et al.*,1996; Vazquez & Givnish, 1998; Grytnes, 2003), elevational zonation of vegetation types (Fram & Gradstein,1991) and environmental gradients *viz.*, climate, productivity, biotic interaction, habitat heterogeneity and history (Givnish, 1999; Willig *et al.*, 2003; Currie & Francis, 2004; Gonzalez-Espinosa *et al.*, 2004;) as part of the efforts to understand the ecosystem effects on biodiversity and conservation (Vetaas & Grytnes,2002). In the Himalaya, an elevational transect includes vegetation from tropical monsoon forest to alpine meadow and scrub, constituting an unusually extensive elevational and vegetational gradients (Singh & Singh, 1992). The studies on altitudinal gradient of floristic diversity are relatively few in the Himalaya (Bhattarai & Vetaas, 2003).

In the Indian Himalayan Region (IHR), a few studies on the altitudinal gradient for IHR taking different factors into consideration (Kharkwal *et al.*, 2005; Behera & Kushwaha, 2007; Chawla *et al.*, 2008; *etc.*) are available.But, these are mostly confined to the West Himalaya, putting directly an emphasis on the importance for such type of studies in other parts of IHR including the Himachal Himalaya. The State Himachal Pradesh is very well known for its typical topography, large altitudinal range, diverse habitats, representative, natural, unique and socio-economically important biodiversity is also facing high pressures. A perusal of literature indicated that except for a few studies (Chawla *et al.*, 2008) focused on altitudinal gradient from ecological aspect in Himachal Himalaya, no research has been conducted on assessment of floristic diversity along an altitudinal gradient particularly in the central part of Himachal Pradesh which is floristically very rich and varied. The review of literature indicated that in the Chailchowk-Rohanda-Kamrunag Area (CRKA) of Mandi district, studies have not been conducted so far on the assessment of floristic diversity.Therefore, this study has been focused on the assessment of vegetation along an altitudinal gradient to understand the status of the floristic diversity.

STUDY AREA

The study area (31° 27.79′-31°33.98′N Latitudes and 76° 59.46′-77° 03.21′ E Longitudes) comprises the stretch of the district from Chailchowk to Kamrunag via Ruhanda (Fig. 4.1). The area covered is approximately 558 Km^2. It is a mountainous region with acute unevenness of terrain from 1300m amsl at Chailchowk to 3050m amsl at Kamrunag peak. The study area falls in Nachan and Suket forest divisions of Mandi district, which is bounded in the north by Kangra district, in the east by Kullu district, in the south by Shimla and Solan districts and in the west by Bilaspur and Hamirpur districts. Population in this area lives in small villages and houses scattered across the hills and valleys. The representative villages of the study area are Ratheri, Dhagwain, Matogalu, Kutachi, Sanjala, Badhu, Bharmot, Shillnu, Shakoor, Ruhanda and Khanad. The geology of the area comprises of Granite Gneiss, Leucogranite, Phyllite, Minor Limestone, Pebbly Quartzite, Slate, Grit, Streaky and Banded Gneisses. The area has a sub-tropical/mild temperate climate in the Chailchowk region which changes to typical temperate and sub-alpine climate types as one move to Kamrunag region. Altogether, the climate is temperate with well-marked three seasons viz., summer (mid April-mid June), rainy (monsoon) (mid June-September) and winter (October-March) seasons. The higher reaches of Rohanda and Kamrunag hills get precipitation in the form of snow during the winter season. Climatically the area is unique; the temperature ranges between -4°C to 38°C.

MATERIALS AND METHODS

Survey, Sampling and Identification of the Species

Surveys were conducted between 1300-3050m *amsl*in CRKA in all the seasons of the years from 2006-2008. The rapid sampling was done for floristic inventory. The samples of the vascular plants were collected and for each species, information on altitudinal range, habit, habitat (s), *etc.* was gathered. The species were identified with the help of flora (Chowdhery & Wadhwa, 1984; Aswal & Mehrotra, 1994; Dhaliwal & Sharma, 1999 and Singh & Rawat, 2000). All the identified species were listed and analyzed for floristic diversity following Samant *et al.*, (1998).

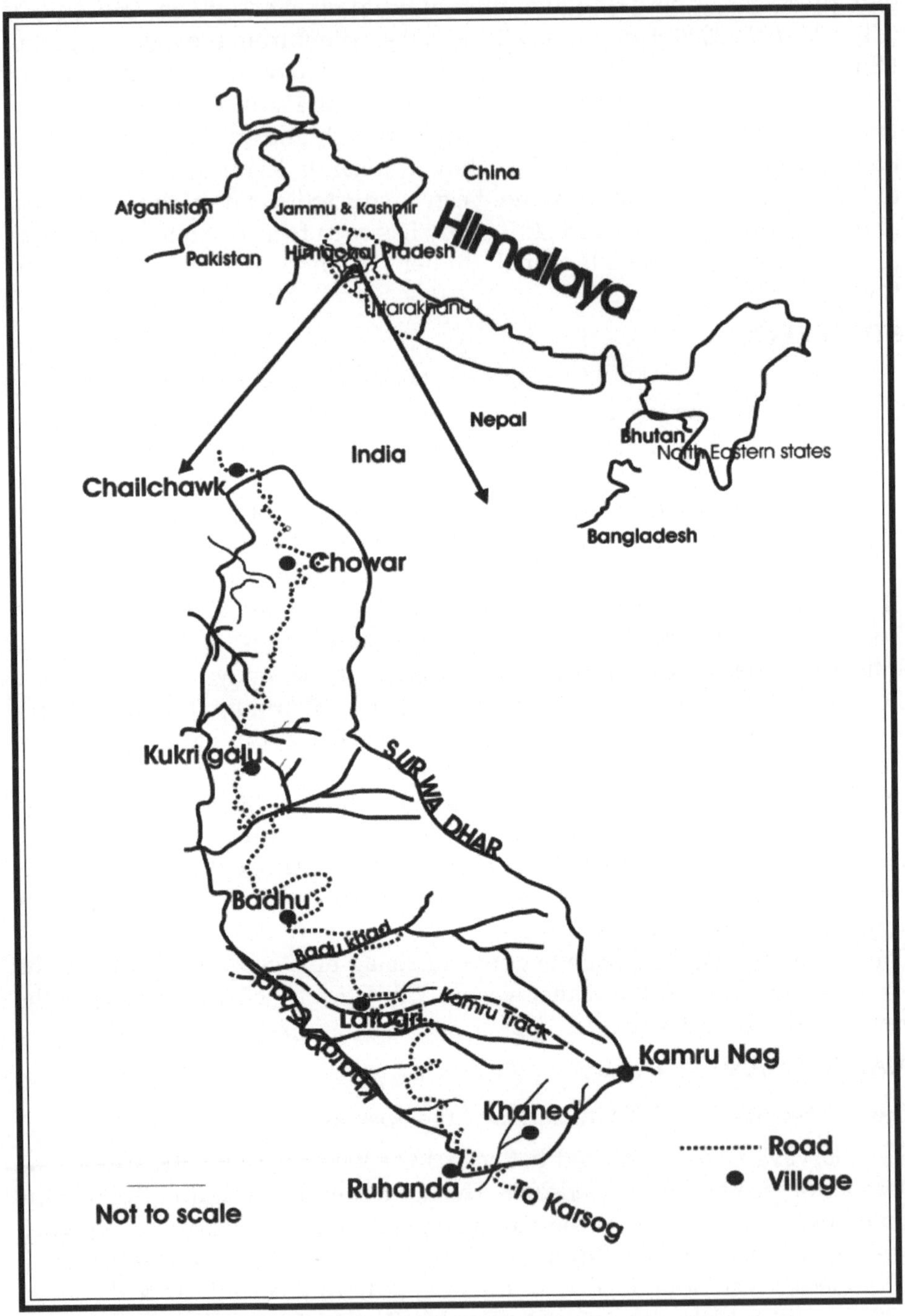

Fig. 4.1: Map of the Study Area

Nativity of the species indicates first record/origin of the species (Anonymous, 1883-1970; Samant *et al.*, 1998). The nativity of the species has been identified following Anonymous (1883-1970), and Samant *et al.* (2000). The species having their origin from Himalayan region have been considered as natives. In case of pteridophytes the species distributed in the Himalayan Region only, have been considered as native to the Himalayan region whereas remaining species have been considered as non-natives.

Endemism encompasses taxonomic units of any rank or taxa usually isolated by geographical, ecological and temporal barriers (Nayar, 1996). Endemism of the species has been identified based on distribution of the species (Samant *et al.*, 1998, 2000). The species restricted to the IHR have been considered as endemic whereas those with extended distribution to neighbouring countries/states considered as near endemic. The distribution pattern of the native and endemic species has been identified based on the survey and occurrence of the species (Samant *et al.*, 2001).

RESULTS

Species Diversity

A total of 620 species of vascular plants *i.e.*, Angiosperms (113 families, 332 genera and 548 species), Gymnosperms (02 families, 05 genera and 06 species) and Pteridophytes (16 families, 26 genera and 66 species) were recorded from CRKA. Of the total species, 75species were trees, 105 shrubs, 374 herbs and 66 pteridophytes (Table 4.1).

Table 4.1: Taxonomic Description of Floristic Diversity in CRKA

Taxonomic Group	Families	Genera	Species	Herbs	Shrubs	Trees
Angiosperms	113	332	548	374	105	69
Gymnosperms	02	05	06	–	–	06
Pteridophytes	16	26	66	66	–	–
Total	**131**	**363**	**620**	**440**	**105**	**75**

Among the angiosperm families, 113 families were found in the altitudinal zone 1300-1800m, while 103 families in the zone 1801-2800m and 60 families above 2800mwere recorded. Thirty four angiospermic families had wide range of altitudinal distribution *i.e.*, they were found throughout the study area starting from the lowest altitude of 1300m to the upper limit of the study area *i.e.*, 3050m. Asteraceae (51 spp.); Poaceae (36 spp.); Lamiaceae (35 spp.); Rosaceae (29 spp.); Fabaceae (24 spp.); Orchidaceae (19 spp.); Ranunculaceae (18 spp.); Scrophulariaceae, Apiaceaeand Cyperaceae (13 spp., each); Urticaceae (12 spp.); Polygonaceae and Moraceae (10 spp., each) were recorded with major contribution to the flora of the present study area. Thirty six families *i.e.*,Agavaceae, Alliaceae, Apocynaceae, Aristolochiaceae,

Begoniaceae, Bombacaceae, Cannabaceae, Coriariaceae, Corylaceae, Cuscutaceae, Ehretiaceae, Grossulariaceae, Haemodoraceae, Hippocastanaceae, Juglandaceae, Lardizabalaceae, Linaceae, Loganiaceae, Loranthaceae, Lythraceae, Melastomataceae, Myricaceae, Myrsinaceae, Orobranchaceae, Papaveraceae, Parnassiaceae, Phytolaccaceae, Podophyllaceae, Punicaceae, Sabiaceae, Santalaceae, Saururaceae, Schisandraceae, Symplocaceae, Thymelaeaceae and Trillidiaceaewere recorded to be monotypic. Among genera, 276 genera were found in the altitudinal zone 1300-1800m, 277 genera in the 1801-2800m zone and 117 genera >2800m zone. *Ficus* (09 spp.); *Carex* and *Desmodium* (07 spp., each); *Artemisia, Hypericum, Impatiens, Clematis, Rubus, Persicaria* and *Viburnum* (05 spp., each); were the dominant genera. Eight (08) genera *viz., Arabidopsis, Capsella, Cynoglossum, Silene, Mentha, Leptodermis, Valeriana* and *Asplenium* showed distribution throughout the study area *i.e.,* from 1300-3050m. Among gymnosperms, only 01 family was recorded in the zone 1300-1800m, 02 families, each in the zones, 1801-2800m and >2800m, respectively. Only 01 gymnospermic family showed a wide range of altitudinal distribution *viz.,* Pinaceae was found from 1300-3050m. The families Pinaceae (05 spp.) and Genus, *Pinus* (02 spp.) were dominant. Among the genera, 02 genera were distributed in the zone 1300-1800m, 05 genera in 1801-2800m and 02 genera >2800m zones. Taxaceae was the monotypic family. Among the Pteridophytes, 12 families were recorded in the zone 1300-1800m, 15 families in the zone 1801-2800m and 13 families >2800m zone. Six (06)pteridophytic families were found throughout the study area. The families, Polypodiaceae (14 spp.); Dryopteridaceae (11 spp.); Athyriaceae (08 spp.); Aspleniaceae (05 spp.) and Pteridaceae (05 spp.) and genera, *Polystichum* (07 spp.); *Lepisorus* (06 spp);*Asplenium*and*Athyrium* (05 spp., each) and*Adiantum, Dryopteris, Polypodioides*and *Pteris* (04 spp., each) were species rich (Appendix).Nineteen (19) pteridophytic genera were restricted between 1300-1800m, 24 genera in 1801-2800m and 14 genera >2800m zones. Only 01 genus*viz., Asplenium* was found throughout the study area. Blechnaceae, Botrychiaceae, Cryptogrammaceae, Onocleaceae and Selaginaceae were the monotypic familiesamong pteridophytes.

ALTITUDINAL DISTRIBUTION

The altitudinal distribution of the floristic diversity has been presented (Fig. 4.2). Maximum number of species (*i.e.,* 512 spp.) was recorded in the altitudinal zone, 1801-2800m. The diversity decreased with the increasing altitude. The representative species of altitudinal zone, 1300-1800m were *Pinus roxburghii, Myrica esculenta, Quercus leucotrichophora, Quercus glauca, Rhododendron arboreum, Daphniphyllum himalayense, Berberis lycium, Carissa opaca, Flemingia strobilifera, Cinnamomun tamala, Zanthoxylum armatum,Randia tetrasperma,Vitex negundo, Dioscorea bulbifera, Ajuga bracteosa, Urena lobata* and

Viola canescens; altitudinal zone, 1801-2800m were *Cedrus deodara, Alnus nitida, Cornus capitata, Cornus macrophylla, Neolitsea pallens, Pinus wallichiana, Quercus floribunda, Picea smithiana,Ilex excelsa,Carpinus viminea,Prinsepia utilis, Asparagus racemosus, Berberis aristata, Skimmia laureola, Daphne papyracea, Hedychium spicatum,Botrychium ternatum, Habenaria intermedia*and the altitudinal zone >2800m were *Dactylorhiza hatagirea, Taxus baccata* subsp. *wallichiana,Acer acuminatum, Abies pindrow, Delphinium vestitum, Quercus semecarpifolia, Podophyllum hexandrum, Polygonatum cirrhifolium, Corydalis cornuta, Impatiens glandulifera, Malaxis muscifera, Potentilla atrosanguinea* and *Viburnum cotinifolium.*

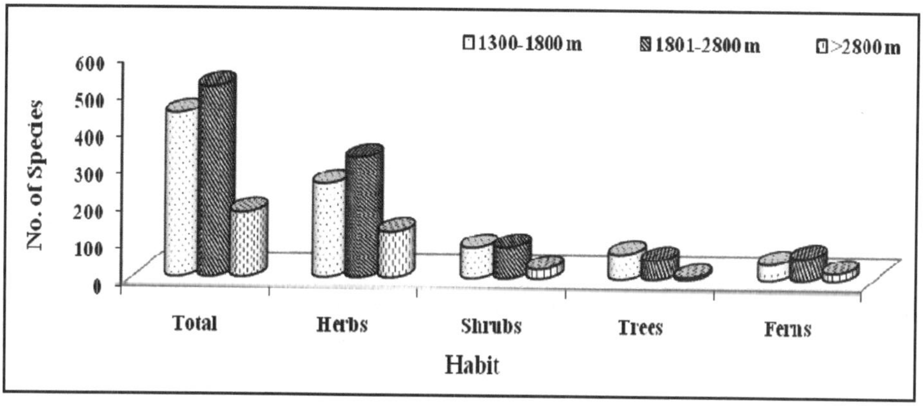

Fig. 4.2: Altitudinal Distribution of Vascular Plants in CRKA

Some of the species had wide range of distribution viz., *Arabidopsis thaliana, Capsella bursa-pastoris, Cynoglossum glochidiatum, Silene conoidea, Mentha longifolia, Leptodermis lanceolata, Valeriana jatamansi* and *Asplenium dalhousiae* which were found throughout the study area.

NATIVITY AND ENDEMISM

In general, in the Chailchowk-Rohanda-Kamrunag Area (CRKA), of the total 620 species recorded, 292 species were native to the Himalayan Region, remaining species were non-natives. 02 species were endemic and 137 species near endemic to the Indian Himalayan Region. A total of 455 species were quantified in the CRKA of which 50.6% species were native to the Himalaya. 0.43% was endemic and 23.5% were near endemic to the IHR.

The altitudinal distribution of the native, non-native and endemic species have been presented in Fig. 4.3. Maximum number of native (237 spp.), nearendemic (131 spp.) and endemic (02 spp.) specieswere recorded in the altitudinal zone 1801-2800m, followed by 1300-1800m zone whereasmaximum number of non-native species (*i.e.*, 275 spp.) were recorded in the altitudinal zone 1300-1800m and the number of non-natives decreased with the increasing altitude.

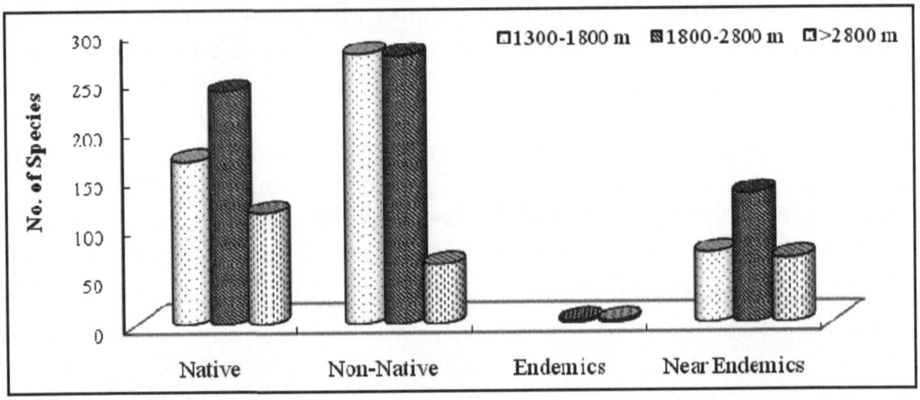

Fig. 4.3: Altitudinal Distribution of Native, Non-native, Endemicand Near Endemic Species in CRKA

The reported endemic species were *Pimpinella acuminata* and *Scrophularia himalensis* and the not able near endemics were *Ajuga brachystemon, Berberis lycium, Bergenia ligulata, Cinnamomum tamala, Cirsium wallichii, Sarcococca saligna, Schisandra grandiflora, Quercus floribunda, Habenaria edgeworthii, Rhamnus purpureus, Abies pindrow, Picea smithiana, Skimmia laureola, Hedychium spicatum* and *Viola canescens*. Among the pteridophytes, *Athyrium rupicola, A. rubricaule* and *Lepisorus kashyapii* were near endemics. The notable native species were *Acer acuminatum, Chaerophyllum villosum, Begonia picta, Cornus capitata, Cinnamomum tamala, Persea duthiei, Dactylorhiza hatagirea, Roscoea alpina, Cedrus deodara, Taxus baccata* subsp. *wallichiana*. *Ageratum conzoides* and *Lantana camara* were the two non-native plants which were found dominant in 1300-1800m zone, *Cynoglossum glochidiatum*and*Hackelia uncinata* were the non-native plants dominant in 1801-2800m zone and above.

DISCUSSION

Floristic Inventory

In the Indian Himalayan Region, a lot of work has been done on the flroa at district and state level. However, focused studies on the floristic diversity rich areas are meager and require detailed investigatons (Samant *et al.*, 2001). In view of the above fact, CRKA which represents sub-tropical, temperate and sub-alpine vegetation was selected and explored for the floristic diversity. The present investigation recorded 620 species of vascular plants *i.e.*, Angiosperms (113 families, 332 genera and 548 species), Gymnosperms (02 families, 05 genera and 06 species) and Pteridophytes (16 families, 26 genera and 66 species) for the first time from the area. Occurrence of 620 species of vascular plants indicatedthat the environmental conditions are favourable for the growth and development of the floristic elements. Number of species are comparatively lesser than earlier reported in Flora of Kullu (930 spp.), Flora of Lahaul & Spiti (985 spp.), Flora of Great Himalayan

National Park (GHNP) (832 spp.) and Flora of Mandi Forest Division (1027 spp.).The number of species recorded in a comparatively small geographical area indicated comparatively high richness of floristic diversity in the area. Asteraceae, Poaceae and Lamiaceae were the dominant families.Asteraceae is also the most dominant family in Lahaul-Spiti, Himachal Pradesh, high altitude regions of western Himalaya and Bhabha valley (Chowdhery & Wadhwa, 1984; Aswal & Mehrotra, 1994; Chawla *et al.*, 2008)whereas *Ficus, Carex* and *Desmodium* were the dominant genera. Dominance of these genera has been also reported by other workers (Aswal & Mehrotra, 1994; Dhaliwal & Sharma, 1999 and Singh & Rawat, 2000).

The mid altitudinal range (*i.e.*, 1801-2800m) represented the highest species richness(*i.e.*, 512spp.). Similar trends have also been reported from Grytnes (2003) in other temperate forests.The distribution of species richness along elevational gradient is governed by a series of interacting biological andclimatic factors. The reduction in species in higher altitudinal zone could be attributed to loss of habitat diversity (Bhattarai & Vetaas, 2003) andeco-physiological constraints such as reduced growing season, low temperature and low ecosystem productivity in high elevation (Korner, 1998) and of lower altitudinal zone to anthropogenic disturbances. The number of species was less in the lower altitudinal zone in CRKA due to intense agriculture and other anthropogenic pressures. Moreover, the mid altitudinal zone favoured co-existense of a large number of species which were common to low as well as high altitudinal zones (Lomolino, 2001). Thirty four angiosperm families had wide range of altitudinal distribution indicating the adaptive nature of different families with increasing altitudes.

NATIVITY AND ENDEMISM

In Himachal Pradesh, 90.6% species are natives, leaving 9.4% of the total species to be exotic in comparison to just 5% exotics in the year 1987-1988, directly implying that exotics have doubled their population in a time span of 15 years or so (Kohli *et al.*, 2004). The occurrence of present share of exotics and their naturalization cannot be considered safe for native and endemic flora from ecological and socio-economic perspectives. Though the protected areas are managed for preservation of native fauna and flora and management practices favour the long term sustainability/health of these systems but the unprotected areas are more prone to invasions. Presence of non-natives in India and the Himalaya is known, which is largely attributed to migration over geological time periods.

The tropical, sub-tropical and temperate forests support many resources to human population. Hence, the degree of anthropogenic pressure is very high in the forests, compared to the sub-alpine and alpine area of the IHR. This has lead decrease in population of the native and endemic species.The study area has 50.6% native species, 23.5% near endemic and 0.43% endemicspecies. Representation of 49.4% non-native species and relatively low percentage of endemic species in the CRKA indicated the high degree of disturbance because of the high anthropogenic pressures.Also, the high percentage of non-native species indicated habitat alterations and changes in vegetation pattern.The high percentage of the native and endemic species at higher elevations is due to low anthropogenic pressure and severe climatic conditions compared to the mid and lower elevations where high anthropogenic pressure and mild climatic conditions support the speciation of the non-native species. Hence keeping in view the vast floristic diversity and native and endemic species this study would help for developing management plan for the Chailchowk- Rohanda- Kamrunag area of Mandi district.

APPENDIX

Diversity, Distribution, Nativity and Endemism of Vascular Plants in CRKA, Mandi district

Family/Taxa	Local Name	AR(m)	Habitat/s	HF	Nativity	End
Angiosperms						
Acanthaceae						
*Adhatoda zeylanica*Medik.	Basunti	1300-1500	2, 4	Sh	As Trop	
Aechmanthera gossypina (Nees)Nees	–	1500-2200	1, 2, 9	Sh	Ind Or	–
Barleria cristata L.	–	1300-2000	1, 2, 3, 4	H	Ind Or Burma	–
Dicliptera roxburghiana Nees	–	1300-2300	1, 2	H	Ind Or	–
Goldfussia dalhousiana Nees	–	1300-2100	1, 3, 4	H	Reg Himal	–
Justicia japonica Don	–	1300-2000	1, 8	H	As et Afr Trop	–
Strobilanthes atropurpureus Nees	Mashna	1300-2400	1, 2, 3, 5, 7	H	Reg Himal	NE
S. wallichii Nees	–	2000-3050	1, 7	H	Reg Himal	NE
Aceraceae						
Acer oblongum Wall.	Parange	1300-1800	1, 7	T	Reg Himal	–
A. acuminatum Wall. ex D.Don	–	2600-3050	1, 7	T	Reg Himal	NE
A. cappadocicum Gled.	–	2000-2800	1, 3	T	As Min	–
Achyranthaceae						
Achyranthes aspera L.	Putkanda	1300-2500	1, 2, 3, 5	H	As Trop	–
A. bidentata Bl.	Putkanda	1300-2000	1, 2, 5, 9	H	Reg Trop	–
Agavaceae						
Agave angustifolia Haw.	–	1300-1600	1, 2, 4	Sh	Mexic	–
Amaranthaceae						
Cyathula capitata Moq.	–	1600-2000	1, 4	H	Reg Himal	–
C. tomentosa (Roth) Moq.	–	1300-2200	2, 3	H	Reg Himal	–

(Contd...)

Family/Taxa	Local Name	AR(m)	Habitat/s	HF	Nativity	End
Alliaceae						
Allium rubellum Bieb.	–	1300-1700	1, 4	H	Europe Oriens Sibir	–
Anacardiaceae						
Pistacia integerrima Sw.	Kakare	1300-2200	2, 3	T	Reg Himal Aegypt Persia	–
Rhus cotinus L.	Chulli	1300-1800	1, 2, 3	Sh	Reg Medit Oriens Reg Himal China	–
R. javanica L.	Titri	1300-2200	1, 2, 3, 4	T	Reg Himal China Ins Sandvic	–
R. wallichii Hk. f.	–	1300-2200	1, 8	T	Reg Himal	NE
Apiaceae						
*Bupleurum candollii*Wall. ex DC.	–	2800-3050	1, 4	H	Reg Himal	NE
B. falcatum L.	–	1600-3050	1, 3, 4	H	Europe Oriens As Bor Reg Himal	–
B. tenue Buch. – Ham. ex D. Don	–	1300-2200	1, 2, 3, 4	H	Reg Himal	–
Centella asiatica (L.) Urb.	Brahmi	1300-1600	2, 4	H	Reg Trop et Sub Trop	–
Chaerophyllum reflexum Lindl.	Khelti	2100-3050	3, 6	H	Reg Himal	–
C. villosum Wall. ex DC.	–	2500-3050	1, 4, 6	H	Reg Himal	NE
Heracleum candicans L.	Badiyach	1800-2800	1, 8	H	Reg Himal	–
Hydrocotyle javanica Thunb.	–	1300-2000	1, 5	H	Java	–
Pimpinella acuminata (Edgew.) Cl.	–	2000-3050	1, 5	H	Reg Himal	E
P. diversifolia DC.	–	1500-2500	2, 3, 4, 5	H	Reg Himal	–
Sanicula elata Buch.-Ham. ex D.Don	–	2500-3050	1, 2	H	Europe As Bor Afr Austr	–
Selinum tenuifolium Wall.	Bhutkeshi	2800-3050	1, 2	H	Reg Himal	NE
S. vaginatum (Edgew.) Cl.	–	2900-3050	1, 6	H	Reg Himal	–
Apocynaceae						
*Carissa opaca*Stapf ex Haines	Garne	1300-1600	1, 2, 4	Sh	Reg Himal	–
Aquifoliaceae						
Ilex dipyrena Wall.	Tarkuch	2000-2800	1, 2, 4, 7	T	Reg Himal	–
I. excelsa (Wall.) Hk.	–	1600-2400	1, 2	T	Reg Himal	–
Araceae						
*Acorus calamus*L.	Bauch	1300-2200	5	H	Reg Bor Temp	–

(Contd...)

Family/Taxa	Local Name	AR(m)	Habitat/s	HF	Nativity	End
Arisaema intermedium Bl.	–	2100-3050	1, 3	H	Reg Himal	NE
*A. jacqmontii*Bl.	–	2200-3050	1, 2, 3, 4, 5, 6, 7, 8	H	Reg Himal	NE
A. tortuosum (Wall.) Schott	Biskaphar	1300-2200	1, 2, 3, 4, 5	H	Reg Himal	–
Colocasia affinis Schott	–	1300-2000	1, 2, 3	H	Reg Himal	–
Araliaceae						
Aralia cachemirica Decne.	–	2500-3050	2, 3	H	Reg Himal	NE
Hedera nepalensis Koch.	Mathodi, Grumru	1300-2500	1, 2, 3, 5, 7	Sh	Europe Afr Bor As Temp	–
Aristolochiaceae						
Aristolochia dilatata Br.	–	1800-2500	1, 2, 3	Sh	Ind Or	–
Asclepiadaceae						
Cryptolepis buchananii Roem. & Schultes	–	1300-1800	1, 3	Sh	Ind Or	–
Marsdenia roylei Wt.	–	1800-2500	2, 5	H	Reg Himal	NE
Asparagaceae						
Asparagus filicinus Buch.-Ham. ex D.Don	Sansarpali	2000-2800	1, 3	H	Reg Himal Burma	–
A. racemosus Willd.	Sansarpali	1300-1700	1, 2	H	Ind Or Afr TropAustr	–
Asteraceae						
*Achillea millefolium*L.	Fye	1800-3050	1, 2, 3, 6	H	Europe	–
Ageratum conyzoides L.	–	1300-2000	1, 2, 4, 9	H	Reg Trop	–
Ainsliaea aptera DC.	Durwa	2000-3050	1, 2, 3	H	Reg Himal	NE
A. latifolia (D. Don) Sch.–Bip.	–	2000-3050	1, 2	H	Reg Himal	–
Anaphalis busua DC.	–	2000-2600	1, 2, 4, 7	H	Reg Himal	–
A. contorta Hk.f.	–	1800-2700	1, 2, 3, 4	H	Reg Himal	–
A. triplinervis (Sims.) Cl.	–	1500-3050	1, 2, 3	H	Reg Himal	–
Arctium lappa L.	–	2000-3050	6, 8	H	Europe	–
Artemisia japonica Thunb.	–	1300-1600	1, 2, 4	H	Japan	–
A. nilagirica (Cl.) Pamp.	Kubsh	1300-2700	1, 2, 3, 5, 7, 9	H	Reg Temp Bor	–
A. parviflora Roxb. ex D.Don	–	1300-2200	1, 2	H	Ind Or Burma	–
A. roxburghiana Bess.	Drubaha	2000-3050	1, 2	H	Reg Himal	NE
A. vestita Wall. ex DC.	Kubsh	1800-3050	2, 4	H	Reg Himal China	–
Aster himalaicus Cl.	–	2000-2800	3, 8	H	Reg Himal	NE
*A.peduncularis*Wall. ex Nees	–	2000-3050	1, 7	H	Reg Himal	NE

(Contd...)

Family/Taxa	Local Name	AR(m)	Habitat/s	HF	Nativity	End
Bidens biternata Merr. & Sherf.	–	1300-1600	2, 4	H	Reg Trop	–
B. pilosa L.	–	1500-2200	1, 2, 3, 4, 9	H	Ind Occ Am Austr	–
Blumea laciniata (Roxb.) DC.	–	1300-2000	2, 4	H	Ind Or Malaya China	–
Carpesium pedunculosum Wall. ex DC.	–	2000-3050	1, 2, 3, 4, 6, 9	H	Europe As Temp	–
Centipeda minima (L.) A.Br. & Asch.	–	1300-1700	1, 2, 4	H	As et Austr Trop Ins Pacif	–
Cicerbita macrorhiza (Royle) Beauv.	–	2100-3050	1, 3	H	Reg Himal	–
Cirsium wallichii DC.	–	1800-2500	1, 2, 3, 4, 5, 6	H	Reg Himal	NE
Conyza stricta Willd.	–	1300-2200	1, 2, 4	H	Ind Or Afr Trop	–
Cyathocline purpurea Kuntz	–	1300-1800	2, 5	H	Ind Or	–
Erigeron bonariensis L.	–	1300-1700	1, 2, 5, 9	H	Am Austr	–
E. canadensis L.	–	1300-2000	2, 4, 5, 9	H	Amphig	–
E. karvinskianus DC.	–	1600-2200	2, 7	H	Maxic	–
E. multiradiatus (DC.) Cl.	–	1300-2200	1, 4	H	Reg Himal	–
Eupatorium adenophorum Spreng.	–	1300-2200	1, 2, 4	Sh	Jameic Maxic	–
Galinsoga ciliata Blake	–	1300-1600	2, 4	H	Am Bor	–
G. parviflora Cav.	–	1500-2500	4, 5	H	Mexic North Am	–
Gerbera gossypina (Royle) Beauv.	–	1300-2500	1, 2, 3, 4, 9	H	Reg Himal	NE
Gnaphalium affine D.Don	–	1900-2600	1, 2, 3, 4, 9	H	Reg Magell	–
G. hypoleucum DC.	Brunn	1300-2200	1, 2, 3, 4, 9	H	As Trop	–
G. luteoalbum L.	Gorbagare	1300-2500	2, 8	H	Cosmop	–
Inula cappa DC.	Gadush	1600-2500	1, 2	H	Reg Himal JavaChina	–
I. cuspidata Hk.f.	–	1300-1600	1, 2	Sh	Reg Himal	–
Lactuca longifolia DC.	–	1600-2500	1, 4	H	Reg Himal	–
Myriactisnepalensis Less.	–	1800-3050	1, 3, 4, 5, 7, 9	H	Reg Himal As Centr	–
Prenanthes brunoniana Wall. ex DC.	Dudhli	1500-3050	1	H	Reg Himal	NE
Rhynchospermum verticillatum Rein.	–	1800-2800	1, 5, 6, 7	H	Java	–
Saussurea heteromalla (D.Don) Hand.-Mazz.	–	2200-2800	2, 4	H	Reg Himal	NE

(Contd...)

Family/Taxa	Local Name	AR(m)	Habitat/s	HF	Nativity	End
Senecio chrysanthemoides DC.	–	2500-3050	3, 7	H	Reg Himal	–
S. graciliflora DC	–	2000-3050	1, 2	H	Reg Himal	NE
S. nudicaulis Buch.-Ham.	–	1500-2100	1, 2, 4	H	Reg Himal	–
S. rufinervis DC.	–	2000-3050	1, 3	H	Reg Himal	NE
Solidago virga- aurea L.	–	1800-2800	1, 2, 3, 4	H	Reg Bor Temp	–
Sonchus asper Hill.	–	1300-2200	1, 2, 4	H	Cosmop	–
S. oleraceus L.	–	1300-1800	2, 4	H	Cosmop	–
Tagetes minuta L.	–	1500-1800	2, 3, 4, 5	H	Am Trop	–
Taraxacum officinalis Webb.	–	1300-2800	1, 2, 4, 5, 7	H	Am Trop	–
Balsaminaceae						
Impatiens amphorata Edgew.	–	1300-1800	2, 5	H	Reg Himal	–
I. glandulifera Royle	–	2200-3050	1, 2, 3 6, 7	H	Reg Himal	–
I. racemosa Hk. F.	–	1600-2700	5	H	Reg Himal	NE
I. scabrida DC.	–	1300-2600	1, 2, 3, 5	H	Reg Himal	NE
I. sulcata Wall.	–	2000-3050	1, 3, 4, 5, 9	H	Reg Himal	NE
Begoniaceae						
Begonia picta Sm.	–	1500-2000	1, 2, 3	H	Reg Himal	NE
Berberidaceae						
Berberis aristata DC.	Kasmal	1800-2800	1, 2, 4, 7	Sh	Ind Or	NE
B. asiatica Roxb. ex DC.	Kasmal	1300-1700	1, 2	Sh	Reg Himal	–
B. jaeschkeana Sehneid.	Kasmal	2700-3050	1, 2	Sh	Reg Himal	NE
B. lycium Royle	Kasmal	1300-2200	1, 2, 3, 4, 5, 9	Sh	Reg Himal	NE
Betulaceae						
Alnus nepalensis D.Don	Kosh	1300-2200	1, 5, 9	T	Reg Himal	–
A. nitida (Spach) Endl.	Kosh	1600-2500	5	T	Reg Himal	NE
Betula alnoides Buch.-Ham. ex Don	–	1400-2200	1, 2	T	Reg Himal Japan	–
Bombaceae						
*Bombax ceiba*L.	Semal	1300-1600	1, 2	T	Am Austr	–
Boraginaceae						
Cynoglossum glochidiatum Wall. ex Benth.	–	1300-3050	1, 2, 3, 5, 6, 8	H	Ind Or Burma	–
C. zeylanicum (Hornem.) Thunb. ex Lehm.	–	1300-2200	1, 2, 4, 6	H	Ind Or Malaya	–
Hackelia uncinata (Benth.) Fisher	–	2500-3050	1, 2, 4, 7	H	Reg Himal	–
Brassicaceae						

(Contd...)

Family/Taxa	Local Name	AR(m)	Habitat/s	HF	Nativity	End
*Arabidopsis mollissima*Schulz.	–	2200-3050	1, 2, 4	H	Reg Himal Sibir	–
A. stricta Busch.	–	2000-3050	1, 2, 4	H	Reg Himal Sibir	–
A. thalliana L.	–	1300-3050	1, 2, 4	H	Reg Temp	–
Capsella bursa-pastoris (L.) Medik	–	1300-3050	1, 2, 4	H	Reg Temp	–
Thlaspi arvense L.	–	1300-2500	1, 4	H	Europe As Bor	–
Buxaceae						
Buxus wallichiana Baill.	Shamshad	1800-2700	1	T	Europe Oriens As Temp	–
Sarcococcasaligna (Don) Muell. Arg.	Charabri/ Troddi	1400-2800	1, 2, 3, 4, 5, 6, 7, 9	Sh	Reg Himal Ind Or Malaya	NE
Caesalpiniaceae						
Bauhinia variegata L.	Kariyala/ Kachnar	1300-1500	1	T	Ind Or Burma China	–
Caesalpinia bonduc (L.) Roxb.	–	1300-1600	1, 2	Sh	Cosmop Trop	–
Cassia mimosoides L.	–	1300-1800	2, 4	H	Cosmop Trop	
Campanulaceae						
Campanula argyrotricha Wall. Ex DC.	–	2800-3050	2, 3	H	Reg Himal	NE
C. colorata Wall.	–	1300-2600	1, 2, 3	H	Ind Or Afghan	–
C. latifolia L.	–	2600-3050	1, 2	H	Europe Oriens As Temp	–
Codonopsis ovata Benth.	–	2800-3050	1, 7	H	Reg Himal	–
Cannabaceae						
Cannabis sativa L.	Bijya	1300-2000	1, 2, 4, 6, 9	H	As Centr Reg Himal Bor Occ	–
Caprifoliaceae						
Lonicera angustifolia Wall. ex DC.	–	2700-3050	1, 7	Sh	Reg Himal	NE
L. myrtillus Hk.f.	–	2800-3050	1, 3	Sh	Europe Oriens As Temp	–
L. obovata Royle ex Hk.f.	–	2800-3050	1, 3	Sh	Reg Himal	NE
L. quinquelocularis Hardw.	Jamnu	1300-2800	1, 3, 4	Sh	Reg Himal	–
Viburnum cotinifolium Don	Dab	1600-2500	1, 2, 3, 8	Sh	Reg Himal	NE
V. erubescens Wall. ex DC.	–	2000-3050	1, 7	Sh	Reg Himal Ind Or	–
V. grandiflorum Wall. ex DC.	Padara	2700-3050	1, 2	Sh	Reg Himal	NE
V. mullaha Buch. -Ham. ex Don	–	1600-2500	1, 2, 3	Sh	Reg Himal	–
V. nervosum D.Don	Tilenal	2200-3050	1, 7	Sh	Reg Himal	NE

(Contd...)

Family/Taxa	Local Name	AR(m)	Habitat/s	HF	Nativity	End
Caryophyllaceae						
Drymaria cordata Edgew. & Hk.	–	1300-2100	1, 4, 5	H	Cosmop Trop	–
Gypsophila cerastiodes D. Don	–	1700-2700	1, 2, 3, 4, 7	H	Reg Himal	NE
Silene conoidea L.	–	1300-3050	4, 7	H	Europe Oriens	–
S. edgeworthii Bacq.	Jhunjhunu	1800-3050	1, 6, 7	H	Reg Himal	NE
S. gonosperma Bacq.	–	2800-3050	1, 7	H	Europe Oriens	–
Stellaria himalayensis Majumdar	–	2000-3050	1, 2, 3, 6	H	Reg Himal	NE
S. involucrata Wall.	–	2000-2600	1, 7	H	Reg Himal	NE
S. media (L.) Vill.	Bariyala	1300-2000	1, 7	H	Reg Temp	–
S. monosperma D.Don	–	1700-2700	1, 7	H	Reg Himal	–
Celastraceae						
Euonymus tingens Wall.	chindwara	1700-2100	1, 4, 7	T	Reg Himal	–
E. pendulus Wall.	Chopru	1700-2200	1, 4, 7	T	Reg Himal	NE
Maytenus rufa (Wall. ex Roxb.) Raju & Babu	–	1300-1700	2, 4	T	Ind Or	–
Chenopodiaceae						
Chenopodium album L.	–	1300-2500	1, 4, 6	H	Reg Temp et Trop	–
C. foliosum (Moench) Asch.	–	1500-3050	1, 4, 6	H	Reg Bor et Austr	–
Commelinaceae						
Commelina paludosa Bl.	–	1300-2000	4, 7	H	Ind Or Malaya	–
Cyanotis cristata (L.)D.Don	–	1500-2000	1, 2, 4	H	Ind Or Malaya	–
C. vaga L.	–	1300-2000	1, 2, 3, 4, 5	H	Ind Or Malaya	–
Coriariaceae						
Coriaria nepalensis Wall.	Fanai	1300-2000	2, 4	Sh	Reg Himal China	–
Cornaceae						
Cornus capitata Wall.	Kreeva	1500-2000	1, 2, 3, 7	T	Reg Himal	NE
C. macrophylla Wall.	Khrembal	1500-2800	1, 3, 7, 9	T	Reg Himal	–
C. oblonga Wall.	Diyan	1800-2800	1, 5, 7	Sh	Reg Himal	–
Corylaceae						
Carpinus viminea Lindl.	Khirk	1800-2600	1, 7	T	Reg Himal	–
Crassulaceae						
Crassula indica Dcne.	–	1800-2800	2, 7	H	Reg Himal	–
Sedum indicum (Dcne.) Hamet.	–	2600-3050	1, 2, 3	H	Reg Himal	–

(Contd...)

Family/Taxa	Local Name	AR(m)	Habitat/s	HF	Nativity	End
Cucurbitaceae						
Melothria heterophylla (Lour.)Cogn.	–	1300-2000	1, 2, 4	H	As Trop et Sub Trop	–
*Trichosanthes tricuspidata*Lour.	–	1300-2300	1, 2	H	Cochinch	–
Cuscutaceae						
Cuscuta reflexa Roxb.	–	1300-2200	1, 4, 7	H	Ind Or	–
Cyperaceae						
Carex aristata Till. & Taylor	–	1300-2000	1, 2, 4, 6, 8	H	Reg Himal As Trop	–
C.cruciata Wall.	–	1300-2200	1, 2, 5, 7, 8, 9	H	Ind Or	–
C. filicina Nees	–	1500-3050	1, 2	H	Ind Or Malaya	–
C. foliosa D.Don	–	1900-3050	1, 2	H	Reg Himal	–
C. nubigena D. Don	–	2000-3050	1, 2, 4, 5	H	Ind Or	–
C. setigera D. Don	–	2500-3050	1, 2	H	Reg Himal	NE
C. squarrosa L.	–	1500-3050	1, 5	H	Am Bor	–
Cyperus compressus L.	–	1300-2000	1, 2	H	Cosmop Trop	–
C. niveus Retz.	–	1300-1800	1, 2	H	Ind Or	–
C. squarrosus L.	–	1300-2000	1, 2, 3, 4	H	Ind Or	–
Eriophorum comosum Wall. ex Nees	–	1300-2600	2, 4, 5	H	Ind Or	–
Fimbristylis dichotoma (L.) Vahl	–	1300-2000	1, 3	H	Europe Austr Afr Bor	–
F. glomerata Nees	–	1300-2000	1, 3, 7	H	Amphig Trop	–
Dioscoreaceae						
Dioscorea belophylla Voigt. ex Haines.	Tardi	1300-1800	1, 2, 4	H	Guiana	–
D. bulbifera L.	Tardi	1300-2000	1, 2, 4	H	As Trop	–
D. deltoidea Wall. ex Kunth	–	1600-2800	1, 2, 3, 4, 7	H	Ind Or	–
Dipsacaceae						
Dipsacus mitis D.Don	–	2200-3050	1, 2, 4	H	Reg Himal	–
Morina longifolia Wall. ex DC.	–	2900-3050	1, 7	H	Reg Himal	NE
Ehretiaceae						
Ehretia acuminata R.Br.	Bakli/ Banchaula	1300-2000	2, 4	T	As et Austr Trop	–
Elaeagnaceae						
Elaeagnus conferta Roxb.	Geai	1300-1800	1, 2, 4, 7	Sh	Ind Or	NE
E. parvifolia Wall. ex Royle	Geai	1600-2400	1, 5	T	Japan	–
Ericaceae						
Lyonia ovalifolia (Wall.) Drude	Airean, Ehran	1300-2000	1, 2, 3, 5	T	Reg Himal Japan	–

(Contd...)

Family/Taxa	Local Name	AR(m)	Habitat/s	HF	Nativity	End
Rhododendron arboreum Sm.	Brash	1400-2200	1, 2, 3, 5, 7, 9	T	Reg Himal Ceylon	–
Euphorbiaceae						
Daphniphyllum himalayense Muell.-Arg.	Kaula	1600-2400	1, 5, 7	T	Reg Himal	–
Euphorbia helioscopia L.	–	1300-1800	1, 4	H	Europe et As Bor	–
E. pilosa L.	–	2000-3050	1, 4, 8	H	Europe As Bor	–
E. prolifera Buch.-Ham. ex D.Don	–	1300-1800	1, 4	H	Reg Himal	–
Glochidion velutinum Wt.	Salambra	1300-1800	1, 2, 4	T	Ind Or	–
Mallotus philippensis Mull.	Kambal	1300-1500	1, 2, 4	T	As et Austr Trop	–
Phyllanthus parvifolius Buch.-Ham.	–	1400-2100	1, 5	Sh	Reg Himal	NE
Ricinus communis L.	Arand	1300-1600	2, 4, 7	Sh	Reg Trop	–
Sapium insigne Trin.	Dudhla	1300-1900	2, 3	T	Ind Or	–
Fabaceae						
Astragalus chlorostachys Lindl.	–	1500-3050	1, 3	Sh	Reg Himal	NE
Crotalaria albida Heyne ex Roth.	–	1300-1800	1, 2, 4	H	Ind Or	–
Desmodium concinum DC.	Chagla	1300-2000	1, 2, 8	Sh	Reg Himal Burma	–
D. elegans DC.	Chagla, Kathi	1300-2500	1, 2, 3, 5, 7, 9	Sh	Reg Himal China	–
D. gangeticum (L.) DC.	Chagla	1300-2200	2, 4, 8	Sh	As Trop Austr	–
D. microphyllum (Thunb.) DC.	–	1300-2000	1, 2, 4	H	As Trop Austr	–
D. motorium Merrill.	–	1300-1600	2, 4, 8	H	As Trop	–
D. multiflorum DC.	–	1500-2000	1, 2	H	Reg Himal	–
D. triquetrum DC.	–	1600-2500	2, 4	H	As Trop	–
Flemingia semialata Roxb.	–	1300-1700	1, 2, 3, 4	Sh	As Trop	–
F. strobilifera R.Br.	–	1300-2000	1, 2	H	Ind Or Malaya	–
Indigofera heterantha Wall. ex Brand.	Kali Kathi	1600-2800	1, 2, 3, 4, 5, 7, 9	Sh	Reg Himal	–
I. dosua Buch. -Ham. ex D.Don	–	1300-1600	1, 2	H	Reg Himal	–
Lespedeza gerardiana Grah. ex Baker	–	1600-2800	1, 2, 3, 4	Sh	Reg Himal	NE
Medicago lupulina L.	–	1300-2000	2, 4, 6, 8	H	Geront Bor Temp	–
Parochetus communis Buch.-Ham. ex D.Don	–	1800-2800	1, 5	H	Ind Or Malaya Afr Trop	–

(Contd...)

Family/Taxa	Local Name	AR(m)	Habitat/s	HF	Nativity	End
Robinia pseudoacacia L.	Robinia	1300-2000	1, 4	T	Am Bor	–
Shuteria involucrata Wt. & Arn.	–	1300-2600	1, 3	H	Ind Or	–
S. vestita Wt. & Arn.	–	1400-2600	1, 3	H	Ind Or	–
Trifolium pratense L.	–	2000-2500	4, 5	H	Europe As Temp	–
T. repens L.	–	1300-2500	1, 6, 8	H	Geront Bor Temp	–
Trigonella emodi Royle ex Benth.	–	2000-3050	1, 2, 4, 6, 7, 8	H	Reg Himal	–
Vicia rigidula Royle	–	2800-3050	1, 7	H	Reg Himal	–
Vigna vexillata (L.) A.Rich.	–	2000-2800	1, 2, 4	H	Geront Trop	–
Fagaceae						
Quercus floribunda Thunb.	Mohru	2000-2900	1, 2	T	Reg Himal	NE
Q. glauca Thunb.	Banni	1400-1800	1, 2	T	Reg Himal Japan	–
Q. leucotrichophora Cam.	Baan	1300-2500	1, 2, 3, 4, 5, 7	T	Reg Himal	–
Q. semecarpifolia Sm.	Kharsu	2500-3050	1, 2, 3, 7	T	Reg Himal	–
Fumariaceae						
Corydalis cornuta Royle	–	2000-3050	1, 2, 3, 6	H	Reg Himal	–
Dicentra roylei Hk.f. &Th.	–	1600-3050	1	H	Reg Himal	–
Fumaria indica Pugsley	–	1300-1800	1, 2, 4	H	Europe Afr Bor	–
Gentianaceae						
Gentiana aprica Dcne.	–	1800-2500	1, 8	H	Reg Argent	–
G. carinata Griseb.	–	2800-3050	2, 8	H	Reg Himal	NE
Halenia elliptica D.Don	Pitpapra	2800-3050	1, 4, 8	H	Reg Himal	–
Swertia angustifolia Buch. - Ham. ex D.Don	–	1600-2400	1, 4	H	Reg Himal	–
S. cordata (G.Don) Wall.ex Cl.	Charaite	2000-3050	1, 2	H	Reg Himal	NE
S. paniculata Wall.	Charaite	2000-2600	1, 2, 3, 4, 8	H	Reg Himal	NE
Geraniaceae						
Geranium collinum Steph. ex Willd.	–	1500-1900	1, 2	H	Europ Or As Bor	–
G. nepalense Sw.	Jibru ghass	1500-2500	1, 3, 4, 5, 6, 9	H	Ind Or China	–
G. pratense L.	–	2200-3050	1	H	Europe As Bor	–
G. wallichianum D.Don ex Sw.	–	2600-3050	1, 2, 3, 5, 6, 8	H	Reg Himal	NE
Grossulariaceae						
Ribes glaciale Wall.	–	2800-3050	1	Sh	Reg Himal	–

(Contd...)

Family/Taxa	Local Name	AR(m)	Habitat/s	HF	Nativity	End
Haemodoraceae						
Ophiopogon intermedius D.Don	–	1500-2400	1, 2, 3, 7	H	Ind Or	–
Hippocastanaceae						
Aesculusindica Coleb. ex Camb.	Khanor	1800-2600	1	T	Reg Himal	NE
Hydrangeaceae						
Deutziacorymbosa R. Br.	Chururu	2000-2900	1, 3	Sh	China	–
D. staminea R. Br.	Brudi	1500-1800	1, 2, 3, 4, 7	Sh	Reg Himal	NE
Hydrangea anomala D.Don	–	1500-2200	7	Sh	Reg Himal Malaya China	–
Hypericaceae						
*Hypericum elodeoides*Choisy	–	2000-2800	1, 3	H	Reg Himal Burma	–
H. japonicum Thunb. ex Murr.	–	1600-2600	3, 4	H	As Temp Or AustrAs	–
H. oblongifolium Choisy	Kharau	1300-2200	1, 5, 7	Sh	Reg Himal	NE
H. perforatum L.	–	1900-2400	1, 2	H	Europe As Bor	–
H. uralum Buch.-Ham.	Bani Wakra	1800-2500	1, 5	Sh	Reg Himal China Japan	–
Hypoxidaceae						
Curculigo orchioides Gaertn.	–	1300-2000	1, 2, 4	H	As Trop	–
Hypoxis aurea Lour.	–	1600-2000	1, 2, 4, 8	H	Cochinch	–
Juglandaceae						
Juglans regia L.	Akhrot	1600-2000	1, 4, 7	T	As Occ Reg Himal	NE
Juncaceae						
Juncus bufonius L.	–	1500-2500	2, 6, 8	H	Amphig	–
J. himalensis Klotz. & Garcke	–	2800-3050	1, 2, 4	H	Reg Himal	NE
Lamiaceae						
Ajuga brachystemon Maxim.	Neel kanthi	1300-2500	1, 2, 4, 5, 7, 8	H	Reg Himal	NE
A. bracteosa Wall. ex Benth.	Neel kanthi	1300-2600	1, 2, 4, 5, 7, 8	H	Afr Trop Ind Or As	NE
A. parviflora Benth.	–	1300-2000	1, 2, 4, 7	H	Reg Himal	NE
Clinopodium umbrosum. Koch	–	1300-2700	1, 2, 4	H	Oriens Ind Or	–
Colebrookia oppositifolia Sm.	Banse	1300-1700	1, 2, 4	Sh	Ind Or Burma	–
Craniotome furcata (Link) Kuntze	–	1800-2600	2, 4	H	Reg Himal	–
C. versicolor Rchb.		1800-2600	1, 3	H	Reg Himal	–
Elsholtzia flava (Benth.) Benth.	Jaunkra	1600-2000	1, 2, 4	H	Reg Himal	NE

(Contd...)

Family/Taxa	Local Name	AR(m)	Habitat/s	HF	Nativity	End
E. fruticosa (Don) Rehd.	Pothi,	1600-2200	1, 2, 4	Sh	Reg Himal	–
E. strobilifera Benth.	–	1600-2700	1, 2	H	Reg Himal	–
Leonurus cardiaca L.	–	1800-2600	1, 2, 4, 8	H	Reg Bor Temp	–
Leucas capitata Desf.	–	1600-2200	1, 2	H	Ind Or	–
L. lanata Benth.	–	1300-2800	1, 2, 3, 6	H	Ind Or China	–
Mentha longifolia (L.) Huds.	Podina	1300-3050	4, 6	H	Europe As Bor	–
M. piperita L.	–	1300-1800	1	H	Europe As et AfrBor	–
Micromeria biflora Buch.-Ham.	–	1300-2100	1, 2, 4, 5	H	Ind Or Arab Afr Trop	–
Nepeta govaniana Benth.	–	2400-3000	1, 2, 4	H	Reg Himal	NE
N. leucophylla Benth.	–	1300-2200	1, 6	H	Reg Himal	NE
`*N. royleana* Stew.	–	2000-2800	1, 8	H	Reg Himal	–
Origanum vulgare L.	Bantulsi	1600-3000	1, 2, 4, 5, 7, 8	H	Europe As	–
Phlomis bracteosa Royle ex Benth.	–	2000-3050	1, 3, 6, 7	H	Reg Himal	NE
Plectranthus coesta Buch.-Ham. ex D.Don	Chichri	2000-2500	1, 2, 3, 4, 5	H	Reg Himal Burma	–
P. mollis Spr.	–	1300-1500	1, 4	H	Ind Or	–
P. rugosus Wall.	–	1500-2600	2, 4	Sh	Reg Himal	–
P. striatus Benth.	–	2000-2600	1, 4	H	Reg Himal	–
Pogostemon benghalense (Burm.f.) Kuntz	–	1800-2300	1, 2, 4	Sh	Ind Or	NE
Prunella vulgaris L.	Patindu	2000-2800	1, 2, 4, 8	H	Reg Temp	–
Roylea cinerea Baill.	Karnait	1300-1700	1, 4	Sh	Reg Himal	–
Salvia lanata Roxb.	Guadra	1300-2200	1, 2, 3, 4, 6	H	Reg Himal	NE
S. moorcroftiana Wall. ex Benth.	–	2000-3050	2, 4, 8	H	Reg Himal	NE
S. nubicola Wall.	–	1400-2200	2	H	Europe Austr Oriens Reg Himal	NE
Scutellaria scandens Buch.-Ham. ex D.Don	–	1300-2100	1, 4	H	Reg Himal	NE
Stachys sericea Wall.	–	1600-2800	1, 3, 4, 5, 6, 8	H	Reg Himal As Bor	–
Teucrium royleanum Wall. ex Benth.	–	1600-2200	1, 2, 4, 8	H	Reg Himal	NE
Thymus linearis Benth.	Ban jira	2000-3050	1, 2, 4, 8	H	Europe As et Afr Bor	–
Lardizabalaceae						
Holboelia latifolia Wall.	–	1600-2000	1	Sh	Reg Himal	–

(Contd...)

Family/Taxa	Local Name	AR(m)	Habitat/s	HF	Nativity	End
Lauraceae						
Cinnamomum tamala Nees & Ebern	–	1300-1600	1, 5	T	Reg Himal	NE
Neolitsea pallens (D.Don) Momi. & Hara ex Hara	Pangain, Paror	1800-2800	1, 2, 4, 5, 7	T	Reg Himal	–
Persea duthiei (King. ex Hk.f.) Kostern.	Badrol	1400-2000	1, 2, 7	T	Reg Himal	NE
P. gamblei (King. ex Hk.f.) Kostern.	Badrol	1300-1500	1, 5	T	Reg Himal	NE
P. odoratissima (Nees) Koster.	Badrol	1600-2000	1, 2	T	Ind Malaya China	–
Liliaceae						
Polygonatum cirrhifolium (Wall.) Royle	Salam-Mishri	2500-3050	1	H	Reg Himal As Bor	–
P. verticillatum (L.) Al.	Salam-Mishri	2000-3050	1, 2, 3, 4	H	Europe As Bor	–
Smilacina purpurea Wall.	–	2800-3050	1, 3, 7	H	Reg Himal	–
Linaceae						
Reinwardtia indica Dumort.	Piyan	1300-1800	1, 2, 5	H	Ind Or	NE
Loganiaceae						
Buddleja crispa Benth.	Snehali	1300-1800	2, 3, 4	Sh	Reg Himal Burma	–
Loranthaceae						
Viscum album L.	Rhini	1300-2000	10	Sh	Europe As Temp	–
Lythraceae						
Woodfordia fruticosa (L.) Kurz.	Dhwe	1400-1700	1, 2, 4	Sh	As et Afr Trop	–
Malvaceae						
*Malva verticillata*L.	–	1300-2000	1, 2, 6, 8	H	Europe As et Afr Bor	–
Sida cordata (Burm.f.) Borss.	–	2000-2300	1, 2, 4	H	Ind Or	–
Urena lobata L.	–	1300-1600	1, 2, 4	Sh	Reg Trop	–
Mimosaceae						
*Albizzia chinensis*Merr.	Ohi	1300-1700	1,2	T	Ind Or	–
A. julibrissin Durazz.	–	1600-2200	1, 2	T	As Afr Trop	–
A. lebbek Benth.	Siris	1300-1500	1, 2	T	Geront Trop	–
Melastomataceae						
Osbeckia stellata Buch.-Ham. ex Don	Kubsh	1400-2000	1, 2, 8	Sh	Reg Himal	NE
Meliaceae						
Melia azedarach L.	Darek	1300-1700	1, 2	T	Reg Himal	–

(Contd...)

Family/Taxa	Local Name	AR(m)	Habitat/s	HF	Nativity	End
Toona ciliata Roem.	Tooni, Tun	1300-1600	1, 5	T	Malaya Austr	–
T. serrata (Royle) Roem.	Darlein	1400-2200	1, 5	T	Malaya Austr	–
Menispermaceae						
Cissampelos pariera L.	–	1300-2000	1, 2	H	Reg Trop	–
Stephania glabra (Roxb.) Miers.	–	1300-1600	1	H	As Trop	–
Moraceae						
Ficus nemoralis Wall. ex Mir	Dudla	1600-2000	1, 2	T	Reg Himal	NE
F. palmata Forsk.	Fegra	1300-1800	1, 2	T	Afr Trop Arab Ind Or	–
F. pumila L.	–	1300-2000	1, 2	T	Afr Trop Arab Ind Or	–
F. religiosa L.	Pipal	1300-1500	1, 2	T	Ind Or	–
F. roxburghii Wall.	Tremal/ Thraimbal	1300-1600	1, 2	T	Reg Himal Burma	–
F. rumphii Bl.	–	1300-1600	1, 2, 7	T	Reg Himal Malaya	–
F. sarmentosa Ham. ex Sm.	Denbere	1300-2000	1, 2, 3, 7	Sh	Reg Himal	–
F. semicordata Buch.-Ham. ex Sm.	–	1300-1600	1, 2, 3	T	Reg Himal	–
F. subincisa Buch.-Ham. ex Sm.	–	1300-1600	1, 2	T	Reg Himal	–
Morus serrata Roxb.	Cheemu	1300-1800	1, 4, 5	T	Reg Himal	NE
Myricaceae						
Myrica esculenta Buch.-Ham. ex Don	Kaphal	1400-2400	1, 2, 3, 4	T	As Trop et Sub Trop	–
Myrsinaceae						
Myrsine africana L.	Kanaru	1600-2500	1, 2, 3	Sh	Reg Himal Afr Austr et Trop Ins Azor	–
Oleaceae						
Jasminum dispermum Wall.	Banmalti	1500-2000	1, 4, 7	Sh	Reg Himal	–
J. humile L.	Banmalti	1600-3050	1, 7	Sh	Reg Himal	–
J. officinale L.	Banmalti	1800-2900	1, 2, 3	Sh	Ind Bor Occ China	–
Onagraceae						
Circaea alpina L.	–	2200-3050	1, 2, 3	H	Europe As Bor Am Bor	–
Epilobium angustifolium L.	–	1800-3050	1, 3	H	Europe As Bor Am Bor	–
E. latifolium L	–	1900-3050	1, 3	H	Reg Bor et Arct	NE

(Contd...)

Family/Taxa	Local Name	AR(m)	Habitat/s	HF	Nativity	End
Oenothera rosea Herit. ex Ait.	–	1300-2000	2, 4, 9	H	Am Bor Occ Peruv	–
Orchidaceae						
Calanthe plantaginea Lindl.	–	1800-2600	1	H	Reg Himal	NE
*C. tricarinata*Lindl.	–	1500-2500	1, 2	H	Reg Himal	–
Cephalanthera longifolia (L.) Fritsch.	–	2200-3050	1, 3	H	Europe Afr Bor As Temp	–
Dactylorhiza hatagirea (D.Don) Soo	–	2900-3050	4, 8	H	Reg Himal	NE
Epipactis giganteum Dougl. ex Hk.	–	2400-3050	1, 2	H	Am Bor As Temp	–
E. heleborine (L.) Crantz	–	1600-2200	1, 2, 3	H	Reg Himal	–
Goodyera biflora Hk.f.	–	1800-2600	1	H	Reg Himal	NE
G. repens (L.) R.Br.	–	2400-2800	1, 2	H	Reg Himal	–
Habenaria edgeworthii Hk.f. ex Coll.	–	2000-2800	1, 2, 3, 7	H	Ind Or	NE
H. intermedia Don	Sirab	1600-2000	1, 2, 7	H	Reg Himal	NE
H. marginata Hk.f. ex Collett	–	1300-1500	1, 2	H	Ind Or	–
H. pectinata (Sm.) D.Don	–	1500-2000	1, 2	H	Reg Himal	NE
Herminium lanceum Thunb. ex Swartz.	–	1800-3050	1, 2, 7	H	Java	–
Listera pinetorum Lindl.	–	2600-3050	1, 3	H	Reg Himal	–
L. tenuis Lindl.	–	2800-3050	1, 2	H	Reg Himal	–
Malaxis acuminata Don	–	1600-2200	1, 2, 7	H	Reg Himal	–
M. muscifera (Lindl.) Kuntze	–	2800-3050	1, 5	H	Reg Himal	–
Satyrium nepalense D.Don	–	1600-2500	4, 8	H	Ind Or	–
Spiranthes spiralis Koch.	–	1600-2200	4, 8	H	Europe As Temp	–
Orobranchaceae						
Orobranche alba Stephan ex Willd.	–	2500-3000	2, 7	H	Europe Or As Bor	–
Oxalidaceae						
Oxalis corniculata L.	Malori	1300-2200	1, 2, 5	H	Amphig Temp et Trop	–
O. latifolia Hk.f.	–	1500-2500	1, 4, 7, 8	H	Mexic	–
Papaveraceae						
Argemone mexicana L.	–	1300-1500	1, 2, 4	H	Am Bor Mexic	–
Parnassiaceae						
Parnassia nubicola Wall. ex Royle	–	2700-3050	1, 8	H	Reg Himal	NE

(Contd...)

Family/Taxa	Local Name	AR(m)	Habitat/s	HF	Nativity	End
Phytolaccaceae						
Phytolacca acinosa Roxb.	Zharka	2000-2500	3, 7	H	Reg Himal China	–
Plantaginaceae						
Plantago himalaica Pilg.	Isabgol	2900-3050	1, 4, 6	H	Reg Himal	NE
P. lanceolata L.	Isabgol	2000-2800	1, 4, 5, 6	H	Reg Himal	–
Poaceae						
Agrostis munroana Aitch.	–	2500-3050	1, 2, 3, 5	H	Afgan	–
A. pilosula Trin.	–	2000-2800	1, 2, 3	H	Reg Himal Or	NE
Apluda mutica L.	Mushkneti	1400-2500	1, 2, 3, 4, 5, 7	H	As Trop Pdynes Austr	–
Arthraxon lancifolius Hochst.	–	1300-2000	2, 4, 7	H	Ind Or	–
A.lanceolatus Hochst.	–	1500-2400	2, 4, 7	H	Ind Or Abyss Japon	–
Arundinella nepalensis Trin.	Garein	1300-2000	1, 4, 7	H	Ind Or	–
A. pumila Steud.	–	1300-1800	1, 4, 7	H	Abyss	–
Avena sativa L.	Jaoi	1300-2000	1, 2, 4	H	Terr Temp	–
Bothriochloa intermedia Cam.	Palwan	1300-1700	2, 4	H	Oriens Afr et As Trop Austr	–
B. pertusa (L.) Cam.	–	1700-2000	1, 2, 4	H	Sicil As et Afr Trop Austr	–
Bromus japonicus Thunb. ex Murr.	–	2000-3050	1, 2, 3	H	Japan	–
Chrysopogon gryllus (L.) Trin.	–	1600-2000	1, 4, 5, 8	H	Reg Trop et Sub Trop Afr Europe Austr	–
C. serrulatus Trin.	–	1300-2000	1, 4, 5, 8	H	Ind Or Afr Trop	–
Cymbopogon distans (Nees) Wats.	–	1800-2200	1, 7, 8	H	Ind Or	–
C. martini (Roxb.)Wats.	Dantu ghass	1300-1600	1, 8	H	Reg Trop	–
Cynodon dactylon (D) Pers.	Doob	1300-2500	1, 2, 5	H	Cosmop	–
Dactylis glomerata L.	–	2000-3050	2, 3	H	Europe As Bor	–
Eleusine indica Gaertn.	–	1300-1800	1, 4, 7	H	Cosmop Trop et Sub Trop	–
Eragrostis pilosa L.	–	1300-1800	1, 4, 7	H	Reg Calid	–
E. tenella Roem. & Schult.	–	1500-2000	1, 2, 4, 5	H	As et Afr Trop	–
E. unioloides Nees ex Steud	–	1400-1900	1, 2, 9	H	Ind Banca	–
Festuca rubra L.	Jau	1600-2500	2, 4	H	Reg Bor Temp etArct	–
Heteropogon contortus L.	Kumbri	1300-1700	4, 7, 8	H	Ind Or	–
Imperata cylindrica Raeusch.	–	1300-1900	4, 5, 8	H	Reg Calid	–

(Contd...)

Family/Taxa	Local Name	AR(m)	Habitat/s	HF	Nativity	End
Oplismenus compositus L.	–	1300-2000	1, 2, 4, 7	H	Cosmo Trop	–
O. undulatifolius (L.) Beauv.	–	1800-2400	1, 2, 3, 7	H	Cosmo Trop	–
Poa alpina L.	–	2500-3050	1, 6	H	Reg Bor et Arct	–
P. annua L.	–	1600-2000	1, 4	H	Reg Bor Temp	–
P. pratensis (L.) Gaud.	–	1800-3050	1, 7	H	Reg Bor Temp	–
Pogonatherum paniceum Hack.	–	1300-2000	3, 5, 8	H	As Trop	–
Polypogon fugax Nees ex Steud	–	1300-2100	1, 5	H	Austr	–
Saccharum spontaneum L.	Surah	1300-2000	1, 2, 3, 4, 9	H	Geront Trop	–
Setaria glauca L.	Siuh	1300-2500	4, 7	H	Europe As Temp	–
Sinarundinaria falcata Chao & Renv.	–	1300-2200	1, 2, 3, 7	Sh	Reg Himal	–
Themeda anathera (Nees ex Steud.) Hack.	Bhagadey	1300-2000	1, 2, 7	H	Ind Or	–
Thysanolaena maxima Kuntze	–	1300-1600	5, 7	H	As Trop	–
Podopyllaceae						
Podophyllum hexandrum Royle	Ban Kakri	2900-3050	1, 3, 5, 7	H	Reg Himal	–
Polygonaceae						
Bistorta amplexicaulis (D. Don) Greene	–	1500-2600	1, 2, 3, 4, 6, 7	H	Reg Himal	–
Fagopyrum debotrys (Don) Hara	–	1600-2800	1, 4	H	Reg Himal China	–
F. esculentum (L.) Moench	–	1300-2000	1, 4	H	Europe As Bor	–
Persicaria capitata (Buch.-Ham. ex D. Don) Gross	–	1300-2000	1, 2, 3, 4, 5, 6, 9	H	Reg Himal	–
P. hydropiper (L.) Spach.	–	1300-2200	3, 5	H	As et Afr Trop et Sub Trop	–
P. nepalense Meisn.	Nalora	1600-2000	1, 2, 3, 9	H	As et Afr Trop et Sub Trop	–
P. plebium R.Br.	–	1300-2200	3, 5, 7	H	Geront Trop et Temp	–
P. recumbens Royle ex Bab.	–	1800-2500	1, 2, 6	H	Reg Himal	NE
Rumex hastatus Don	Malori	1300-1800	2, 3, 5, 9	H	Reg Himal	–
*R. nepalensis*Spr.	Malora	1800-3050	1, 2, 4, 5, 6	H	As Occ Ind Or Malaya Afr	–

(Contd…)

Family/Taxa	Local Name	AR(m)	Habitat/s	HF	Nativity	End
Primulaceae						
Androsace rotundifolia Hardw.	–	1800-2800	1, 2, 3, 4, 5	H	Reg Himal	NE
A. sarmentosa Wall.	–	2200-3050	1, 4	H	Reg Himal	NE
Lysimachia chenopodioides Watt ex Hk.	–	2000-2800	1, 4	H	Reg Himal	–
L. ferruginea Edgew.	–	1300-2500	1, 4, 7	H	Reg Himal China Austr	–
L. lobelioides Wall.	–	1600-2200	1, 2	H	Reg Himal Java	–
*Primula denticulata*Sm.	Kauri	1800-3050	1, 2, 3, 6, 7	H	Reg Himal	–
Punicaceae						
Punica granatum L.	Daru	1300-1800	1, 2, 7	T	Europe Austr Maurit	–
Ranunculaceae						
Actaea spicata Wall. exRoyle	–	2200-2600	1, 7	H	Reg Bor Temp	–
Anemone obtusiloba D.Don	–	2500-3050	1, 2, 6	H	Reg Himal	NE
A. rivularis Buch.-Ham. ex DC.	Mamiri	2200-3050	1, 2, 4, 6	H	Ind Or	–
A. rupicola Camb.	–	2800-3050	1, 2	H	Reg Himal	–
A.vitifolia Buch.-Ham. ex DC.	–	1800-2800	1, 4, 6, 8	H	Reg Himal	–
Aquilegia pubiflora Wall. ex Royle	–	2500-3050	1, 2, 3	H	Reg Himal Ind Or	NE
Clematis acuminata DC.	Bel kangu	2000-2800	1, 5	Sh	Reg Himal	NE
C. barbellata Edgew.	–	2800-3050	1, 2, 3, 4, 5	Sh	Reg Himal	NE
C. buchananiana DC.	–	1400-2000	1, 2, 5	Sh	Reg Himal	–
C. graveolens Lindl.	–	1500-2400	1, 2	Sh	Reg Himal	–
C. montana Buch.-Ham. ex DC.	–	1800-2600	1, 2	Sh	Reg Himal	–
Delphinium denudatum Wall. ex Hk. f. & Th.	–	2700-3050	1, 4, 6	H	Reg Himal	NE
D. vestitum Wall. ex Royle	Kelulu	2800-3050	1, 4, 6	H	Reg Himal	NE
Ranunculus diffusus L.	–	1600-2800	1, 2, 4, 5, 6	H	Ind Or Malaya	–
R. hirtellus Royle ex D.Don	–	2500-3050	1, 6	H	Reg Himal	–
R. laetus Wall. ex D.Don	–	2000-3050	1, 5	H	Reg Himal	–
Thalictrum foliolosum DC.	Mamiri	1500-2600	1, 2, 3, 5	H	Reg Himal	NE
T. secundum Edgew.	Katmeena	2600-3050	1, 3, 6	H	Reg Himal	NE
Rhamnaceae						

(Contd...)

Family/Taxa	Local Name	AR(m)	Habitat/s	HF	Nativity	End
Rhamnus prostrata Jacq. ex Parker	–	1800-2300	1, 4, 7	Sh	Himal Bor Occ	–
R. purpureus Edgew.	–	1400-2000	1, 2	Sh	Reg Himal	NE
R. triqueter Wall.	–	1300-2200	1, 2	Sh	Reg Himal	NE
R. virgatus Roxb.	Chathau	1400-2200	1, 2, 4	Sh	Ind Or Bor	–
Rosaceae						
Agrimonia pilosa Ledeb.	Kanaula	1600-2800	1, 2, 3, 4, 5, 6, 9	H	Reg Bor Temp	–
Cotoneaster acuminatus Lindl.	Chinchri	2800-3050	1, 2, 3	Sh	Reg Himal	–
C. bacillaris Wall. ex Lindl.	Rhiunsh	1600-2200	1, 2	Sh	Reg Himal	NE
C. microphyllus Wall. ex Lindl.	Chinchri	2000-3050	1, 2, 4	Sh	Reg Himal	–
Duchesnea indica Focke	–	1600-2500	1, 2, 3, 4, 5, 9	H	Ind Or Malaya China	–
Fragaria nubicola L.	–	1400-1800	1, 2, 5, 6	H	Reg Temp	–
Filipendula vestita Wall. ex G.Don	–	2800-3050	1, 2, 5	H	Reg Himal	–
Geum elatum Wall. ex G.Don	–	2800-3050	1, 2, 4, 5	H	Reg Himal	NE
Potentilla argyrophylla Wall. ex Lehm.	–	2500-3050	1, 7	H	Reg Himal	NE
P. atrosanguinea Lodd.	–	2800-3050	1, 2, 3, 4, 6, 8	H	Reg Himal	NE
P. fulgens Wall. ex Hk.f.	Dora	1800-3000	4, 8	H	Reg Himal	NE
Prinsepia utilis Royle	Bekhal	1600-2600	1, 2, 4, 5	Sh	Reg Himal	–
Prunus cerasoides Don	Paja	1300-2200	1	T	Reg Himal	–
P. cornuta Steud.	Jammu	2100-3050	1, 5	T	Himal Occ	–
Pyrus pashia Buch.-Ham. ex Don	Kainth	1300-1800	1, 2, 3, 4, 5	T	Reg Himal	–
Rosa macrophylla Lindl.	–	2200-3050	1, 2, 3, 4, 7	Sh	Reg Himal China	NE
R. moschata L.	Kuja/Shami	1300-1800	1, 2, 3, 4, 7, 9	Sh	Reg Himal China	–
R. sericea Lindl.	–	2000-3050	1, 2	Sh	Reg Himal	–
Rubus biflorus Buch.-Ham. ex Sm.	Akhaey	1500-2500	1, 2	Sh	Reg Himal	–
R. ellipticus Don	Akha	1500-1800	1, 2, 3, 4, 5, 9	Sh	Ind Or	–
R. foliolosus D.Don	Akha	2700-3050	1, 2, 3, 7	Sh	Reg Himal	–
R. niveus Thunb.	–	1800-2600	1, 3	Sh	Reg Himal	–
R. paniculatus Sm.	Kala akha	1500-2600	1, 4	Sh	Reg Himal	NE
Sibbaldia cuneata Hor. ex Kuntz	–	2800-3050	1, 2	H	Reg Bor et Austr	–
Sorbaria tomentosa (Lindl.) Rehd.	–	2500-3050	3, 5, 7	Sh	Reg Himal As Bor	–

(Contd...)

Family/Taxa	Local Name	AR(m)	Habitat/s	HF	Nativity	End
Sorbus lanata (D. Don) Sch.	–	1900-2800	1, 2, 3	T	Reg Himal	–
Spiraea bella Sims.	–	2700-3050	1, 3	Sh	Reg Himal	–
S. canescens Don	Khusti	2000-2700	1, 2, 3, 4	Sh	Reg Himal	NE
S. cantoniensis Lour.	–	1800-2200	1, 4	Sh	China	–
Rubiaceae						
*Galium aparine*L.	–	1500-2800	1, 2, 3	H	Reg Bor Temp et Magell	–
*G. asperifolium*Wall.	–	1800-3050	1, 2, 3, 4, 5	H	Reg Himal	–
G. rotundifolium L.	–	2200-3050	1, 2, 3, 4, 5, 8	H	Europe As Temp	–
Kohautia gracilis DC.	–	1300-1700	1, 2	H	Ind Or	–
Leptodermis lanceolata Wall.	Bilan	1300-3050	1, 2	Sh	Reg Himal	NE
Randia tetrasperma (Roxb.) Benth.	Jhagdu ghass	1300-2200	1, 2, 3, 4, 5	Sh	Reg Himal	NE
Rubia cordifolia L.	–	1300-2400	1, 2	H	As Trop et Temp Afr Trop	NE
Rutaceae						
Boenninghausenia albiflora (Hk.) Reichb.	Pissumar	2000-2900	1, 2, 3, 4, 5, 9	H	Reg Himal Japan	–
Skimmia laureola (DC.) Zucc.	Ner	2500-3050	1, 2, 4	Sh	Reg Himal	NE
Zanthoxylum armatum DC.	Trimbar	1300-1800	2, 4, 7	Sh	Reg Himal China	–
Sabiaceae						
Meliosma dilleniifolia Walp.	–	1800-2600	1, 2	Sh	Reg Himal	–
Salicaceae						
Populus ciliata Wall. ex Royle	Pahari pipal	1300-1600	1, 2	T	Reg Himal	–
Salix acmophylla Boiss.	Bhashal	1400-2000	1, 5	T	Oriens Ind Or	–
S. babylonica L.	Majnu	1500-2000	1	T	Reg Caucas As Bor	–
S. denticulata Anderss.	Buins	2000-3050	1	Sh	Reg Himal	NE
S. tetrasperma D. Don	Buins	1500-2400	1,5	T	Ind Or Malaya	–
Santalaceae						
Osyris quadripartita Salzm. ex Decne.	–	1800-2200	1, 2	Sh	As et Afr Trop	–
Saururaceae						
Houttuynia cordata Thunb.	–	1500-2000	1, 5	H	As Temp	–

(Contd...)

Family/Taxa	Local Name	AR(m)	Habitat/s	HF	Nativity	End
Saxifragaceae						
Astilbe rivularis Buch.-Ham. ex Don	–	1800-2800	2, 3, 5	H	Reg Himal	–
Bergenia ligulata (Wall.) Engl.	Pashanved	1500-2000	1, 2, 3, 5	H	Reg Himal	NE
Saxifraga brunonis Wall. ex Seringe	–	1800-2800	3, 7	H	Reg Himal	NE
S. parnassifolia D.Don	–	2800-3050	3, 7	H	Reg Himal	NE
Schisandraceae						
Schisandra grandiflora Hk.f. & Th.	–	2000-3050	2, 7	Sh	Reg Himal	NE
Scrophulariaceae						
Euphrasia himalaica Wettst.	–	2800-3050	2, 4	H	Reg Himal	NE
Lindenbergia indica Vatke.	–	1300-1800	4, 5, 7	H	Ind Or	–
L. macrostachya (Benth.) Benth.	–	1500-2200	1, 4, 7	H	Reg Himal China	–
Mazus surculosus D.Don	–	1600-2800	1, 2, 4, 5	H	Ind Or	–
Pedicularis bicornuta Klotz. ex Klotz. & Garcke	–	2500-3050	1, 4, 7	H	Reg Himal	NE
P. pectinata Wall. ex Benth.	–	2500-3050	2, 7	H	Reg Himal	NE
P. punctata Dcne.	–	2900-3050	1, 8	H	Reg Himal Persia	–
Scoparia dulcis L.	–	1500-1800	4, 7	H	Reg Trop	–
Scrophularia calycina Benth.	–	1300-1800	3, 7	H	Reg Himal	NE
S. himalensis Royle ex Benth.	–	2200-3050	3, 7	H	Reg Himal	E
Verbascum thapsus L.	Gaddi Tamaku	1300-2800	1, 2, 4	H	Europe Afr Reg Himal	–
Veronica javanica Bl.	Bariyala	1300-2200	1, 5	H	Reg Himal Malaya	–
Wulfenia amherstiana Wall. ex Benth.	–	2800-3050	1, 3, 5, 7	H	Reg Himal	NE
Smilacaceae						
Smilax aspera L.	–	1400-2000	1, 2, 7	Sh	Europe Oriens Ind Or	–
S. vaginata Dcne.	–	2700-3050	1, 2, 3, 7	Sh	Reg Himal	–
Solanaceae						
Datura innoxia Mill.	–	1300-1600	4, 7	H	Geront Trop	–
*D. stramonium*L.	Datura	1300-1700	4, 7	H	Cosmo Trop et Temp	–
Nicotiana tabacum L.	–	1300-1800	4, 7	H	Am Austr	–
Solanum indicum L.	–	1300-1800	1, 2, 4	H	Reg Trop	–
S. nigrum L.	–	1400-2500	1, 2, 4, 5	H	Amphig	–

(Contd...)

Family/Taxa	Local Name	AR(m)	Habitat/s	HF	Nativity	End
S. xanthocarpum Sch. & Wendl.	–	1300-2000	1, 2, 4, 5	H	Geront Trop	–
Symplocaceae						
Symplocos chinensis (Lour.) Drace	Lodge	1500-2000	1, 2	T	Reg Himal Burma China Japan	–
Thymelaeaceae						
Daphne papyracea Wall. ex Stued.	Patrori	1800-2800	1, 2, 3, 4, 5, 7	Sh	Reg Himal	NE
Tiliaceae						
Grewia oppositifolia Buch.-Ham. ex D.Don	Bihul	1300-1600	1, 2, 4	T	Reg Himal	NE
Tillaea pentandra Royle ex Edgew.	–	1300-1800	2, 3, 5	H	Ind Or Afr Trop	–
Trillidiaceae						
Trillidium govanianum Kunth	–	2800-3050	1	H	Reg Himal	NE
Ulmaceae						
Celtis australis L.	Khirk	1300-2000	1, 2, 3, 5, 7	T	Europe As Temp Ind Or	–
Ulmus wallichiana Planch.	–	1600-2000	1, 2	T	Ind Or	NE
Urticaceae						
*Boehmeria platyphylla*D.Don	Siar	1300-1800	1, 2, 3, 5	Sh	As et Afr Trop Ins Pacif	–
Debregeasia longifolia (N. Burman) Wedd.	–	1300-2000	1, 4	Sh	Ind Or	–
D. salicifolia (Don) Rendl.	Siaru	1500-2300	1, 2, 5, 9	Sh	As et Afr Trop	–
Elatostema sessile Forst. & Forst.	–	1300-1800	5, 7	H	Ind Or	–
Girardinia diversifolia (Forsk.) Gaud.	Bichhbuti	1500-2400	1, 2, 3, 4, 5	H	Ind Or Malaya	–
Lecanthus peduncularis. Wedd	–	2600-3050	1, 2, 3, 5, 7	H	Ind Or	–
Parietaria debilis Frost.	–	1300-2000	1, 2, 4, 5	H	Reg Trop et Sub Trop	–
Pilea scripta (Buch.-Ham. ex Don) Wedd.	Chamrali	1600-2000	1, 2, 3, 5, 7	H	Reg Himal	–
P. umbrosa Wedd.	–	1800-2600	1, 7	H	Reg Himal	–
Urtica dioica Jacq. ex Wedd.	Bicchu buti	1300-2300	1, 2, 4, 5	H	Reg Bor Temp	–
U. hyperborea Jacq. ex Wedd.	–	1300-2100	1, 2, 4	H	Reg Himal	–
U. parviflora Roxb.	–	2000-3050	1, 2	H	Reg Himal	–
Valerianaceae						

(Contd...)

Family/Taxa	Local Name	AR(m)	Habitat/s	HF	Nativity	End
Valeriana hardwickii Wall.	Nihani/Nakh	2000-3050	1, 2, 7	H	Reg Himal Malaya	–
V. jatamansi Jones	Nihani	1300-3050	1, 2, 3, 4, 5, 7, 9	H	Reg Himal	–
Verbenaceae						
Caryopteris foetida (Don) Robin	Rumri	1300-2000	1, 7	Sh	Reg Himal	NE
Duranta repens L.	–	1300-1600	1, 2, 4, 7	Sh	Am Trop	–
Lantana camara L.	Ujarru	1300-1500	2, 4, 7	H	Am Trop	–
Vitex negundo L.	Banha	1300-1600	1, 2, 4	Sh	As Trop	–
Violaceae						
Viola biflora L.	Banafsha	2800-3050	1, 7	H	Reg Bor Temp	–
V. canescens Wall.	Banafsha	1300-2500	1, 2, 3, 4, 7, 9	H	Ind Or Malaya	NE
V. pilosa L.	Banafsha	1800-2600	1, 2, 4, 7	H	Ind Or Malaya	–
Vitaceae						
Cissus repanda Vahl	–	1400-1600	1, 2	Sh	Ind Or	–
Parthenocissus semicordata (Royle) Planch.	Kramru	1500-2600	1, 2, 3, 7	Sh	Ind Or	NE
Tetrastigma obtectum Planch. ex Franch.	–	1300-2200	1, 2, 3	Sh	Reg Himal Burma China	–
T. serrulatum(Roxb.) Planch.	–	1500-2200	1, 2, 3, 5, 9	H	Ind Or	–
Zingiberaceae						
Globba racemosa Sm.	–	1300-1700	1, 5	H	Reg Himal	–
Hedychium spicatum Buch.-Ham. ex Sm.	Ban halder, Shau	1300-2200	1, 2, 3, 4, 5, 7	H	Reg Himal	NE
Roscoea alpina Royle	–	2500-3050	2, 3, 4, 8	H	Reg Himal	NE
R. procera Wall.	–	1800-2800	2, 7	H	Reg Himal Burma	–
Gymnosperms						
Pinaceae						
Abies pindrow Spach.	Tosh	2200-3050	1, 2, 3	T	Reg Himal	NE
Cedrus deodara (Royle ex D. Don) G. Don	Kelo, Diar	1500-2300	1, 2, 3, 5	T	Reg Himal	NE
Picea smithiana (Wall.) Boiss.	Rai	2000-2600	1, 2, 4, 5	T	Reg Himal	NE
Pinus roxburghii Sarg.	Chir	1300-2200	1, 2, 3, 4, 5	T	Reg Himal	NE
P. wallichiana A.B. Jack.	Kail	2000-2800	1, 2, 3, 4, 5	T	Reg Himal	NE
Taxaceae						
Taxus baccata L. subsp. *wallichiana* (Zucc.) Pilger	Rakhala/ Talispatra	2400-3050	1,2,3	T	Reg Himal	–

(Contd…)

Family/Taxa	Local Name	AR(m)	Habitat/s	HF	Nativity	End
Pteridophytes						
Adiantaceae						
Adiantum capillus- veneris L.	Barin	1300-2200	1, 2, 3, 4	H	–	–
A. edgeworthii Hk.	–	1600-2000	1, 2, 3, 4, 7	H	–	–
A. lunulatum Burm.	–	1300-1700	2, 4, 7	H	–	–
A. venustum D. Don	–	1800-3050	1, 2, 3, 5	H	–	–
Aspleniaceae						
Asplenium dalhousiae Hk.	–	1300-3050	1, 2, 3, 5	H	–	–
A. varians D.Don	–	2000-3050	2, 3, 7	H	–	–
A. tenuicaule Hayata	–	1500-3050	2, 3, 7	H	–	–
A. trichomanes L.	–	1600-2600	2, 3, 7	H	–	–
A. yunnanense Franch.	–	1800-2500	2, 3, 7	H	–	–
Athyriaceae						
Athyrium atkinsonii Bedd.	–	2800-3050	1, 2, 3, 4	H	–	–
A. attenuatum Tagawa	–	2800-3050	1, 2, 3, 4, 7, 9	H	–	–
A. fimbriatum Moore.	–	2000-2800	1, 4, 5	H	–	–
A. rupicola (Edgeworth ex Hope) C.Chr.	–	1800-2400	1, 2, 7	H	–	NE
A. rubricaule (Edgew. ex Cl.)Bir	–	2800-3050	1, 2, 3	H	–	NE
Deparia allantodioides Kato.	–	1800-3050	1, 7	H	–	–
Diplazium esculentum (Retz.) Sw.	Linger	1300-1800	1, 2, 4, 5	H	–	–
D. spectabile Ching.	–	1800-2400	1, 2	H	–	–
Blechnaceae						
Woodwardia unigemmata (Mak.) Nakai	–	1600-2400	1, 2, 4	H	–	–
Botrychiaceae						
Botrychium ternatum (Thunb.) Swartz.	–	2000-2800	2, 4	H	–	–
Cryptogrammaceae						
Onychium contiguum Wall.	–	1600-2800	1, 2, 3, 5, 7, 8	H	–	–
Davalliaceae						
Araiostegia beddomei Ching.	–	2700-3050	1, 2, 3, 5, 7	H	–	–
A. delavayi Ching	–	2700-3050	1, 2	H	–	–
A. pseudocystopteris (Kunze) Copel.	–	2200-2800	1, 2, 5	H	–	–
Dryopteridaceae						

(Contd...)

Family/Taxa	Local Name	AR(m)	Habitat/s	HF	Nativity	End
Dryopteris cochleata C. Chr.	–	1300-1600	2, 7	H	–	–
D. juxtaposita Chr.	–	1300-2600	1, 2, 3, 4, 7	H	–	–
D. panda (Cl.) Chr.	–	2700-3050	1, 3, 7	H	–	–
D. sparsa Kuntz	–	1800-2900	2, 4, 7	H	–	–
Polystichum lachenense Bedd.	–	2900-3050	1, 3, 7	H	–	–
P. lentum (D.Don) Moore	–	1600-2600	1, 2, 3, 7	H	–	–
P. longipaleatum Chr.	–	1800-2500	1, 2, 7	H	–	–
P. mehrae Fraser-jenk. & Khul.	–	1500-2600	1, 2, 3, 7	H	–	–
P. nepalense (Spreng.) C.Chr.	–	2000-2800	2, 5	H	–	–
P. piceopaleceum Tagawa	–	1800-2800	1, 2, 7	H	–	–
P. squarrosum(D.Don) Fee	Barna	1600-2400	1, 2, 3, 5, 7	H	–	–
Equisetaceae						
Equisetum debile (Roxb. ex Vauch.) Hauke	Khasra ghass	1300-2000	1, 5	H	–	–
E. arvense L.	–	1800-3050	1, 5	H	–	–
Hemionitidaceae						
Coniogramme falcata D.Don	–	2000-2800	1, 3	H	–	–
C. intermedia Hier.	–	2000-2600	1, 2	H	–	–
Onocleaceae						
Woodsia cycloloba Hand. – Mazz.	–	2800-3050	1, 3, 7	H	–	–
Polypodiaceae						
Lepisorus amaurolepidus (Sledge) Bir & Trikha	–	1400-2200	1, 3, 7	H	–	–
L. contortus (Christ) Ching.	–	2000-2800	1, 3, 7	H	–	–
L. kashyapii Mehra	–	2100-2600	1, 3, 7	H	–	NE
L. pseudonudus Ching.	–	1800-3050	1, 3, 7	H	–	–
L. nudus (Hk.) Ching.	–	1500-2500	1, 2, 5, 7, 10	H	–	–
L. tenuipes Ching.	–	1300-2200	1, 3, 7	H	–	
Phymatopteris stracheyi Serm.	–	2500-3050	1, 3, 7	H	–	–
Polypodioides amoena (Wall. ex Mett.) Ching	–	1800-2400	1, 2, 3, 4, 7, 10	H	–	–
P. lachnopus Ching.	–	1800-2500	1, 3, 5, 7, 10	H	–	–
P. microrhizoma Ching.	–	2000-2600	1, 3, 7, 10	H	–	–
P. subamoena (H.) Ching	–	2000-2600	1, 2, 3, 7, 10	H	–	–

(Contd…)

Family/Taxa	Local Name	AR(m)	Habitat/s	HF	Nativity	End
Polypodium polypodioides (L.) Hitch.	–	1800-2000	1, 2, 3, 7, 10	H	–	–
Pyrrosia beddomeana Ching.	–	1300-1600	1, 10	H	–	–
P. stricta (Kunze) Holtt.	–	1400-1800	1, 3, 10	H	–	–
Pteridiaceae						
Pteridium aquilinum (L.) Kuhn.	–	1600-2500	1, 2, 4	H	–	–
Pteris biaurita L.	Puai	1500-2000	1, 3, 7	H	–	–
P.cretica L.	Puai	1300-2000	1, 2, 3, 4, 5, 7	H	–	–
P.quadriaurita Bedd.	Puai	1800-2400	1, 2, 3, 7	H	–	–
P. vittata L.	–	1300-1600	1, 2, 4, 5, 7	H	–	–
Selaginaceae						
Selaginella chrysocaulos (Hk. et Grev.) Spring	–	1300-1800	1, 2, 7	H	–	–
Sinopteridaceae						
Cheilanthes albo-marginata Cl.	Dangtulli	1300-1800	1, 2, 3, 4, 5, 7	H	–	–
C.dalhousiae Hk.	–	2000-2800	1, 3, 4, 7	H	–	–
C.dubia Hop.	–	1300-1700	1, 2, 3, 7	H	–	–
Thelypteridaceae						
Phegopteris connectilis Watt.	–	2600-3050	1, 3, 5, 7	H	–	–
P. punctata (Thunb.) Bedd.	Baran	1800-2200	1, 3, 5, 7	H	–	–
Pseudophegopteris levingei Ching.	–	2200-3050	1, 2, 3, 7	H	–	–
Thelypteris palustris (Salisb.) Schott	–	2400-3050	1, 5, 3, 7	H	–	–

Abbreviations used: AR=Altitudinal range; HF=Habit forms; End=Endemism; H =Herb; Sh =Shrub; T =Tree; Reg Himal = Himalayan Region; Ind Or =Indian Oriental; Bor =Borealis; Temp =Temperate; Arct =Arctic; et =And; As =Asia; Centr =Central; Afr = Africa; Geront =Gerontia; Trop =Tropical; Amphig =Amphigaea; Austr =Australia; Am =America; N.Zel =New Zealand; Orient =Oriental; Cosmop =Cosmopolitan; Occ =Occidentalis; Afghan =Afganistan; Turkist =Turkistan; Arab =Arabia; Subtrop =Subtropical; Hisp =Hispan; Min =Minor; Polynes =Polynesia; Madag =Madagascar; Alger =Algeria; E =Endemic; NE =Near Endemic; 1=Shady Moist; 2=Dry; 3=Rocky; 4=Degraded; 5=Riverine; 6=Camping site; 7=Bouldary; 8=Open slope; 9=Landslide and 10=Epiphyte

REFERENCES

Anonymous 1883-1970. Index Kewensis Plantarum Phanerogamarum Vol. 1-2 (1883-1885) and 15 Suppl. (1886-1970). Clarendron Press, Oxford.

Aswal, B.S. and Mehrotra, B.N. 1994. Flora of Lahaul-Spiti (A Cold Desert in North-West Himalaya). Bishen Singh Mahendra Pal Singh, Dehradun.

Behera, M.D. and Kushwaha, S.P.S. (2007): An Analysis of Altitudinal Behaviour of Tree Species in Subansiri District, Eastern Himalaya. Biodiversity and Conservation, 16: 1851-1865.

Bhattarai, K.R. and Vetaas, O.R. (2003): Variation in Plant Species Richness of Different Life Forms Along a Subtropical Elevation Gradient in the Himalayas, East Nepal. Journal of Global Ecology and Biogeography, 12: 327-340.

Chawla, A., Rajkumar, S., Singh, K.N., Lal, B., Thukral, A.K. and Singh, R.D., 2008. Plant Species Diversity Along an Altitudinal Gradient of Bhabha Valley in Western Himalaya. Journal of Mountain Science, 5: 157-177.

Chowdhery, H.J. and Wadhwa, B.M. (1984):Flora of Himachal Pradesh, Vols. 1-3. Botanical Survey of India, Calcutta.

Currie, D.J. and Francis, A.P. (2004): Regional Versus Climate Effect on Taxon Richness in Angiosperms: Reply to Qian and Ricklefs. Amarican Nature, 163: 780-785.

Dhaliwal, D.S. and Sharma, M. (1999): Flora of Kullu District (Himachal Pradesh). Bishen Singh Mahendra Pal Singh, Dehradun.

Fram, J.P. and Gradstein, S.R. (1991): An Altitudinal Zonation of Tropical Rain Forests Using Bryophytes. Journal of Biogeography, 18: 669-678.

Givnish, T.J. (1999): On the Causes of Gradients in Tropical Tree Diversity. Journal of Ecology, 87: 193-210.

Grytnes, J.A. (2003): Species-richness Patterns of Vascular Plants Along Seven Altitudinal Transects in Norway. Ecography. 26: 291-300.

Gonzalez-Espinosa, M., Rey-Benayas, J.M., Ramirez-Marcial, N., Huston, M.A. and Golicher, D. (2004): Tree Diversity in the Northern Neotropics: Regional Patterns in High Diverse Chiapas, Mexico. Ecography, 27: 741-756.

Lieberman, D., Lieberman, M., Peralta, R. and Hartsharn, G.S. (1996): Tropical Forest and Composition on a Large Scale Altitudinal Gradient in Costa Rica. Journal of Ecology, 84: 137-152.

Lomolino, V.M. (2001): Elevation Gradients of Species-density: Historical and Prospective View. Journal of Global Ecology and Biogeography, 10: 3-13.

Kharakwal, G., Mehrotra, P., Rawat, Y.S. and Pangtey, Y.P.S. 2005. Phytodiversity and Growth form in Relation to Altiudinal Gradient in the Central Himalaya Region (Kumaon) of India. Current Science, 89 (5): 873-878.

Kohli, R.K., Dogra, K.S., Batish, D.R. and Singh, H.P. (2004): Impact of Invasive Plants on the Structure and Composition of Natural Vegetation of Northwestern Indian Himalayas. Weed Technology, 18: 1296-1300.

Korner, C. (1998): A Re-assessment of High Elevation Tree Line Positions and Their Explanation. Oecologia, 115: 445-459.

Nayar, M.P. (1996): Hotspots of Endemic plants in India, Nepal and Bhutan. Tropical Botanic Garden and Research Institute, Thiruvananthapuram, India.

Pant, B.R. (2003): Degrading Environment and Growing Population of the Indian Himalaya. ENVIS Bulletin: Himalayan Ecology, 11(1): 26-37.

Singh, J.S. and Singh, S.P. (1992): Forest of Himalaya: Structure, Functioning and Impact of Man. Gyanodya Prakashan, Nainital.

Samant, S.S., Dhar, U. and Palni, L.M.S. (1998): Medicinal Plants of Indian Himalaya: Diversity Distribution Potential Values. Gyanodaya Prakashan, Nainital.

Samant, S.S., Joshi, H.C. and Arya, S.C. (2000): Diversity, Nativity and Endemism of Vascular plants in Pindari Area of Nanda Devi Biosphere Reserve-II. Himalayan Bioshere Reserve, 2(1 & 2): 1-29.

Samant, S.S., Joshi, H.C., Pant, S. and Arya, S.C. (2001): Diversity, Nativity and Endemism of Vascular Plants in Valley of Flowers National Park. Himalayan Bioshere Reserve, 3(1&2): 1-17.

Singh, P.B. (1992): Flora of Mandi Forest Division, Himachal Pradesh, India. Ph.D. Thesis.H.N.B. Garhwal University, Srinagar, Garhwal.

Veenendaal, E.M., Swaine, M.O., Agyeman, V.K., Blay, D., Abebrese, I.K. and Mullins, C.E. (1996): Differences in Plant and Soil Water Relations in and Around a Forest Gap in West Africa during the Dry Season may Influence Seedling Establishment and Survival. Journal of Ecology, 83: 83-90.

Vazquez, J.A. and Givnish, T.J. (1998): Altitudinal Gradient in the Tropical Forest Composition, Structure and Diversity in the Sierra de Manantla'n. Journal of Ecology, 86: 999-1020.

Vetaas, O.R. and Grytnes, J.A. (2002): Distribution of Vascular Plant Species Richness and Endemic Richness Along the Himalayan Elevational Gradient in Nepal. Journal of Global Ecology and Biogeography, 11: 291-301.

Willig, M.R., Kaufman, D.M. and Stevens, R.D. (2003): Latitudinal Gradients of Biodiversity: Pattern Process, Scale and Synthesis. Annals of Review of Ecology Evolution and Systematics, 34: 273-309.

Pages: 78-87

BIODIVERSITY, BIOTECHNOLOGY AND ENVIRONMENTAL CONSERVATION

Edited by: Dr. Pawan Kumar 'Bharti'; Mr. Govinda Bhandari

ISBN: 978-93-5056-750-0

Edition: 2015

Published by: Discovery Publishing House Pvt. Ltd., New Delhi (India)

CHAPTER 5

Natural Regeneration Status of Silver Fir and Spruce Forests in Himachal Pradesh

Dinesh Gupta[1*]; DP Sharma[2] and GS Shamet[3]

ABSTRACT

Silver fir (*Abies pindrow* Royle.)and spruce (*Picea smithiana* Wall.) commonly referred as high level conifers, cover extensive areas in north-west Himalayan states of Himachal Pradesh, Jammu and Kashmir and Uttraknand and occupy about 31.15% of total area under coniferous forests and account for 48.8% of the total growing stock.Regeneration survey was carried out in Periodic Block-I of Naggar (Forest Division), Nohra (Rajgarh Forest Division) and Kotgarh (Kotgarh Forest Division) Forest Range of Himachal Pradesh. Overall per cent regeneration was better at Kullu (91.68), followed by Kotgarh (74.69) and Rajgarh (72.47).

1 Himachal Pradesh State Biodiversity Board, Himachal Pradesh State Council for Science Technology and Environment, 34 SDA Complex, Kasumpti, Shimla - 171 009, Himachal Pradesh, (India).

2 Department of Silviculture and Agroforestry, Dr. Y.S. Parmar University of Horticulture and Forestry, Nauni, Solan - 173 230, Himachal Pradesh, (India).

3 College of Forestry, Dr. Y.S. Parmar University of Horticulture and Forestry, Nauni, Solan - 173 230, Himachal Pradesh, (India).

INTRODUCTION

Silver fir and spruce commonly referred as high level conifers, cover extensive areas in north-west Himalayan states of Himachal Pradesh, Jammu and Kashmir and Uttraknand. They occupy about 31.15% of total area under coniferous forests and account for 48.8% of the total growing stock in these states (Singh & Singh, 1984). Together these species cover 15640 hectare in Himachal Pradesh (Balu, 2000). These forests are very valuable resource as they play an important role in improving the economy of these states, and help soil and water conservation in catchment area of major rivers (Kumar *et al.*, 2005). These species extend throughout the western Himalaya from Afghanistan to Nepal chiefly from 2200m to 3500m above mean sea level, but sometimes descend and are found in cool ravines.

The commercial exploitation of these forests was planned after First World War. In the past there was a keen demand for it for packing cases because wood is light, practically odourless and whitish in colour. Demand of fir and spruce wood is increasing for the feeding the paper and pulp, rayon, hard wood and clipboard industries. Selected timber of spruce has also been found to be quite suitable for manufacture of gliders (Dhillon, 1961).

Regeneration in silver fir and spruce forests, which have been felled extensively since the Second World War, has practically failed. Natural regeneration is generally difficult to obtain in the fir and spruce forests of Himachal Pradesh (Agarwala & Datta, 1968). The different silvicultural requirement of silver fir (shade demander) and spruce (moderate light demander) were realized very early by Parmand and Wright, 1922 and different silvicultural treatments were advocated for true management of forests (Kaushik, 1954). Seedling of both fir and spruce are slow growing, require good light for their proper development, and often suffer from a dense canopy of trees or bush growth.Artificial regeneration has now been introduced with good success to limited extent. It has been reasonably established that silver fir and spruce can be raised artificially by planting the nursery raised seedlings of 23cm to 30cm size. The time taken to raise plants of these sizes in the nursery is from 3.5 to 4.5 years in high level nurseries (Agarwala & Datta, 1968).

With the imposition of a ban on green felling since 1985 and absence of management practices, these forests might have suffered from absence of regeneration as well as normal distribution of growth in the forests. The known poor response of fir and spruce forests to regeneration, under the present circumstances at all is not desirable as far the scientific management of the forests in concerned. There is a need to understand the growth distribution under present condition, so that suitable management practice with ensured regeneration and proper yield regulation could be evolved.

MATERIALS AND METHOD

Study Area

The study area falls under Kullu, Rajgarh and Kotgarh Forest Division of Himachal Pradesh (Table 5.1). The description of the study area is given as under.

Table 5.1: Details of Locations in Kullu, Rajgarh and Kotgarh Study Area

Forest Division	Forest Range	Compartment	Periodic Block (PB)	Area (ha)	Aspect
Kullu	Naggar	C-I (b)	PB-I	25.49	North-west
Rajgarh	Nohra	C-I (c)	PB-I	78.00	South
Kotgarh	Kotgarh	C-60	PB-I	72.90	West and north west

Location

Kullu

The Kullu district forms a transitional zone between the lesser and great Himalaya and lies between 1263 to 6495m above mean sea level.The track lies between north latitude 31° 45′N to 32°26′ N and east longitude 76° 59′ E to 77°50′ E. Silver fir and spruce are the main species, with the former predominating on higher reaches and latter available at lower elevation. Scattered deodar is present on rocks and precipitous slope while kail may be observed on exposed spurs and ridges.

Rajgarh

The study was confined to silver fir and spruce forest of Rajgarh forest division, which is situated between 77°15′ to 26°13′ E longitude and 30° 30′40″ to 30°14′55″ N latitude. The track is mountainous varying in altitude between 1000m to 3,400m above mean sea level. The slopes are steep to very steep with precipitous rocks. The silver fir and spruce forests are confined between 2,400m to 3,200m elevation thus occupy the highest slopes of ridges in Rajgarh and Nohra range and are next to deodar, kail and chil in order and importance. In general in fir forests the proportion of spruce is higher than silver fir. In the past working plan, these forests were worked under concentrated regeneration felling but regeneration was unsatisfactory.

Kotgarh

The Kotgarh Forest Division lies between 31°08′40″ to 31°42′50″ N latitude and 72°18′50″ to 77°0′58″ E longitude. All the fir, spruce forests having pure crop or 60 per cent or more in composition in a compartment and suitable for working under concentrated regeneration felling. The forests are very much under-stocked and there is preponderance of mature to over mature trees. Natural regeneration in these forests is very much poor and more over heavy grazing and indiscriminate felling in the past has caused great damage to these forests.These forests are managed under Indian irregular shelterwood system with a rotation age of 120 years and regeneration period of 30 years.

Regeneration Survey

Observations on regeneration were made in periodic block I of each at three locations with a recording unit (quadrat) size of 2 × 2 m (4 sq m).The data thus collected was analyzed using the formulae given by Chacko (1965) as follows:

$$\text{Recruits (r)/ha} = 2500\sum_{i=1}^{n} ri/m$$

$$\text{Unestablished regeneration (u)/ha} = 2500\sum_{i=1}^{n} ui/m$$

$$\text{Established regeneration (e)/ha} = 2500\sum_{i=1}^{n} ei/m$$

Where

n – Number of sampling units

m – Total number of recording units in survey

ri – Total number of recruits in each sampling unit

ui – Total number of unestablished plants in each sampling unit

ei – Total number of established plants in each sampling unit

$$\text{Weighted Average height (m)} = \frac{\text{Total height of unestablished regeneration + (Number. of established plants × establishment height)}}{\text{Total unestablished plants + total established plants}}$$

On the basis of above estimates following indices were calculated:

$$\text{Establishment index } (I_1) = \frac{\text{Weighted average height}}{\text{Establishment height}}$$

$$\text{Stocking index } (I_2) = 1/2500 \times \frac{\text{Unestablished regeneration/ha}}{4} + \text{Established regeneration/ha}$$

Established stocking per cent = 100 ($I_1 \times I_2$)

Regeneration success (%) = Stocking index (I_2) X 100

Solar Radiation (influx)

Relative light illumination was recorded by lux meter. The measurement of solar radiation was taken under and outside the canopy during day time and the value in percentage of light intensity under the canopy to that in open was calculated (Rao, 1998) as:

$$\text{Solar influx (\%)} = \frac{\text{Total solar radiation beneath the canopy}}{\text{Total solar radiation in open}} \times 100$$

Depth of Organic Matter

To record the depth of humus layer, a horizontal cut was given by a sharp knife through the humus layer and thickness of the humus was read on a graduated scale placed in front of the sharp cut.

Soil pH

A composite soil sample from all the five quadrate in each sample plot (40m × 30m) was made by collecting soil from surface 0-10cm depth and sub surface 15 to 20cm depth. The soil samples thus collected were air dried, crushed, passed through 2mm sieve and stored in cloth bags for pH analysis. A sub-sample of 20 gm of air dried soil sample was thoroughly mixed in 50ml of distilled water (Jackson 1973). The pH of the soil water suspension was then estimated with help of digital pH meter.

Results

The regeneration status of fir and spruce forest at three locations i.e. Kullu, Kotgarh and Rajgarh forest was studied by recording data on number of recruits, unestablished and established regeneration in the regeneration block (PB-I). The results are presented in table 5.2.

The result revealed that Kotgarh observed maximum recruits (4250/ha) followed by Rajgarh (3667/ha) and Kullu (3168/ha). The unestablished regeneration was recorded maximum at Kullu (5500/ha) followed by Rajgarh (4583/ha) and Kotgarh (3001/ha) whereas, established regeneration was maximum at Kotgarh (1117/ha) followed by Kullu (917/ha) and Rajgarh (666/ha).Per cent regeneration was higher at Kullu (91.68) then Kotgarh (74.69) and Rajgarh (72.74).

The Kullu site observeddominance of *Picea smithiana* at 84, 89 and 72.7 per cent of recruits, unestablished and established regeneration, respectively over rest of the tree species. The regeneration of *Abies pindrow* was completely absent. *Pinus wallichiana* recorded 10.5 per cent recruits and unestablished and established regeneration at 3 and 27.2 per cent respectively. The recruits

(5.2%) for deodar were though recorded yet regeneration under eunestablished and established regeneration categories was absent. However, *Quercus dilatata* was able to report 7.5 per cent unestablished regeneration, failed to show any recruits, and established regeneration. Out of 91.68 per cent regeneration *Picea smithiana* contributed 75.85 per cent followed by *Pinus wallichiana* (11.66%) and *Quercus dilatata* (4.16%).

Table 5.2: Regeneration Status of Fir/Spruce Forests in PB-I

Species	Recruits No./ha (%)	Unestablished No./ha (%)	Established No./ha (%)	Per cent Regeneration
Kullu				
Picea smithiana	2667(84.0)	4917(89.0)	667(72.7)	75.85
Cedrus deodara	167(5.2)	–	–	–
Pinus wallichiana	334(10.5)	166.6(3.0)	250(27.2)	11.66
Quercus dilatata.	–	416.6(7.5)	–	4.16
Total	**3168**	**5500.2**	**917**	**91.68**
Kotgarh				
Abies pindrow	2583(60.8)	167(5.5)	167(14.9)	8.53
Picea smithiana	833(19.6)	2667(88.9)	783(70.09)	57.99
Pinus wallichiana	167(3.9)	–	167(14.9)	6.68
Quercus semicarpifolia	417(9.8)	167(5.5)	–	1.67
Taxus baccata	250(5.8)	–	–	–
Total	**4250**	**3001**	**1117**	**74.69**
Rajgarh				
Picea smithiana	2667(72.7)	3833(83.6)	583(87.5)	61.65
Pinus wallichiana	333(9.1)	–	–	0
Quercus dilatata	–	250(5.5)	–	2.5
Rhododendron arborium	250(6.8)	333(7.2)	83(12.5)	6.65
Quercus semicarpifolia	417(11.3)	167(3.6)	–	1.67
Total	**3667**	**4583**	**666**	**72.47**

The Kotgarh study site reported dominance of recruits, unestablished and established plants with 80.4, 94.4 and 84.99 per cent regeneration respectively, including *Picea smithiana* and *Abies pindrow*. Individually, *Abies pindrow* (60.8%) reported the higher number of recruits than *Picea smithiana* (19.6%). However, *Picea smithiana* observed higher unestablished (88.9%) and established (70.09%) regeneration than 5.5 and 14.9 per cent for *Abies pindrow* in the corresponding regeneration categories. *Picea smithiana* also had highest per cent regeneration (57.99). *Quercus semicarpifolia, Taxus baccata and Pinus wallichiana* reported 9.8, 5.8 and 3.9 per cent recruits. The *Quercus semicarpifolia* and *Taxus baccata* failed to report any established regeneration.

The Rajgarh site observed dominance of *Picea smithiana* regeneration with recruits, unestablished and established regeneration at 72.7, 83.6 and

87.5 per cent respectively, over rest of tree species. Any kind of regeneration for *Abies pindrow* was absent. *Quercus semicarpifolia, Pinus wallichiana* showed 11.3, 9.1 and 6.8 per cent recruits respectively, and recruit and established regeneration was missing for *Quercus dilatata*. The unestablished and established regeneration was found to be absent for *Pinus wallichiana*. *Picea smithiana* dominated in per cent regeneration (61.65) over rest of the tree species.

Established Stocking Per cent

Data pertaining to established stocking per cent is presented in table 5.3. Overallstocking was higher at Kullu (21.06%) than Kotgarh (20.43%) and Rajgarh (20.23%). Among all tree species, *Picea smithiana* showed highest established stocking at Kotgarh (19.13%) and followed by Kullu (17.25) and Rajgarh (17.24).

Table 5.3: Establishment Index, Stocking Index and Established Stocking Percent of Fir/Spruce Forests

Species	Establishment Index (I_1)	Stocking Index (I_2)	Established Stocking Per cent ($100 \times I_1 \times I_2$)
Kullu			
Picea smithiana	0.23	0.76	17.25
Pinus wallichiana	0.20	0.12	2.48
Quercus dilatata	0.32	0.04	1.33
Total	**0.75**	**0.92**	**21.06**
Rajgarh			
Picea smithiana	0.28	0.62	17.24
Rhododendron arborium	0.36	0.07	2.16
Quercus dilatata	0.19	0.03	0.48
Quercus semicarpifolia			
Total	**1.05**	**0.74**	**20.23**
Kotgarh			
Abies pindrow	0.11	0.08	0.91
Picea smithiana	0.33	0.58	19.13
Pinus wallichiana	0.01	0.07	0.07
Quercus semicarpifolia	0.19	0.02	0.32
Total	**0.64**	**0.75**	**20.43**

Humus Depth, Soil pH and Solar Influx

The reported humus depth, soil pH and solar influx under different stocking at three sites are given in table 5.4. Rajgarh reported higher humus depth (5.14 cm) followed by Kotgarh (4.35 cm) and Kullu (2.80 cm). The pH did not show much variation at three sites (6.80-6.90). However, Kullu having highest stocking (21.06%) and per cent regeneration (91.68) reported lowest solar influx of 21.96 followed by Rajgarh (20.23%) and Kotgarh (20.43%) with solar influx of 28.09 and 60.50 and respectively.

Table: 5.4: Humus Depth, Soil pH Under Different Stocking at Kullu, Rajgarh and Kotgarh

Site	Per cent Regeneration	Established Stocking Per cent	Humus Layer (cm)	Soil pH	Solar Influx (%)
Kullu	91.68	21.06	2.80	6.83	21.96
Rajgarh	72.47	20.23	5.14	6.80	28.09
Kotgarh	74.69	20.43	4.35	6.90	60.50

DISCUSSION

Recruits reported at Kotgarh (4250/ha) were much higher than Rajgarh (3667/ha) and Kullu (3168/ha), whereas unestablished and established regeneration was seen higher at Kullu (5500/ha) and Kotgarh (1117/ha), respectively (Table 5.2). Higher quantity of recruits at Kotgarh may be due to adequate number of seed bearers and exposed site conditions as is evident from solar influx values of 60.50% recorded at the site in table 5.4.

Percent regeneration, which is based on unestablished and established regeneration following Chacko (1965), was better at Kullu (91.68%) than other sites. Large number of unestablished seedlings at Kullu has contributed in overall higher regeneration percent (Table 5.2). The established regeneration was maximum at Kotgarh (1117/ha) whereas, unestablished regeneration was maximum at Kullu (5500/ha). It seems that there had been less proportionate conversion of unestablished to established regeneration at Kullu in the past, which may be attributed to higher biotic interference (Grazing and trampling by animals) at the site. The results are supported by the findings of Dhillon, 1961 who has observed considerable damage to young seedlings by animals in fir and spruce forest.

Kullu (75.85%) and Rajgarh (61.65%) noticed adequate regeneration of *Picea smithiana*, whereas, regeneration of *Abies pindrow* was completely absent at both the sites (Table 5.2).The results are against the regeneration description given in working plan of Kullu Forest Division, which report that natural regeneration in these forests is very much poor and more over heavy grazing and indiscriminate felling in the past has caused great damage to these forests. The better percent regeneration at Rajgarh is supported by Shrivastava 1997, who reported that younger regeneration thrives well under selection system with little biotic interference at Rajgarh forest division. *Picea smithiana* (spruce) invades an area earlier than *Abies pindrow* (silver fir) and ultimately spruce may be ousted altogether (Dhillon, 1961). Moreover, spruce is a pioneer species as it is much hardier, requires more light and grows faster than fir (Agarwala and Datta, 1968).

The absence of regeneration of *Abies pindrow* at Kullu may be attributed to extremely low proportion of fir trees, absence of mother trees at low altitude of the compartment (1889-2348m). While its absence at Rajgarh may be explained in the light of absence of mother trees and warm southern aspect. The results are in line with the findings of Gupta (1996), who has reported better regeneration of spruce at lower elevation whereas, for fir it was better at higher elevation. Moreover, *Abies pindrow* is a shade tolerant species in the early years of growth and needs protection against drought and sun (Troup, 1921 and Agarwala and Datta, 1968).

The data on regeneration establishment stocking (Table 5.3) revealed that the establishment stocking of fir and spruce did not show much variation whereas, variation in humus depths was seen among three sites (Table 5.4). Regeneration percent of 91.68, 74.69 and 72.47 with humus depth of 5.14, 4.35 and 2.80cm at Rajgarh, Kotgarh and Kullu, respectively indicate that humus depth had influenced regeneration (Table 3). Effect of undecomposed humus layer on regeneration in fir and spruce forest is well documented by Troup, 1921; Taylor *et al.*, 1934; Glover, 1936; Datta,1958; Dhillon, 1961and Kaul, 1990; and, an inverse relationship between humus layer and regeneration in fir and spruce at Jubbal forest range has been reported by Sharma (2006).

The soil was acidic in all the three sites. The value of pH ranged from 6.83 to 6.90, which did not indicate any effect on regeneration. The impact of light on regeneration is evident from table 5.4, which showed increase in regeneration percent with decrease in solar influx. The solar influx was maximum at Kotgarh (60.50) followed by Rajgarh (28.09) and Kullu (21.96) with regeneration percent of 74.69, 72.47 and 91.68, respectively.

CONCLUSION

The study concludes that natural regeneration of fir is poor as compared to spruce at the selected sites owing to their different silvicultural requirement.Moreover proportionate conversion of recruits and unestablished regeneration to established regeneration is not upto the mark due to biotic interference. There is an intense need to advocate different silvicultural treatments for the true management of fir and spruce forests.

REFERENCES

Agrawala, V.P. and Datta, R.C.1968. Artificial Regeneration of Fir and Spruce in Himachal Pradesh. Proc. Eleventh Silvicultural Conference, Vol. II Dehra Dun. 493-495.

Balu, T.R. 2000. Forest Cover of Himachal Pradesh. *State of Forest Report* pp. 49-51.

Chacko, V.J. 1965. A Manual of Sampling Techniques for Forest Surveys. Manager Publications, Delhi p. 172.

Datta, R.C. 1985. Natural Regeneration of Spruce and Fir. Proc. First Regional Meeting of Silviculturerists, Himalayan Region Kashmir. 13-15.

Dhillon, G.S. 1961. Recent Trends in Natural Regeneration Technique of Silver Fir and Spruce Forests. Proc. Tenth Silvicultural Conference, Vol. (1) 313-321.

Dwivedi, A.P. 1993. Principals and Practices of Silviculture. Surya Publications, 4-B Nashville Road, Dehradun. p. 256.

Glover, H.N. 1936. Practical Problems of Management of the Himalayan Fir Forests. *Indian Forester.* 62(5): 276-282.

Gupta, N.K. 1996. Appraisal of Vegetational Pattern of Shimla District Through Remote Sensing with Special Reference to the Ecology of Fir–spruce Forest. Ph.D. Thesis Dr. YS Parmar UHF, Solan (H.P.). p. 113.

Jackson, M.L. 1973. Soil Chemical Analysis. Prentice Hall of India Pvt. Ltd. New Delhi.

Kaul, P.N. 1970. Natural Regeneration of Silver Fir and Spruce. Proc. State Conference J & K State. pp. 79-84.

Kaushik, R.C. 1954. Management of Spruce (*Picea morinda*) and Fir (*Abies pindrow* and *Abies webiana*) forests. *Indian forester*. 80(2): 78-89.

Kumar, M., Sharma, C.M. and Rajwar, G.S. 2005. The Stability and Diversity Patterns of Vegetation in Tropical Foot hill Forest Along Disturbance Gradient in Garhwal Himalaya. *Annals of Forestry* 13(1): 84-92.

Pramand and Wright, H.L.1922. The Himalayan Spruce and Silver Fir: Note on Their Silvicuture and Regeneration. Proc. Punjab Forest Conference. Lahore. 41-58.

Rao, G.R. 1998. Study on Dynamics of Herbage Layer in Pine and Khair Based Natural Silvipastoral System in North West Himalaya. Ph.D. Thesis, Dr. Y.S.Parmar. UHF, Solan (H.P.) p. 125.

Sharma, Y. 2006. Studies on Stand Parameters and Natural Regeneration Status of Silver Fir and Spruce in Himachal Pradesh. M.Sc. Thesis, Dr. Y.S. Parmar UHF, Solan (H.P) p. 83.

Shrivastava, M.B. 1997. Management of Spruce (*Picea smithiana*) and Silver Fir (*Abies pindrow*) Forests in Western Himalayas. *Indian Journal of Forestry* 20(2): 116-128.

Singh, V. and Singh, R.V. 1984. Silvicultural, Dispersal, Seed Germination and Seedling Establishment in Natural Forest of Silver Fir and Spruce. *Indian Forester.* 110(6): 529-539.

Taylor, R.M., Mehta, M.L. and Hoon, R.C.1934. Investigation of Some Bajrundi Forest Soils With Reference to Regeneration of Fir Spruce (*Picea morinda*). *Indian Forester.* 60(5): 388-401.

Troup, R.S.1921. The Silviculture of Indian Trees. Vol. III. Clarendon Press, Oxford. 1923.

Pages: 88-114

BIODIVERSITY, BIOTECHNOLOGY AND ENVIRONMENTAL CONSERVATION

Edited by: Dr. Pawan Kumar 'Bharti'; Mr. Govinda Bhandari

ISBN: 978-93-5056-750-0

Edition: 2015

Published by: Discovery Publishing House Pvt. Ltd., New Delhi (India)

CHAPTER 6

GC-MS Studies and *in-vitro* and *in-vivo* Biological Activities of Solvent Extracts of Mokkathotapapada Leaves of *Piper betel* L. Cv. Kapoori, a Local Cultivar

Ammani Kandru*; Lydia Swapna Nandam[1]
Harikrishna Ramaprasad Saripalli[2]

ABSTRACT

India is a treasure house of a wide variety of medicinal plants. Some species are found wild, while a number of species have been domesticated by the farmers. India is known to be the richest repository of medicinal plants amongst the ancient civilizations, About 8,000 herbal remedies have been codified in Ayurveda. The recorded medicinal plants in *Rigveda* (5000 BC) – 67species, *Yajurveda* 81 species, *Atharvaveda*(4500-2500 BC) 290 species, *Charak Samhita* (700 BC) and *Sushrut Samhita* (200 BC) had described properties and uses of 1100 and 1270 species respectively, in compounding of drugs and these are still used in the classical formulations, in the Ayurvedic system of medicine. It has been estimated that in India, plant drugs constitute as much

* Department of Botany and Microbiology, Acharya Nagarjuna University, Guntur, Andhra Pradesh, (India).

1 Department of Biology and Biotechnology, C N C S, Aksum University, Axum, Ethiopia, North East Africa.

2 Department of Biology and Biotechnology, C N C S, Aksum University, Axum, Ethiopia, North East Africa.

as 80% of the total drugs. India is the world's 12th biodiversity centre with the presence of over 45000 different plant species. In India, drugs of herbal origin have been used in customary medicines such as *Unani* and *Ayurveda.*

Traditional systems of medicine keep on to be widely practised on many acounts. Many of the green plants synthesizes and bottle a variety of biochemical products, many of which are extractable and used as chemical feed stocks or as raw material for various scientific investigations. In accordance with this information, *Piper betel* L. Cv. Kapoori (a local cultivar), which is commonly considered as a traditional medicinal plant, was taken for the study. Solvent extracts of Mokkathotapapada leaves of *Piper betel* L. Cv. Kapoori made in ether, chloroform, ethanol and methanol were tested for antibacterial activity against *Escherichia coli, Bacillus subtilis, Pseudomonas aeruginosa, Corynebacterium diphtheria, Xanthomonas citrovorum, Proteus vulgaris* and *Staphylococcus aureus.* The ether extracts showed high activity against tested bacteria even at lowest concentrations. Among the solvent extracts, ether extracts of Mokkathotapapada leaves of *Piper betel* L. Cv. Kapoori, exhibited high antibacterial activity compared with other solvent extracts. In case of antifungal studies, solvent extracts of Mokkathotapapada leaves of *Piper betel* L. Cv. Kapoori made in ether, chloroform, ethanol, methanol were tested for antimycotic activity against *Aspergillus niger, Aspergillus fumigatus* and *Candida albicans.* The chloroform and methonolic extracts shown high zones of growth inhibition against fungi.

Helminth infections are the most banal health problems in India; in developing countries they pose a large treat to public. These infections can affect most population in endemic areas with major economic and social consequences. The research study was also undertaken to investigate the phytochemical constituents and anthelmintic activity of different solvent extracts (ethanol, chloroform, methanol and petroleum ether) of the Mokkathotapapada leaves of *Piper betel* L. Cv. Kapoori(a local cultivar) using an adult Indian earthworms, *Pheretima posthuma* as a test worm. Six concentrations (10, 20, 40, 60, 80, 100 mg/ml) of each extracts were studied in the bioassay which involved the determination of time of paralysis and time of death of the worm. Piperazine was used as a reference standard at a concentration of 10 mg/ml. The anthelmintic activity of Mokkathotapapada leaves of *Piper betel* L. Cv. Kapoori revealed that all the solvent extracts exhibited varying degree of activity against both the worms and caused paralysis followed by death at all tested concentrations. Organic solvent extracts of the plant at different concentrations showed dose-dependent vermicidal activities. Among the tested extracts, ethanol and methanolic extracts exhibited more potent activity at higher concentration (100mg/ml) when compared to the reference standard piperazine citrate (10 mg/ml).

Piper betel L. Cv Kapoori (family Piperaceae) is implicated in a variety of ethno-medicinal therapies ranging from oral, skin, gastro-intestinal to respiratory problems. The effect of this plant for cytotoxicity needs to be investigated. Thus, the brine–shrimp lethality studies on the leaves (Mokkathotapapada) were carried out. The different fractions of solvent extracts of Mokkathotapapada leaves were subjected to cytotoxicity studies. The brine-shrimp lethality assay analyzed using the Finney probit method showed that the solvent extracts of the leaves displayed LD_{50} values were dose-dependent, enhanced with increase in concentration. These findings indicate the potential of Mokkathotapapada leaves of the plant as panacea for infectious diseases and also reveal a novel potential in the fight against tumors in man.

The phytochemical composition of non-polar solvent extract, chloroform and polar solvent extract, methanol were further analyzed, qualitatively, by Gas Chromatography - Mass Spectrometry (GC-MS). The phytochemical screening of the extracts revealed that the leaves of *Piper betel* L. Cv. Kapoori contained Alkaloids, Fixed oils, Flavonoids, Glycosides, Phenols, Quinones, Resins, Saponins, Steroids, Tannins, Terpenoids and Xanthoproteins.

The above studied methods confirm that *Piper betel* L. Cv. Kapoori (a local cultivar) contains substances with antibacterial, antimycotic, anthelminthic and antitumor properties. The spectra of activities displayed by the extracts can be attributed to the presence of different Phytochemicals and further analysis of chloroform and methanol extracts specially by using GC-MS studies signifies the potential of *Piper betel* L. Cv. Kapoori (a local cultivar) as a source of therapeutic agents and may provide leads in the ongoing search for commercial extraction of essential components employed for varied purposes.

Key words: Antibacterial activity, Antimycotic activity, Anthelmintic activity, Brine-shrimp lethality, GC-MS Analysis, Mokkathotapapada leaves and *Piper betel* L. Cv. Kapoori.

INTRODUCTION

The use of plants as medicines is as old as human civilization itself. Many of the existing medicinal systems such as Ayurveda, Unani, Homeopathy, Naturopathy, Siddha and other alternative medicinal systems have been utilizing plants as effective source of medicines to cure many diseases. India being the largest producer of medicinal herbs is appropriately called the Botanical Garden of the World. (Ahmedulla and Nayer, 1999). *Piper betel* L. belongs to the family Piperaceae. *Piper betel* L. Cv. Kapoori (a local cultivar) is a tropical Asian vine closely related to the common pepper.

Many researchers have haunt on the red lime betel quid in the past few years. A little information on the Betel leaf was found. The plant is a climber with broad, heart-shaped, dark green and shiny, juicy leaves. It is used as an ornamental plant and is also known for its medicinal properties like antibacterial, antioxidant and stimulant and for arthritis (Kirtikar and Basu, 1998). The betel leaf plant is slender stemmed, branching vine climbing as high as 10-15 feet (Prajapathi, 2003). The Betel leaf itself has a spicy taste and yields an essential oil widely used as a medicine. Other biological activities exemplified for the essential oil include antifungal, antiseptic effects (Evans, Bowers, and Funk, 1984). It was evident that Betel leaves contained rich carotenes (80 IU/g fresh wt.), ascorbic acid (1.94 mg/g fresh wt.) and phenolics. Data on the phenolic compounds of this plant is related to chavicol (Amonkar, *et al.*, 1986), chavibetol, chavibetol acetate (Rimando, *et al.*, 1986) and eugenol (Nagabhushan, *et al.*, 1989).

The principal aim of the work was to study the antibacterial, antifungal, anthelminthic, antitumor activityies and phytochemical analysis of different solvent extracts of Mokkathotapapada leaves of *Piper betel* L. Cv. Kapoori (a local cultivar).

The antibacterial and antifungal activity of Mokkathotapapada leaves of *Piper betel* L. Cv. Kapoori (a local cultivar) in different solvents such as ethanol, chloroform, methanol and petroleum ether against seven species of bacteria and three species of fungi . In the experimental study, different fractions of solvent extracts of Mokkathotapapada leaves of the *Piper betel* L. Cv. Kapoori, a local cultivar have been investigated.

The World Health Organization estimates that two billion people harbor parasitic worm infections. These worms also infect livestock and crops, affecting food production with a resultant economic impact. Despite this prevalence of parasitic infections, the research on the anthelmintic drug is sparse. According to the WHO, only a few drugs are used in treatment of helminthes in humans. Anthelmintics from natural sources could play a key role in the treatment of these parasite infections. In view of this, attempts have been made to study the anthelmintic activity of traditional medicinal plant.

The identification of novel antitumor agents that demonstrate efficacy is necessary to improve medical treatment based on new drugs. The pharmaceutical industries have been working together in this area for several years to try to find novel compounds with good antitumor activity. Brine shrimp (*Artemia salina*) larvae have been reported as an organism that can detect bioactive compounds. Since there is a good correlation between the toxicity on *Artemia salina* and antitumor (J.M. McLaughlin, 1991; S. De Rosa et *al.*, 1994) activity, this test is a good prescreening method for identifying new potential antitumor agents. To our knowledge *P. betel* L. Cv Kapoori, a local cultivar has not been investigated for its biological activity. Cytotoxicity of *Piper betel* L. Cv Kapoori leaf (Mokkathotapapada) extracts were studied in different solvents such as ethanol, chloroform, methanol and petroleum ether against Brine shrimp (*Artemia salina*) larvae.

In the experimental study, different solvent extracts of Mokkathotapapada leaves of the *Piper betel* L. Cv Kapoori,a local cultivar plant have been investigated at different concentrations.

MATERIALS AND METHODS

Plant Collection, Identification and Authentication

The *Piper betel* L. Cv Kapoori (a local cultivar) Mokkathotapapada leaves were collected from Chintalapudi, Ponnur, Guntur district of Andhra Pradesh, India, in January 2011. The plant was identified and authenticated by the taxonomist of Faculty of Botany, Hindu college, Guntur and a voucher specimen (ANU/PB-001) was deposited at Department of Botany, Acharya Nagarjuna University, Nagarjuna nagar, Guntur for future reference.

Chemicals Used

Ethanol, chloroform, methanol and petroleum ether (SD Fine Chemicals, Mumbai) was used during experimental protocol.

Extract Preparation

Fresh plant material was dried at room temperature (28 ±30° c) by exposure to atmosphere. The dried materials were pulverized into very fine powder. The coarse powder was extracted with different organic solvents (both polar and nonpolar) using the soxhlet apparatus. The extract was concentrated to dryness in vacuum.

Bacterial Test Organisms

Escherichia coli (ATCC 25922), *Bacillus subtilis* (ATCC 6633), *Pseudomonas aeruginosa* (ATCC 27853), *Corynebacterium diphtheria* (ATCC 75415)., *Xanthomonas citrovorum* (ATCC 8082), *Proteus vulgaris* (ATCC 638) and *Staphylococcus aureus* (ATCC 25923) obtained from the Department of Pharmaceutical Microbiology and Biotechnology, Hindu College of Pharmacy, Guntur, Andhra Pradesh (Characteristics are listed in Table 6.1) were used in the current study. All the above test bacterial species were maintained on Nutrient Agar medium. 36hr-old bacterial culture was inoculated into Nutrient broth and incubated on a rotary shaker at 35 ± 2°C at 100 rpm. After 36 hours of incubation, the bacterial suspension was centrifuged at 10000 rpm for 15 min. The pellet was resuspended in sterile distilled water and the concentration was adjusted to 1×10^8 cfu/ml using UV Visible Spectrophotometer. By reading the OD of the solution to 0.45Å (610nm) it was used for further studies (NCCLS).

Table 6.1: List of the Selected Test Organisms (Bacteria)

Sl. No.	Name of Organism	Characteristics Features	Disease Caused by Organism
1.	*Escherichia Coli* (ATCC 25922)	Gram -ve rod shaped organism	Gastroenteritis
2.	*Bacillus subtilis* (ATCC 6633)	Gram +ve rod shaped organism	Food poisoning
3.	*Pseudomonas aeruginosa* (ATCC 27853)	Gram –ve rod shaped organism	Wounds and urinary tract infections
4.	*Corynebacterium diphtheria* (ATCC 75415)	Gram +ve rod shaped organism	Diphtheria
5.	*Xanthomonas citrovorum* (ATCC 8082)	Gram –ve rod shaped organism	Urinary tract infections
6.	*Proteus vulgaris* (ATCC 638)	Gram negative rod-shaped bacterium	Urinary tract infections and wound infections
7.	*Staphylococcus aureus* (ATCC 25923)	Facultative anaerobic, gram-positive coccus	Minor skin infections, pneumonia, meningitis, osteomyelitis, endocarditis toxic shock syndrome (TSS)

Antibacterial Assay

Different concentrations of solvent extracts of the Mokkathotapapada leaves of *Piper betel* L. Cv. Kapoori (a local cultivar) were tested for antimicrobial activity by using Antibiotic Sensitivity test (Barry, A.C. 1976, Benson, H.J. 1990). Bacterial suspension was evenly mixed with sterile Agar medium and poured into the sterile Petri plates. After allowing the media to solidify at room temperature, wells of 6mm diameter were bored in the agar with sterile cork borer. Each concentration was checked for antibacterial activity by introducing equal amounts of the sample (40µl) into wells. The method was repeated in five plates. Plates were allowed to stand at room temperature for 1 hour, for extract to diffuse into agar media and then incubated at 37 °C for 24 to 48 hours. The zone of growth inhibition around the wells was measured and diameter of inhibition zone was calculated. Simultaneously, the activity of standard antibiotic Streptomycin (10µg/ml) was studied under similar conditions, so as to compare the degree of inhibition by the solvent extracts. Agar wells fed with corresponding solvents served as control. Minimum Inhibitory Concentration which was determined as the lowest concentration of solvent extracts inhibiting the growth of organisms, was determined based on the readings.

Fungal Test Organisms

Aspergillus niger (NCIM 596), *Aspergillus fumigatus* (NCIM 291) and *Candida albicans* (NCIM 670) obtained from the Department of Pharmaceutical Microbiology and Biotechnology, Hindu College of Pharmacy, Guntur, Andhra Pradesh, (Characteristics are listed in Table 6.2) for use in the study. Fungal colonies were harvested from 9-10 days old cultures, which were maintained on Potato Dextrose Agar. The spores were suspended in sterile distilled water and the spore suspensions were adjusted to 1×10^8 spores/ml (NCCLS).

Table 6.2: List of the Selected Test Organisms (Fungi)

Sl. No.	Name of Organism	Characteristics Features	Disease Vaused by Organism
1.	*Aspergillus niger* (NCIM 596)	Dichotomous branches filamentous	Allergy, Asthma
2.	*Aspergillus fumigatus* (NCIM 291)	Dichotomous branches filamentous	Pulmonary haemorrhage, Pnemonia
3.	*Candida albicans* (NCIM 670)	Dimorphic fungi	Oral thrush, gastritis, cutaneous infections

Antifungal Assay

Different concentrations of solvent extracts of the Mokkathotapapada leaves of *Piper betel* L. Cv. Kapoori (a local cultivar) were tested for antimicrobial activity by using Antibiotic Sensitivity test (Barry, A.C. 1976, Benson, H.J. 1990). Microbial suspension was evenly mixed with sterile agar medium and poured into the sterile Petri plates. After allowing the media to solidify at room temperature, wells of 6mm diameter were bored in the agar with sterile cork borer. Each concentration was checked for antimicrobial activity by introducing equal amounts of the sample (40µl) into the wells. The method was repeated in five plates. Plates were allowed to stand at room temperature for 1 hour in order to facilitate diffusion of extract into agar media and then incubated at 37°C for 24- 48 hours. The zone of growth inhibition around the wells was measured and diameter of inhibition zone was calculated. Simultaneously, the activity of standard antibiotic Nystatin (10µg/ml) was studied under similar conditions, so as to compare the degree of inhibition by the solvent extracts. Agar wells fed with corresponding solvents served as control. Minimum Inhibitory Concentration (MIC) which was determined as the lowest concentration of solvent extracts inhibiting the growth of organisms, was determined based on the readings.

Test organism-Animal

The adult Indian earthworm *Pheretima posthuma* L.Vaill (Annelida) were used to study anthelmintic activity. The earthworms were gathered from moist soil and washed with normal saline to remove all fecal matter and immediately transferred into Tyrode solution. The worms were identified at Department of Zoology, Acharya Nagarjuna University, Nagarjuna nagar, Guntur. Earthworms 3-5 cm in length and 0.1-0.2 cm in width were used for all experimental protocol.

Drugs and Chemicals

Piperazine citrate (Glaxo Smithkline), ethanol, chloroform, methanol and petroleum ether (SD Fine Chemicals, Mumbai) was used during experimental protocol.

Anthelmintic Activity

The anthelmintic assay was performed out as per the method of Ajaiyeoba et al. (2001) with minor modifications. The assay was performed on the adult Indian earthworm *Pheretima posthuma* due to its anatomical and physiological resemblance to the human intestinal roundworm parasite (Vidyarthi, 1967; Chatterjee, 1967). Due to their ready availability, earthworms have been used widely for the initial evaluation of anthelmintic compounds *in vitro* (Sollmann, 1918; Jain et al., 1972; Dash et al., 2002).The earthworms were divided into different groups, each group containing six worms. 50 ml formulations containing four different concentrations of organic solvent extracts of *Piper betel* L. (10, 20, 50, 80 and 100 mg/ml in distilled water) were made. The time of paralysis was figured out when no movement of any sort could be observed except when the worms were shaken vigorously. The times of death of the worms were entered after ascertaining that worms neither moved when shaken vigorously or when dipped in warm water (50°C). Reference standard used was Piperazine citrate (10mg/ml) while water served as a control.

Other Materials

Brine shrimp eggs, *Artemia salina,* were collected from pet shop (Kikaluru, Krishna district) and hatched for two days to let them be matured as nauplii (Meyer, B.N *et al.,* 1988).

Toxicity Assay Using Brine Shrimps, *Artemia salina* Leach

Cytotoxicity of organic solvent extracts of Mokkathotapapada leaves of *Piper betel* L. Cv Kapoori, a local cultivar was evaluated in triplicate using *Artemia salina* Leach. Brine shrimp eggs were hatched in artificial sea water (Kester *et al.* 1967). After 48 hours the phototrophic nauplii were collected and a suspension of about 30-50 nauplii in 100 µl were placed into bijoux bottles containing 900 µl of extract in artificial sea water. Eight final concentrations of the extract ranging from 1-128 µg/ml, at two fold serial increments were used in the assay. The control bijoux bottle contained the nauplii in 1000 µl artificial sea water but devoid of the extract. After 24 hours of incubation, the dead nauplii were counted under a dissecting microscope. Subsequently 200 µl of methanol was added to each bottle and 60 minutes later the total number of nauplii was counted. The brine-shrimp lethality assay analyzed using the Finney probit method.

Phytochemical Screening

The solvent extracts of the leaves of *Piper betel* L. Cv. Kapoori (a local cultivar) were screened for the presence of various phytoconstituents (Kokate, 1986).

Further Phytochemical analysis was carried out for the non-polar solvent extract, chloroform and polar solvent extract, methanol by Gas Chromatography-Mass Spectrometry GC-MS unit of GC-MS-QP 2010 [SHIMADZU]; GC CONDITION- Column Oven Temperature70°C, Injector Temperature 240°C, Injection Mode Split, Split Ratio 10, Flow Control Mode Linear Velocity, Column Flow 1.51 ml/min, Carrier Gas Helium 99.9995% purity, Injection volume 1 microlitre; Column Oven Temperature Programme – Rate: 0-10, Temp: 70 - 300(°C), Hold Time 3-9 (35.0mts total); COLUMN VF-5ms – Length 30.0m , Diameter 0.25mm, Film Thickness 0.25um; MS CONDITION MS - Ion source temp 200 °C , Interface temp 240°C, Scan range 40 – 1000 m/z, Solvent cut time 5mins, MS start time 5(min), MS end time 35 (min), Ionization EI (-70ev), Scan speed 2000, MS LIBRARY- NIST08s, WILEY8, FAME.

RESULTS AND DISCUSSION

Antibacterial Assay

The results of the study are given in Table 6.3 and graphical representations of the each solvent given separately as Graph 6.1, 6.2, 6.3 and 6.4. The results indicate that the ether extracts of Mokkathotapapada leaves of *Piper betel* L. Cv. Kapoori were inhibitory to all the test organisms. The minimum inhibitory concentration was found to be 250µg/ml for all tested bacteria such as *Escherichia coli, Bacillus subtilis, Pseudomonas aeruginosa, Corynebacterium diphtheria, Xanthomonas citrovorum, Proteus vulgaris* and *Staphylococcus aureus*. Among the bacterial species tested *Corynebacterium diphtheria* was found to be highly sensitive to the ether extracts of Mokkathotapapada leaves of *Piper betel* L. Cv. Kapoori, a local cultivar (Graph 6.1). The chloroform extracts of the Mokkathotapapada leaves of *Piper betel* L. Cv. Kapoori were also inhibitory to all the test organisms (Graph 6.2). The minimum inhibitory concentration of chloroform extracts was found to be 500µg/ml for *Corynebacterium diphtheria,* while it was 750µg/ml for *Escherichia coli, Bacillus subtilis, Pseudomonas aeruginosa, Xanthomonas citrovorum, Proteus vulgaris* and *Staphylococcus aureus. Proteus vulgaris* was found to be highly sensitive to the chloroform extracts of Mokkathotapapada leaves of *Piper betel* L. Cv. Kapoori, of all the bacterial species tested.

All the test organisms were found to be susceptible to the ethanol extracts of the Mokkathotapapada leaves of *Piper betel* L. Cv. Kapoori. The minimum inhibitory concentration was found to be 500µg/ml for *Escherichia coli, Bacillus subtilis, Corynebacterium diphtheria, Proteus vulgaris* and

Staphylococcus aureus, while it was 750μg/ml for *Pseudomonas aeruginosa* and *Xanthomonas citrovorum*. Among the bacterial species tested, *Corynebacterium diphtheria* was found to be highly susceptible to the ethanol extracts of Mokkathotapapada leaves of *Piper betel* L. Cv. Kapoori (Graph 6.3). The methanol extracts of Mokkathotapapada leaves of *Piper betel* L. Cv. Kapoori also inhibited all the test organisms (Graph 6.4). The minimum inhibitory concentration was found to be 500μg/ml for *Escherichia coli, Bacillus subtilis, Corynebacterium diphtheria* and *Staphylococcus aureus*. The remaining three bacteria exhibited zones of growth inhibition at 750μg/ml. Of all the test organisms, *Staphylococcus aureus* was found to be highly sensitive to the methanol extracts of Mokkathotapapada leaves of *Piper betel* L. Cv. Kapoori, a local cultivar.

Table 6.3: Inhibitory Activity of Solvent Extracts of Mokkathotapapada Leaves of *Piper betel* L. Cv. Kapoori, a Local Cultivar

Solvent Extract	Product (μg)	Zone of Inhibition (mm)						
		A	B	C	D	E	F	G
Ether	Control	7.00	7.00	7.00	7.00	7.00	7.00	7.00
	250	8.50	8.20	7.50	10.50	9.30	8.10	8.10
	500	13.00	13.00	7.50	23.00	19.00	8.50	8.50
	750	21.00	21.00	12.00	28.00	26.00	11.21	11.21
	1000	30.00	30.00	21.00	36.00	32.00	23.21	21.43
Chloroform	Control	9.00	9.00	9.00	9.00	9.00	9.00	9.00
	250	9.00	9.00	9.00	9.00	9.00	9.00	9.00
	500	9.00	9.00	9.00	10.00	9.00	9.00	9.00
	750	13.00	13.00	18.00	16.00	16.00	15.00	15.00
	1000	18.00	18.00	23.00	23.00	22.00	22.57	21.43
Ethanol	Control	9.00	9.00	9.00	9.00	9.00	9.00	9.00
	250	9.00	9.00	9.00	9.00	9.00	9.00	9.00
	500	11.00	11.00	9.00	11.00	9.00	10.00	10.20
	750	17.00	17.00	13.00	18.00	13.00	12.60	21.43
	1000	23.00	23.00	17.00	26.00	17.00	15.60	23.43
Methanol	Control	8.60	8.60	8.60	8.60	8.60	8.60	8.60
	250	8.60	8.60	8.60	8.60	8.60	8.60	8.60
	500	9.00	9.00	8.60	13.00	8.60	8.60	12.21
	750	12.00	12.00	9.00	17.00	9.00	12.60	21.50
	1000	16.00	16.00	13.00	24.00	14.00	12.60	38.00
Std*		26.03	28.55	13.73	25.81	26.00	17.00	19.08

*Standard: Streptomycin (10μg/ml) for Bacteria

(A) *Escherichia coli* (B) *Bacillus subtilis* (C) *Pseudomonas aeruginosa* (D) *Corynebacterium diphtheria* (E) *Xanthomonas citrovorum* (F) *Proteus vulgaris* (G) *Staphylococcus aureus*.

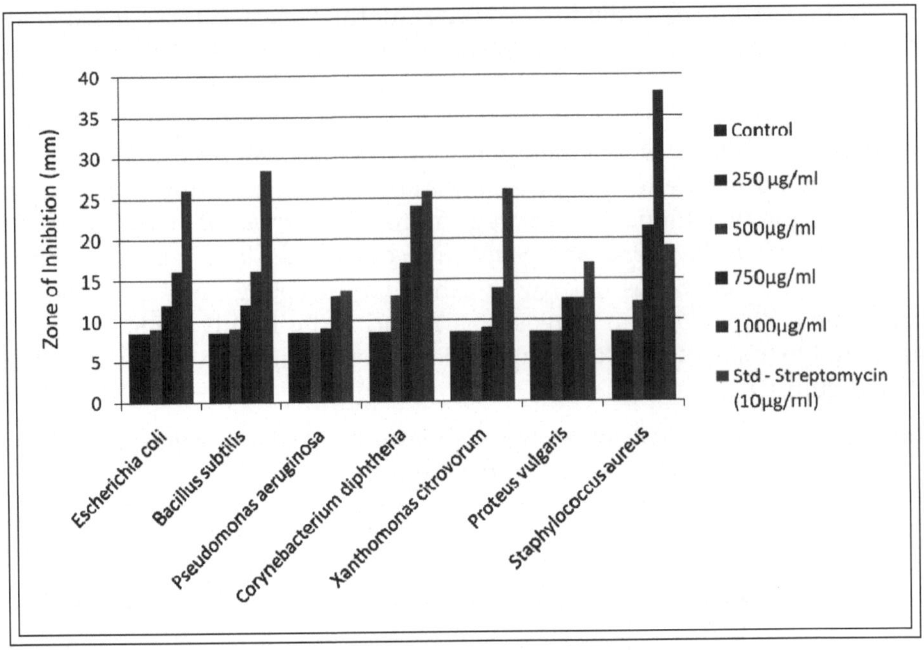

Graph 6.1: Inhibitory Activity of Ether Extracts of Mokkathotapapada Leaves of Piper betel L. Cv. Kapoori, a Local Cultivar

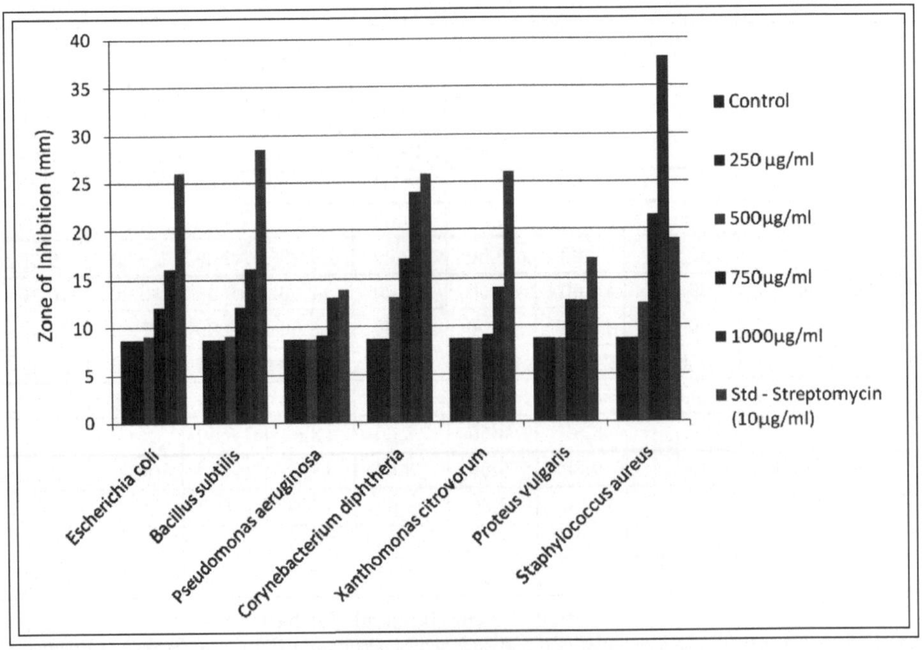

Graph 6.2: Inhibitory Activity of Chloroform Extracts of Mokkathotapapada Leaves of Piper betel L. Cv. Kapoori, a Local Cultivar

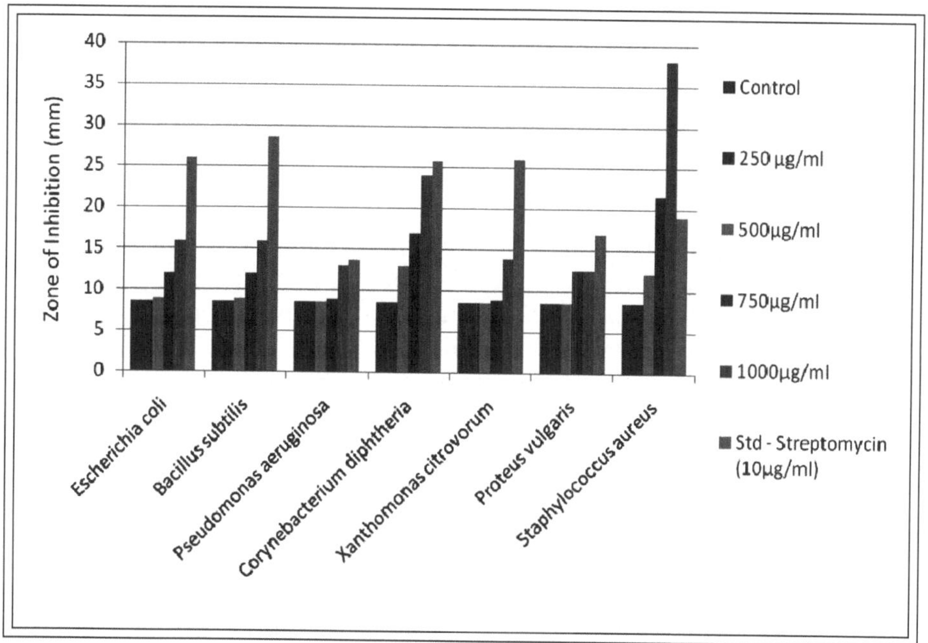

Graph 6.3: Inhibitory Activity of Ethanolic Extracts of Mokkathotapapada Leaves of Piper betel L. Cv. Kapoori, a Local Cultivar

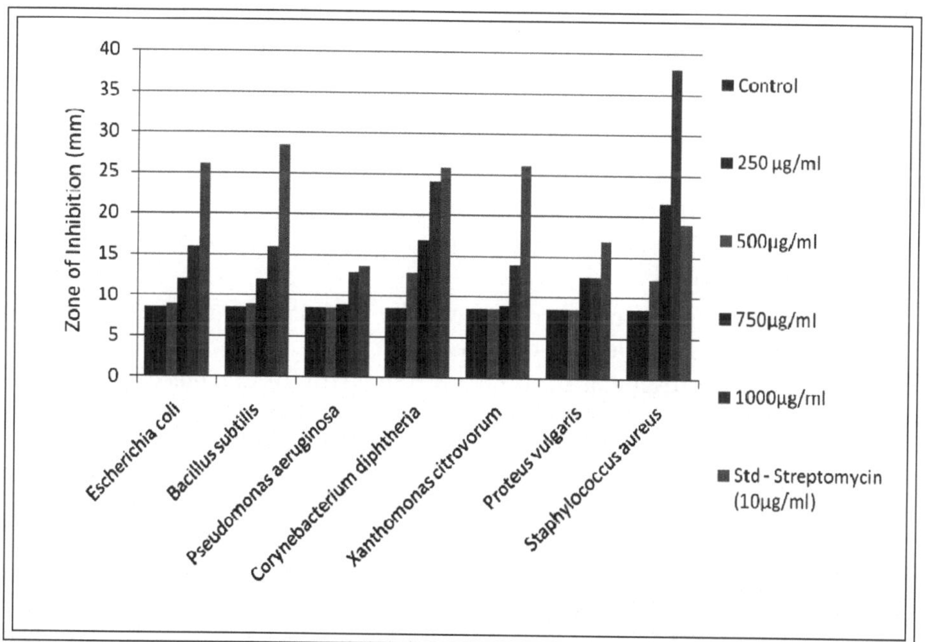

Graph 6.4: Inhibitory Activity of Methanolic Extracts of Mokkathotapapada Leaves of Piper Betel L. Cv. Kapoori, a Local Cultivar

The different solvent extracts of Mokkathotapapada leaves of *Piper betel* L. Cv. Kapoori tested were inhibitory to all the test organisms at various levels. The ethanol and ether extracts showed high activity against bacteria. The chloroform extracts of Mokkathotapapada leaves of *Piper betel* L. Cv. Kapoori showed increased zones of inhibition for the test bacteria *Corynebacterium diphtheria* and *Pseudomonas aeruginosa*. The methanol extract of Mokkathotapapada leaves of *Piper betel* L. Cv. Kapoori were inhibitory to all the test organisms of which, *Corynebacterium diphtheria* was found to be highly sensitive. The ethanol extract also exhibited high activity against the growth of *Corynebacterium diphtheria,* in comparison with other organisms. *Corynebacterium diphtheria* was also found to be highly susceptible to the ether extracts of Mokkathotapapada leaves of *Piper betel* L. Cv. Kapoori, a local cultivar. Among the solvent extracts, ether extracts of Mokkathotapapada leaves of *Piper betel* L. Cv. Kapoori, a local cultivar exhibited high antibacterial activity even at low concentrations. The inhibitory activity of the various solvent extracts was dose-dependent, enhanced with increase in concentration.

Antifungal Assay

Table 6.4 results indicate that the extracts of Mokkathotapapada leaves of *Piper betel* L. Cv. Kapoori are inhibitory to all the test organisms. The minimum inhibitory concentration of the ether extract was found to be 500µg/ml against *Candida albicans* and the remaining two fungi were controlled at 750µg/ml. Among the microbial species tested *Candida albicans* was found to be highly sensitive to the ether extracts of *Piper betel* L. Cv. Kapoori. The chloroform extracts of the Mokkathotapapada leaves of *Piper betel* L. Cv. Kapoori were also inhibitory to all the test organisms. The minimum inhibitory concentration of chloroform extracts was found to be 500µg/ml for *Candida albicans,* while it was 750µ/mlg for *Asperigillus niger* and *Asperigillus fumigatus.* Among the microbial species tested, *Asperigillus niger* was found to be more susceptible to the chloroform extracts of *Piper betel* L. Cv. Kapoori than the other fungi.

All the test organisms were found to be inhibited by ethanol extracts of the Mokkathotapapada leaves of *Piper betel* L. Cv. Kapoori. The minimum inhibitory concentration was found to be 500µg/ml for *Candida albicans,* while it was 750µg/ml for *Asperigillus niger* and *Asperigillus fumigatus.* Among the microbial species tested, *Candida albicans* was found to be highly susceptible to the ethanol extracts of *Piper betel* L. Cv. Kapoori. The methanol extracts of the Mokkathotapapada leaves of *Piper betel* L. Cv. Kapoori also inhibited all the test organisms. The minimum inhibitory concentration was found to be 250µg/ml for *Asperigillus niger, Asperigillus fumigatus* and *Candida albicans.* Among the microbial species tested *Asperigillus niger* was found to be highly sensitive to the methanol extracts of Mokkathotapapada leaves of *Piper betel* L. Cv. Kapoori.

Table 6.4: Inhibitory Activity of Solvent Extracts of Mokkathotapapada Leaves of *Piper betel* L. Cv. Kapoori (a local cultivar)

Solvent Extract	Product (µg)	Zone of Inhibition (mm)		
		Aspergillus niger	***Aspergillus fumigatus***	***Candida albicans***
Ether	Control	15.60	15.60	15.60
	250	15.60	15.60	15.60
	500	15.60	15.60	18.60
	750	28.00	26.00	26.00
	1000	31.00	30.00	32.00
Chloroform	Control	15.60	15.60	15.60
	250	15.60	15.60	15.60
	500	15.60	15.60	20.00
	750	21.60	19.60	24.00
	1000	30.71	28.51	28.00
Ethanol	Control	10.00	10.00	10.00
	250	10.00	10.00	10.00
	500	10.00	10.00	12.00
	750	13.00	12.00	14.00
	1000	15.00	14.20	17.00
Methanol	Control	15.60	15.60	15.60
	250	18.60	18.60	18.60
	500	18.60	18.60	18.60
	750	22.16	20.16	22.12
	1000	39.71	36.51	31.12
Std*		12.66	12.66	17.00

Std* - Standard: Nystatin (10µg/ml)

All the solvent extracts of Mokkathotapapada leaves of *Piper betel* L. Cv. Kapoori (a local cultivar) were inhibitory to all the test organisms (Graphs 6.5, 6.6, 6.7 and 6.8). The chloroform and methanol extracts showed high zones of growth inhibition. The chloroform extracts of Mokkathotapapada leaves of *Piper betel* L. Cv. Kapoori showed increased zones of inhibition for all the test fungi. Of all the fungal organisms selected and tested against chloroform, *Asperigillus niger* was the one that was highly sensitive to chloroform. The methanol extract of Mokkathotapapada leaves of *Piper betel* L. Cv. Kapoori was inhibitory to all the test organisms, of which *Asperigillus niger* was found to be highly sensitive. The ethanol extract of Mokkathotapapada leaves of *Piper betel* L. Cv. Kapoori exhibited high activity against the growth of *Candida albicans* in comparison with other organisms. The ether extracts of Mokkathotapapada leaves of *Piper betel* L. Cv. Kapoori also showed high zones of growth inhibition against *Candida albicans*. The inhibitory activity of different solvent extracts was concentration-dependent and was enhanced with increase in concentration.

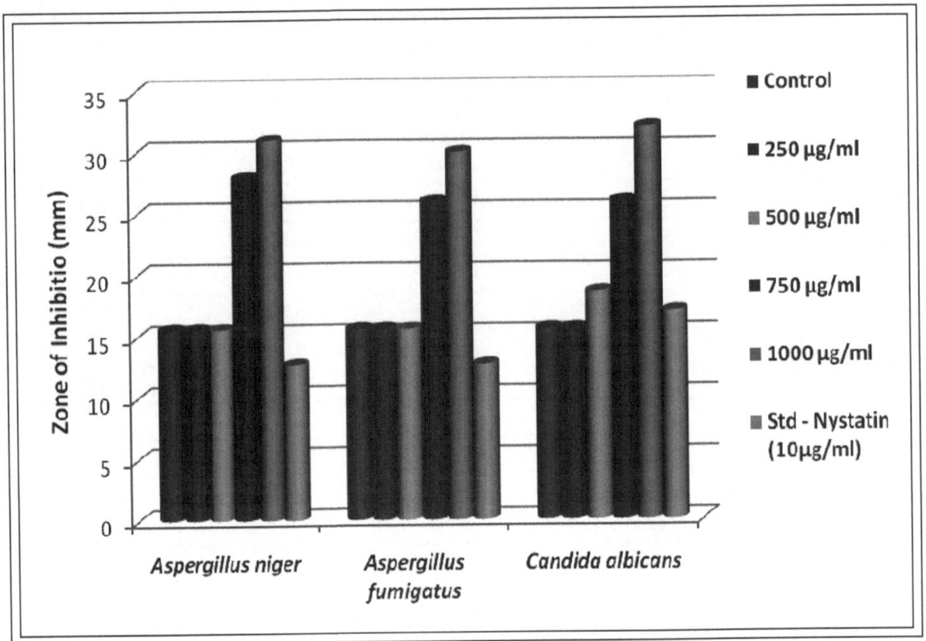

Graph 6.5: Inhibitory Activity of Ether Extracts of Mokkathotapapada Leaves of Piper Betel L. Cv. Kapoori (a local cultivar)

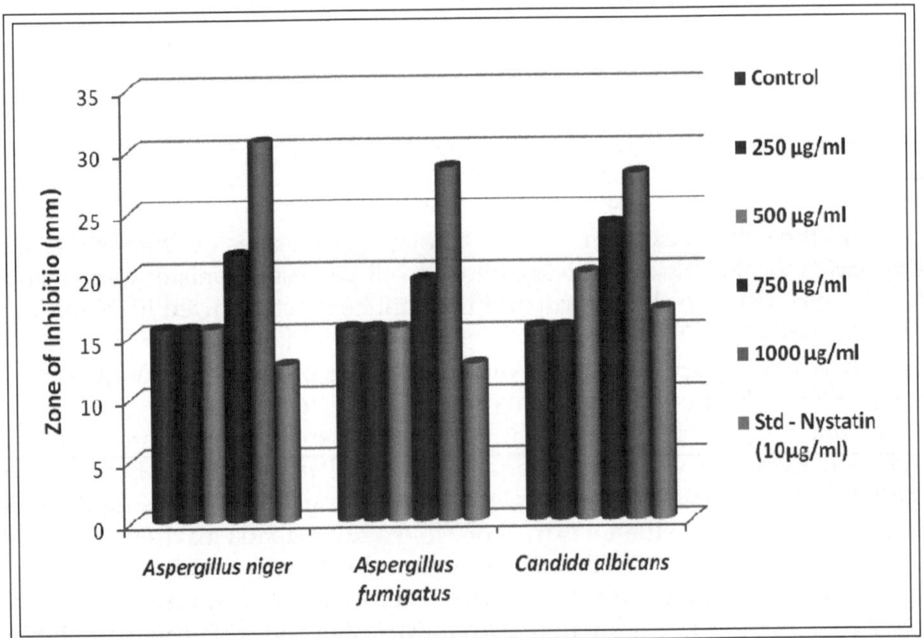

Graph 6.6: Inhibitory Activity of Chloroform Extracts of Mokkathotapapada Leaves of Piper Betel L. Cv. Kapoori (a local cultivar)

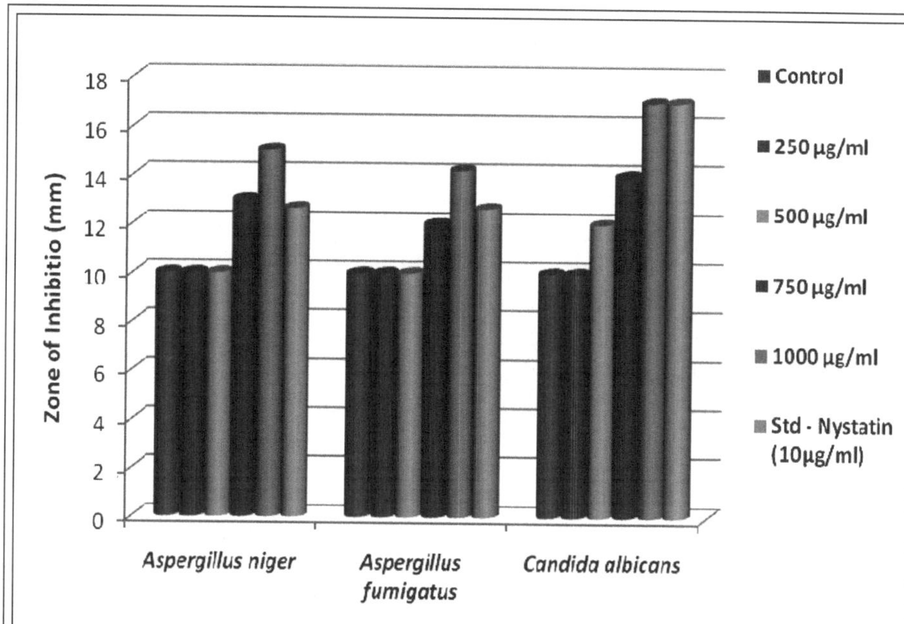

Graph 6.7: Inhibitory Activity of Ethanolic Extracts of Mokkathotapapada Leaves of Piper Betel L. Cv. Kapoori (a local cultivar)

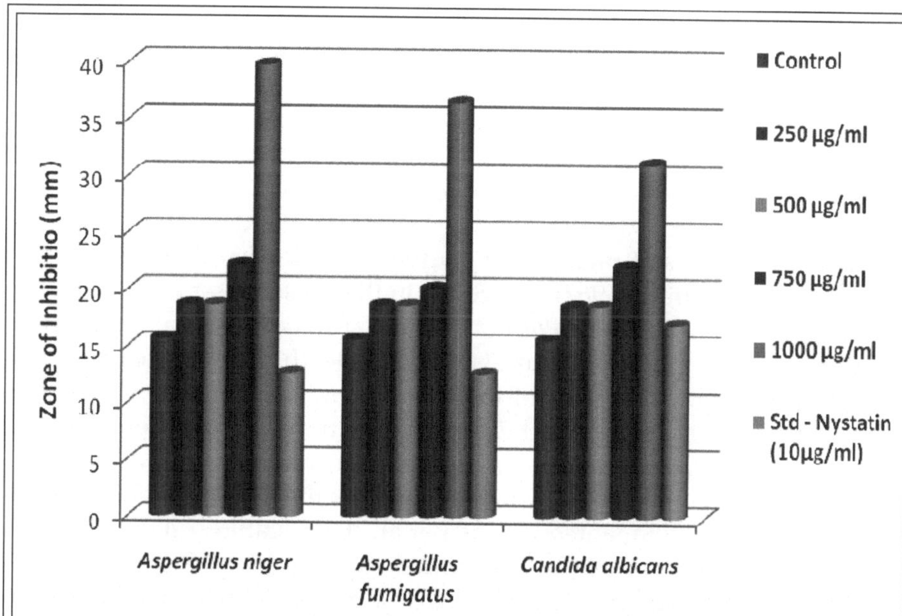

Graph 6.8: Inhibitory Activity of Methanolic Extracts of Mokkathotapapada Leaves of Piper Betel L. Cv. Kapoori (a local cultivar).

Anthelmintic Activity

As shown in table 6.5 The results of anthelmintic activity revealed that petroleum ether, chloroform, ethanol and methanol extracts exhibited varying degree of activity against both the worms and caused paralysis followed by death at all tested concentrations. However, ethanol and methanolic extracts of the plant exhibited more potent activity at higher concentration (100mg/ ml) when compared to the reference standard piperazine citrate (10 mg/ml). The ethanolic extracts of Mokkathotapapada leaves of *Piper betel* L. Cv. Kapoori (a local cultivar) showed dose-dependent anthelmintic activities that caused both paralysis (P) and death (D). The time of paralysis (P) in minutes were 33, 28, 22, 18, 15 and 13; time of death (D) 69, 65, 54, 48, 43 and 31min. In the case of chloroform extract exhibited dose-dependent activities that result both Paralysis and Death in different time (min) intervals such as 42, 34, 30, 27, 24, 20 (P) and 72, 69, 65, 64, 60, 59 (D). Whereas the methanolic extracts possess paralysis (P) in 38, 30, 28, 22, 20, 15min and death (D) in 75, 69, 58, 49, 47 and 38min. While the petroleum ether extract showed paralysis in 39, 34, 30, 28, 25, 22min and death in 89, 84, 75, 65, 62 and 58 min. both the ethanol and methanol extracts showed anthelmintic activity in dose-dependent manner giving shortest time of paralysis (P) and death (D) with 100 mg/ml concentration on the earthworm *P. posthuma*. The ethanolic extract of *Piper betel* L. Cv. Kapoori (a local cultivar) caused paralysis in 13 min and death in 31 min while methanolic extract showed P and D in 15 and 38 min, respectively against the earthworm *P. posthuma*. The reference drug piperazine citrate (10 mg/ml) showed the same at 23 and 60 min. The predominant effect of piperazine citrate on helminth is to cause flaccid paralysis that result in expulsion of the worm by peristalsis. Piperazine citrate shows increasing chloride ion conductance of worm muscle membrane producing hyperpolarisation and reduced excitability that leads to muscle relaxation and flaccid paralysis (Martin, 1985). The anthelmintic activity of the methanol extracts of plants may be due to the presence of polyphenolic compounds (Bate-Smith, 1962). However, in the present assay the extracts of Mokkathotapapada leaves of *Piper betel* L. Cv. Kapoori (a local cultivar) not only demonstrated paralysis, but also caused death of worms especially at higher concentration, 100 mg/ml in shorter time as compared to reference drug piperazine citrate. The anthelmintic activity of the plant extracts may be attributed to the presence of active components such as phenolic compounds, flavonoids, tannins and terpenoids, the anthelmintic properties of which are well documented (Niezen et al., 1995; Lahlou, 2002). From the results reported here, it can be concluded that the plant *Piper betel* L. Cv. Kapoori has significant anthelmintic activity. It would be interesting further to isolate the possible constituents those are responsible for anthelmintic activity and establish the possible mechanism (s) of action.

Table 6.5: Anthelmintic Activity of Solvent Extracts of Mokkathotapapada Leaves of *Piper betel* L. Cv. Kapoori (a local cultivar)

Test Substance	Concentration mg/ml	Time Taken for Paralysis (P) and Death (D) of Worms in Minute	
		Pheretima posthuma L.Vaill	
		P	D
Ethanol Extract	10	33 ± 0.3	69 ± 0.4
	20	28 ± 0.2	65 ± 0.3
	40	22 ± 0.2	54 ± 0.3
	60	18 ± 0.2	48 ± 0.5
	80	15 ± 0.1	43 ± 0.2
	100	13 ± 0.1	31 ± 0.2
Chloroform Extract	10	42 ± 0.2	72 ± 0.2
	20	34 ± 0.3	69 ± 0.2
	40	30 ± 0.3	65 ± 0.1
	60	27 ± 0.4	64 ± 0.1
	80	24 ± 0.4	60 ± 0.1
	100	20 ± 0.5	59 ± 0.3
Methanol Extract	10	38 ± 0.4	75 ± 0.5
	20	30 ± 0.3	69 ± 0.4
	40	28 ± 0.3	58 ± 0.3
	60	22 ± 0.3	49 ± 0.3
	80	20 ± 0.2	47 ± 0.7
	100	15 ± 0.2	38 ± 0.2
Petroleum Ether Extract	10	39 ± 0.4	89 ± 0.9
	20	34 ± 0.3	84 ± 0.7
	40	30 ± 0.2	75 ± 0.7
	60	28 ± 0.2	65 ± 0.7
	80	25 ± 0.7	62 ± 0.6
	100	22 ± 0.9	58 ± 0.5
Std*	10	23 ± 0.7	60 ± 0.5

All values represent Mean ± SEM; n=6 in each group

*Standard: Piperazine citrate 10mg/ml

Brine Shrimp Lethality Bioassay

The solvent extracts of different concentrations of Mokkathotapapada leaves of *Piper betel* L. Cv Kapoori, a local cultivar were tested for toxic activities using brine shrimp lethality bioassay (Graph 6.9). The results are presented in Table 6.6. Finney probit analysis was mentioned in the Appendix.

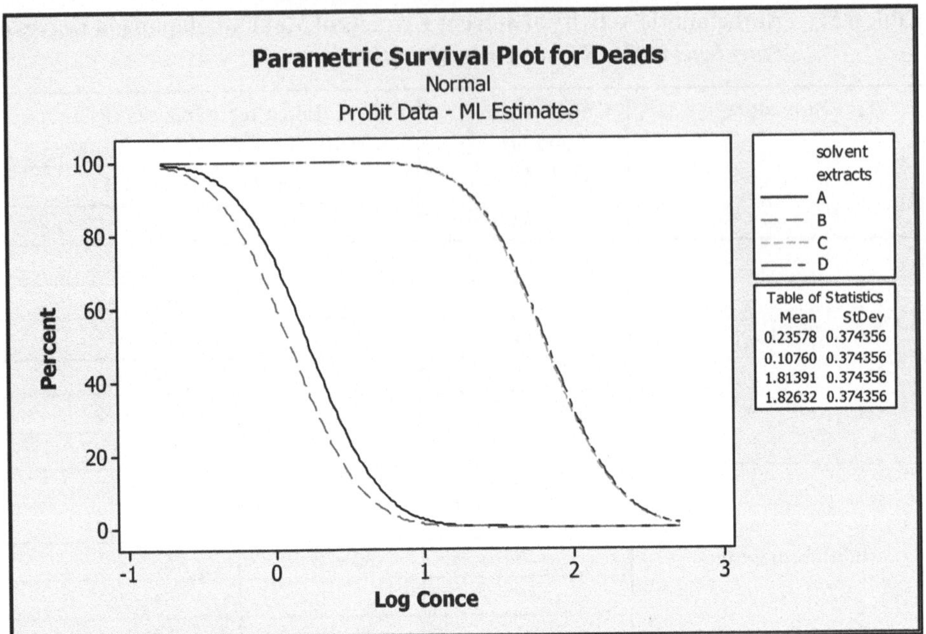

Graph 6.9: Log C versus Average Percentage of Mortality of Nauplii of Solvent Extracts of Mokkathotapapada Leaves of Piper Betel L. Cv Kapoori, a Local Cultivar

(A) Petroleum ether extract (B) Chloroform extract
(C) Methanol extract (D) Ethanol extract

Toxicity tests were carried out in triplicates using *A. salina*. Using the method given in the above, petroleum ether extracts proved to be the most toxic of Mokkathotapapada leaves of *Piper betel* L. Cv Kapoori (local cultivar) extracts tested LC_{50} = 1.72 µg/ml, followed by chloroform extract (1.28 µg/ml), methanol extract (65.15 µg/ml)and ethanol extract (67.03 µg/ml). The extracts were effective at low concentrations, LC_{50} at 1.72 µg/ml indicated toxicity relatively at low concentration. This may undermine its usefulness. Toxicity of samples has been shown to be dependent on the concentration of specific compound(s) in the sample (Svensson *et al.* 2005). The level of toxicity observed in this study may have resulted from presence of multiple compounds in the crude extracts, acting in synergy or independently. Thus, isolation and testing of the pure component may produce lower levels of toxicity.

This finding raises hope for the possibility of developing an antitumor agent from Mokkathotapapada leaves of *Piper betel* L. Cv Kapoori plant extract that can exhibit selective and specific action against *Artemia salina*. Our results seem consistent with the correlation previously established between cytotoxicity and brine shrimp lethality in Mokkathotapapada leaves of the plant extracts. We suggest using this bioassay simultaneously to test natural products for pharmacological activity.

Table 6.6: Toxicity of Solvent Extracts of Mokkathotapapada Leaves of *Piper betel* L. Cv Kapoori, a Local Cultivar Against *Artemia salina* Leach

Log conc. of Extract (µg/ml)	Petroleum Ether Extract			Chloroform Extract			Methanol Extract			Ethanol Extract		
	Total nauplii	Total nauplii killed	% killed	Total nauplii	Total nauplii killed	% killed	Total nauplii	Total nauplii killed	% killed	Total nauplii	Total nauplii killed	% killed
2.107	30	30	100	28	28	100	32	26	81.25	34	28	81.25
1.806	34	34	100	36	36	100	31	19	61.29	30	18	61.29
1.505	36	36	100	42	42	100	30	03	10.00	40	04	10.00
1.204	32	32	100	43	43	100	32	01	3.13	32	01	3.13
0.903	40	36	89.47	38	38	100	32	00	0	42	00	0
0.602	34	24	69.70	50	45	90.20	34	00	0	36	00	0
0.301	32	20	61.29	46	30	66.67	34	00	0	30	00	0
0.001	41	17	40.00	48	20	48.15	31	00	0	28	00	0

LC_{50} *Piper betel* L. Cv Kapoori petroleum ether extract = 1.72 µg/ml;
LC_{50} *Piper betel* L. Cv Kapoori chloroform extract = 1.28 µg/ml;
LC_{50} *Piper betel* L. Cv Kapoori methanol extract = 65.15 µg/ml;
LC_{50} *Piper betel* L. Cv Kapoori ethanol extract = 67.03 µg/ml.

Phytochemical Analysis

The qualitative phytochemical investigation of different solvent extracts of leaves of *Piper betel* L. Cv. Kapoori(a local cultivar) showed the presence of an array of active chemical constituents including Alkaloids, Fixed oils, Flavonoids, Phenols, Terpenoids, Quinones, Resins, Saponins, Steroids, Tannins, Xanthoproteins and Glycosides (Table 6.7) and further investigation of chloroform and methanol extracts using GC-MS analysis revealed active constituents showed in the chromatograms (Fig. 6.1 and Fig. 6.2), The chromatogram of the chloroform extract has a total of ninteen peaks at various retention times, whereas the chromatogram of methanolic extract showed a total of twenty peaks at various retention times.

Table 6.7: Preliminary Phytochemical Screening of Various Extracts of *Piper betel* L. Cv. Kapoori (a local cultivar). Qualitative tests.

Phytochemical Constituents	Ethanolic Extract	Chloroform Extract	Methanolic Extract	Petroleum ether Extract
Alkaloids	Present	Present	Present	Present
Carboxylic acids	Present	–	Present	Present
Coumarins	–	–	–	–
Fixed oils	Present	Present	Present	Present
Flavonoids	Present	Present	Present	Present
Phenols	Present	–	Present	–
Terpenoids	Present	Present	Present	Present
Quinones	Present	–	Present	–
Resins	Present	–	Present	–
Saponins	Present	–	Present	–
Steroids	Present	Present	Present	Present
Tannins	Present	–	Present	–
Xanthoproteins	Present	Present	Present	Present
Glycosides	Present	–	Present	–

Preliminary phyto-chemical screening of plants is very useful for determination of the active constituents in different solvents and their yields. Many primary metabolites lie in their impact as precursors or pharmacologically active metabolites in pharmaceutical compounds (Babeet Singh Tanwer and Rekha Vijayvergia, 2010). The responsibility of antibacterial activity exhibited by the extracts can be attributed to these chemicals. Further phyto-chemical studies are required to determine the purified fractions/ bioactive compounds responsible for the anthelmintic activities of these species, which could serve as useful sources for new antimicrobial agents (Rajesh Kowti *et al.* 2010).

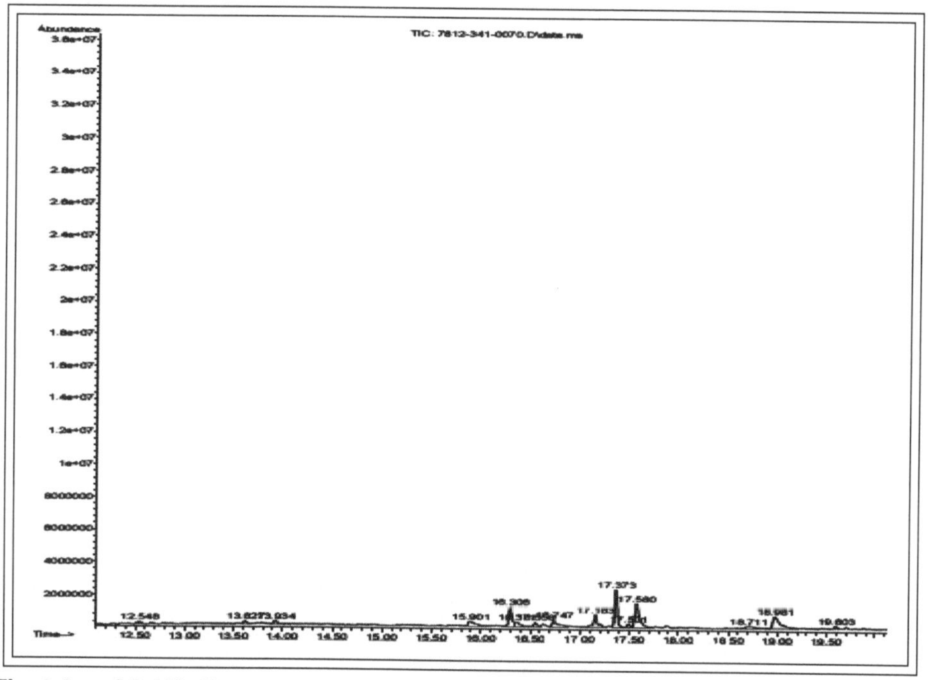

Fig. 6.1: GC-MS Chromatogram of Chloroform Extract of Mokkathotapapada Leaves of Piper Betel L. Cv. Kapoori (A Local Cultivar)

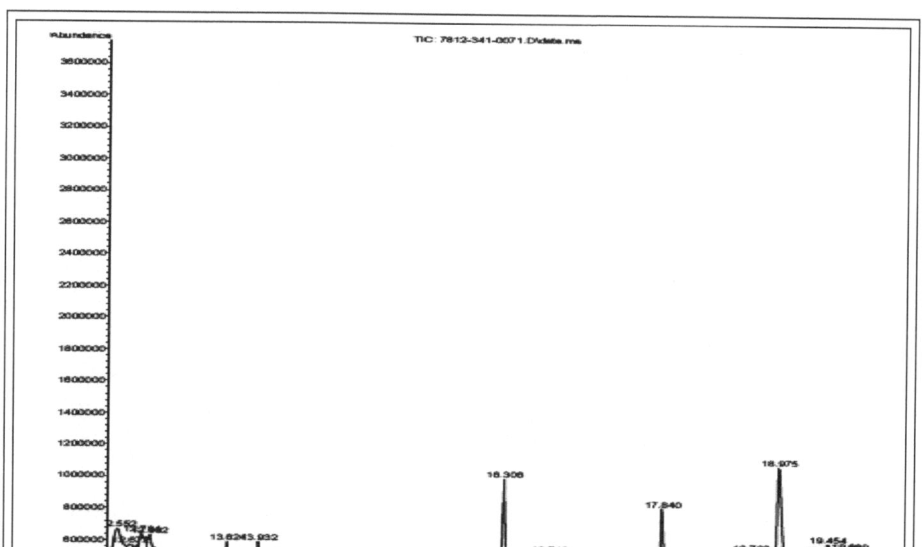

Fig. 6.2: GC-MS Chromatogram of Methanol Extract of Mokkathotapapada Leaves of Piper Betel L. Cv. Kapoori (a Local Cultivar)

A list of GC-MS peaks at the different retention times, area % are given in Table 6.8.

Table 6.8: GC-MS Peaks of Chloroform and Methanol Extracts of Mokkathotapapada leaves of Piper Betel L. Cv. Kapoori (a Local Cultivar)

Sl. No.	Chloroform Extract			Methanol Extract		
	Peak	Retention Time (RT) min	Area %	Peak	Retention Time (RT) min	Area %
1.	1	11.089	8.06	1	10.828	15.58
2.	2	11.162	9.49	2	10.973	13.51
3.	3	11.568	2.39	3	11.568	1.36
4.	4	12.541	1.43	4	12.019	1.11
5.	5	13.631	1.17	5	12.556	11.26
6.	6	13.936	1.38	6	12.672	3.11
7.	7	15.896	4.25	7	12.788	5.58
8.	8	16.303	7.29	8	12.861	7.91
9.	9	16.375	2.88	9	13.631	1.89
10.	10	16.564	1.62	10	13.963	1.74
11.	11	16.753	4.42	11	15.896	3.36
12.	12	17.160	6.28	12	16.303	4.09
13.	13	17.378	11.06	13	16.753	3.64
14.	14	17.508	1.12	14	17.842	4.34
15.	15	17.581	12.95	15	18.699	4.99
16.	16	18.714	3.01	16	18.975	10.18
17.	17	18.975	10.63	17	19.396	1.25
18.	18	19.600	0.98	18	19.454	3.10
19.	19	22.591	9.60	19	19.672	1.66
20.				20	22.925	0.32

CONCLUSION

The secondary metabolites produced by plants mostly serve as plant defensive agents against microorganisms, insects and herbivores, in which pytocuratives play a vital role in treating various infectious diseases (S.H.K.R. Prasad, 2009). Researched plant parts in various species include the roots, seeds, latex, lactiferous tubes, stem wood, stem barks, leaves and whole plants. Many studies have suggested that plant species have therapeutic relevance (Hohman, 2004). Healing property of the *Piper betel* L.(Green Gold of India) phenol, allylpyrocatechol against indomethacin-induced stomach ulceration and mechanism of action has been scientifically proved (Bhattacharya *et al*, 2007). The results of the present study suggest that the solvent extracts are effective against the tested organisms. The values of zone of inhibition, paralysis-death and cytotoxicity reveal the medicinal properties of the experimental plant. Some extracts showed better activity than the standard. The results obtained in the present work may also provide a support to the use of the plant in traditional medicine. Further work is needed to isolate the active principle from the plant extracts and to carry out pharmaceutical studies.

APPENDIX

Probit Analysis: Deads, Trial versus Log Conce, solvent extracts

A. Petroleum Ether Extracts Vs Log Concentration of extract (μg/ml)

Distribution: Normal

Response Information

Variable	Value	Count
Deads	Success	229
	Failure	50
Trial	Total	279

Estimation Method: Maximum Likelihood

Regression Table

Variable	Coef	Standard Error	Z	P
Constant	-0.301579	0.163281	-1.85	0.065
Log Conce	1.85104	0.270172	6.85	0.000
Natural Response	0			

Log-Likelihood = -84.624

Goodness-of-Fit Tests

Method	Chi-Square	DF	P
Pearson	3.06111	6	0.801
Deviance	4.07022	6	0.667

Tolerance Distribution

Parameter Estimates

Parameter	Estimate	Standard Error	95.0% Normal CI Lower	95.0% Normal CI Upper
Mean	0.162924	0.0724729	0.0208799	0.304969
StDev	0.540238	0.0788515	0.405832	0.719157

B. Chloroform extract Vs Log Concentration of extract (μg/ml)

Distribution: Normal

Response Information

Variable	Value	Count
Deads	Success	282
	Failure	49
Trial	Total	331

Estimation Method: Maximum Likelihood

Regression Table

Variable	Coef	Standard Error	Z	P
Constant	-0.303435	0.162825	-1.86	0.062
Log Conce	2.72752	0.411818	6.62	0.000

Natural
Response 0
Log-Likelihood = -79.599
Goodness-of-Fit Tests

Method	Chi-Square	DF	P
Pearson	1.41332	6	0.965
Deviance	2.04769	6	0.915

Tolerance Distribution
Parameter Estimates

		Standard	95.0% Normal CI	
Parameter	Estimate	Error	Lower	Upper
Mean	0.111249	0.0491129	0.0149899	0.207509
St. Dev	0.366633	0.0553565	0.272717	0.492891

C. Methanol extract Vs Log Concentration of extract (µg/ml)

Distribution: Normal
Response Information

Variable	Value	Count
Deads	Success	49
	Failure	207
Trial	Total	256

Estimation Method: Maximum Likelihood
Regression Table

		Standard		
Variable	Coef	Error	Z	P
Constant	-6.08028	0.867484	-7.01	0.000
Log Conce	3.38166	0.487273	6.94	0.000

Natural
Response 0
Log-Likelihood = -51.731
Goodness-of-Fit Tests

Method	Chi-Square	DF	P
Pearson	2.67129	6	0.849
Deviance	2.79191	6	0.834

Tolerance Distribution
Parameter Estimates

		Standard	95.0% Normal CI	
Parameter	Estimate	Error	Lower	Upper
Mean	1.79802	0.0418077	1.71608	1.87996
St. Dev	0.295713	0.0426102	0.222956	0.392214

D. Ethanol extract Vs Log Concentration of extract (µg/ml)

Distribution: Normal
Response Information

Variable	Value	Count
Deads	Success	51
	Failure	221
Trial	Total	272

Estimation Method: Maximum Likelihood
Regression Table

Variable	Coef	Standard Error	Z	P
Constant	-6.27848	0.847173	-7.41	0.000
Log Conce	3.48087	0.478361	7.28	0.000
Natural				
Response	0			

Log-Likelihood = -54.759

Goodness-of-Fit Tests

Method	Chi-Square	DF	P
Pearson	2.47761	6	0.871
Deviance	2.54259	6	0.864

Tolerance Distribution

Parameter Estimates

Parameter	Estimate	Standard Error	95.0% Normal CI Lower	Upper
Mean	1.80371	0.0397285	1.72585	1.88158
St. Dev.	0.287285	0.0394803	0.219450	0.376088

REFERENCES

Ahmedulla M, Nayer M.P (1999). Red Data Book of Indian Plants. Vol. 4. Calcutta: Botanical survey of India.

Ajaiyeoba, E.O., Onocha, P., and O.T. Olarenwaje (2001). *In vitro* Anthelmintic Properties of *Buchholzia coriaceae* and *Gynandropis gynanadra* Extract. Pharmaceutical Biol. 39(3), 217-220.

Amonkar, A.J., *et al.* (1986). Hydroxychavicol: A New Phenolic Antimutagen from *Betel* Leaf. Food and Chemical Toxicology 24, 12: 1321-1324.

Babeet Singh Tanwer and Rekha Vijayvergia (2010). Phytochemical Evaluation and Quantification of Primary Metabolites of *Alangium salviifolium;* International Journal of Pharma and Bio Sciences; 1(3).

Barry, A.C. 1976. Standard Diffusion Methods for Antibiotic Susceptibility of Common Rapid Growing Bacterial Pathogens. Baltimore, USA: Park Press.

Bate-Smith, E.C., (1962). The Phenolic Constituent of Plants and Their Taxonomic Significance, Dicotylendons. J. Linn Soc Bot, 58, 95-103.

Benson, H.J. 1990. Microbiological Applications, 5th ed. USA: WMC. Brown Publ, 34.

Bhattacharya S, Banerjee D, Bauri A K, Chattopadhyay S, Bandyopadhyay S K (2007). Healing Property of the *Piper betel* L. phenol, Allylpyrocatechol Against Indomethacin-induced Stomach Ulceration and Mechanism of Action, *World J Gastroenterol,* 13(27): 3705-3713.

Chatterjee, K.D. (1967). Parasitology, Protoxoology and Helminthology, Guha Ray Sree Saraswaty Press Ltd., Calcutta, pp. 168-169.

Cowan. M.M. 1999. Plant Products as Antimicrobial Agents. Clin Microbio, Rev; 564-582.

Evans, P.H., Bowers, W.S., and Funk, E.J. 1984. Identification of Fungicidal and Nematocidal Components in the Leaves of *Piper Betel* (Piperaceae). Journal of Food Agricultural and Chemistry 32: 1254-1256.

Hohmann J, Molnár J (2004). Plant Toxins are Promising Molecules for the Therapy, Acta Pharm. Hung, 74, 149-157.

J.M. McLaughlin, 1991. *Crown Gall Tumours on Potato Discs and Brine Shrimp Lethality: Two Simple Bioassays for Higher Plant Screening and Fractionation*. In K Hostettmann, Assays for Bioactivity. Academic Press; San Diego, pp. 2-32.

Kester, D.R., I.W. Duedall, D.N. Connors & R.M. Pytkowicz. 1967. Preparation of Artificial Seawater. *Limnology and Oceanography* 12: 176-179.

Kirtikar, K.R.; Basu, B.D. (1998) Indian Medicinal Plants, 2nd ed.; Bishen Singh Mahendra Pal Singh: Dehradun, India,; Vol. III, pp. 2131-2133.

Kokate C.K. (1986). In: Practical Pharmacognosy, 1st ed. Vallabh Prakashan, New Delhi, p. 111.

Lahlou M. Potential of *Origanum Compactum* as a Cercaricide in Morocco. *Ann. Trop. Med. Parasitol.* 96: 587-593 (2002).

Martin RJ. γ-Aminobutyric acid and Piperazine Activated Single Channel Current from *Ascaris suum* Body Muscle. *Br. J. Pharmacol.* 84: 445-461 (1985).

Meyer, B.N. N.R. Ferringni, J.E. Punam, L.B. Lacobsen, D.E. Nichols, J.L. Mclaughlin, 1988. Brine shrimp: A Convenient General Bioassay for the Active Constituents, Planta Medica, 45: 31-32.

Nagabhushan, M., et al. 1989. Hydroxy-Chavicol: A New Anti-Nitrosating Phenolic Compound from *Betel Leaf*. Mutagenesis 4, 3: 200-204.

National Committe for Clinical Laboratory Standards (1993). Methods for Dilution in Antimicrobial Susceptibility Tests: Approved Standard M2-A5. Villanove. P.A, NCCLS.

Niezen JH, Waghorn GC Charleston WAG and Waghorn GC. Growth and Gastrointestinal Nematode Parasitism in Lambs Grazing Either Lucerne (*Medicago sativa*) or sulla *(Hedysarum coronarium)* which Contains Condensed Tannins. *J. Agri. Sci.* 125: 281-289 (1995).

Parekh J, Jadeja D, Chanda S (2005) Efficacy of Aqueous and Methanol Extracts of Some Medicinal Plants for Potential Antibacterial Activity. Turk J Biol, 29, 203-210.

Prajapathi, N.D., Agro's Dictionary of Medicinal Plants, Agrobios, Jodhpur, 2003, p. 401.

Rajesh Kowti, Harsha. R, Mohammed Gulzar Ahmed, Hareesh AR, Thammanna Gowda SS, Dinesha R, Satish Kumar BP, Irfan Ali M (2010). Antimicrobial Activity of Ethanol Extract of Leaf and Flower of *Spathodea campanulata P.* Beauv; Res J Pharm Biol Chem Sci; 1(3); pp. 691.

Rimando, A.M., et al. 1986. Studies on the Constituents of Philippine *Piper Betel* Leaves. Archives of Pharmacal Research 9, 2: 93-97.

S. De Rosa, A. De Giulio, and C. Iodice, 1994. *J. Nat. Prod.*, 57, 1711.

S.H.K.R. Prasad, N.L. Swapna, D. Rajasekhar, K. Anthonamma and Madan Prasad (2009). Preliminary Phytochemical and Antimicrobial Spectrum of Cultured Tissues of *Physalis minima* (L.), Int. J. Chem. Sci.: 7(4), 2009, 2719-2725.

Sollamann, T. (1918). Anthelmintics: Their Efficacy as Tested on Earthworm. J Pharmacol Exp Ther, 12, 129-170.

Svensson, B.M., L. Mathiasson, L. Martensson & Y. Bergstoms. 2005. *Artemia salina* as Test Organism for Assessment of Acute Toxicity of Leachate Water from Landfills. *Environmental Monitoring and Assesment* 102: 309-321.

Vidyarthi, R.D. (1967). A Text Book of Zoology. S. Chand and Co. New Delhi, pp. 329-370.

Pages: 115-173

BIODIVERSITY, BIOTECHNOLOGY AND ENVIRONMENTAL CONSERVATION

Edited by: **Dr. Pawan Kumar 'Bharti'; Mr. Govinda Bhandari**

ISBN: 978-93-5056-750-0

Edition: **2015**

Published by: **Discovery Publishing House Pvt. Ltd., New Delhi (India)**

CHAPTER 7

RNA Interference
An Overview

Aakansha Goswami[1]; B. Singh[2] and Rizuta Tripathi[3]

INTRODUCTION

RNA interference (RNAi) or Post-Transcriptional Gene Silencing (PTGS) is a conserved biological response to double-stranded RNA that mediates resistance to both endogenous parasitic and exogenous pathogenic nucleic acids, and regulates the expression of protein-coding genes. This natural mechanism for sequence-specific gene silencing promises to revolutionize experimental biology and may have important practical applications in functional genomics, therapeutic intervention, agriculture and other areas.

Our genome operates by sending instructions for the manufacture of proteins from DNA in the nucleus of the cell to the protein synthesizing machinery in the cytoplasm. These instructions are conveyed by messenger

[1] Department of Horticulture, Sardar Vallabhbhai Patel University of Agriculture & Technology, Meerut - 250 110 (UP) (India).

[2] Associate Professor, Department of Horticulture, Sardar Vallabhbhai Patel University of Agriculture & Technology, Modipuram, Meerut - 250 110 (UP) (India).

[3] Department of Biotechnology, Sardar Vallabhbhai Patel University of Agriculture & Technology, Meerut - 250 110 (UP) (India).

RNA (mRNA). In 1998, the American scientists Andrew Fire and Craig Mello published their discovery of a mechanism that can degrade mRNA from a specific gene. This mechanism, RNA interference, is activated when RNA molecules occur as double-stranded pairs in the cell. Double-stranded RNA activates biochemical machinery which degrades those mRNA molecules that carry a genetic code identical to that of the double-stranded RNA. When such mRNA molecules disappear, the corresponding gene is silenced and no protein of the encoded type is made.

RNA interference occurs in plants, animals, and humans. It is of great importance for the regulation of gene expression, participates in defense against viral infections, and keeps jumping genes under control. RNA interference is already being widely used in basic science as a method to study the function of genes and it may lead to novel therapies in the future.

The Flow of Information in the Cell: From DNA via mRNA to Protein

The genetic code in DNA determines how proteins are built. The instructions contained in the DNA are copied to mRNA and subsequently used to synthesize proteins (Fig 7.1). This flow of genetic information from DNA via mRNA to protein has been termed the central dogma of molecular biology by the British Nobel Laureate Francis Crick. Proteins are involved in all processes of life, for instance as enzymes digesting our food, receptors receiving signals in the brain, and as antibodies defending us against bacteria.

Our genome consists of approximately 30,000 genes. However, only a fraction of them are used in each cell. Which genes are expressed (*i.e.* govern the synthesis of new proteins) is controlled by the machinery that copies DNA to mRNA in a process called transcription. It, in turn, can be modulated by various factors. The fundamental principles for the regulation of gene expression were identified more than 40 years ago by the French Nobel Laureates François Jacob and Jacques Monod. Today, we know that similar principles operate throughout evolution, from bacteria to humans. They also form the basis for gene technology, in which a DNA sequence is introduced into a cell to produce new protein.

Around 1990, molecular biologists obtained a number of unexpected results that were difficult to explain. The most striking effects were observed by plant biologists who were trying to increase the colour intensity of the petals in petunias by introducing a gene inducing the formation of red pigment in the flowers. But instead of intensifying the colour, this treatment led to a complete loss of colour and the petals turned white! The mechanism causing these effects remained enigmatic until Fire and Mello made the discovery for which they receive this year's Nobel Prize.

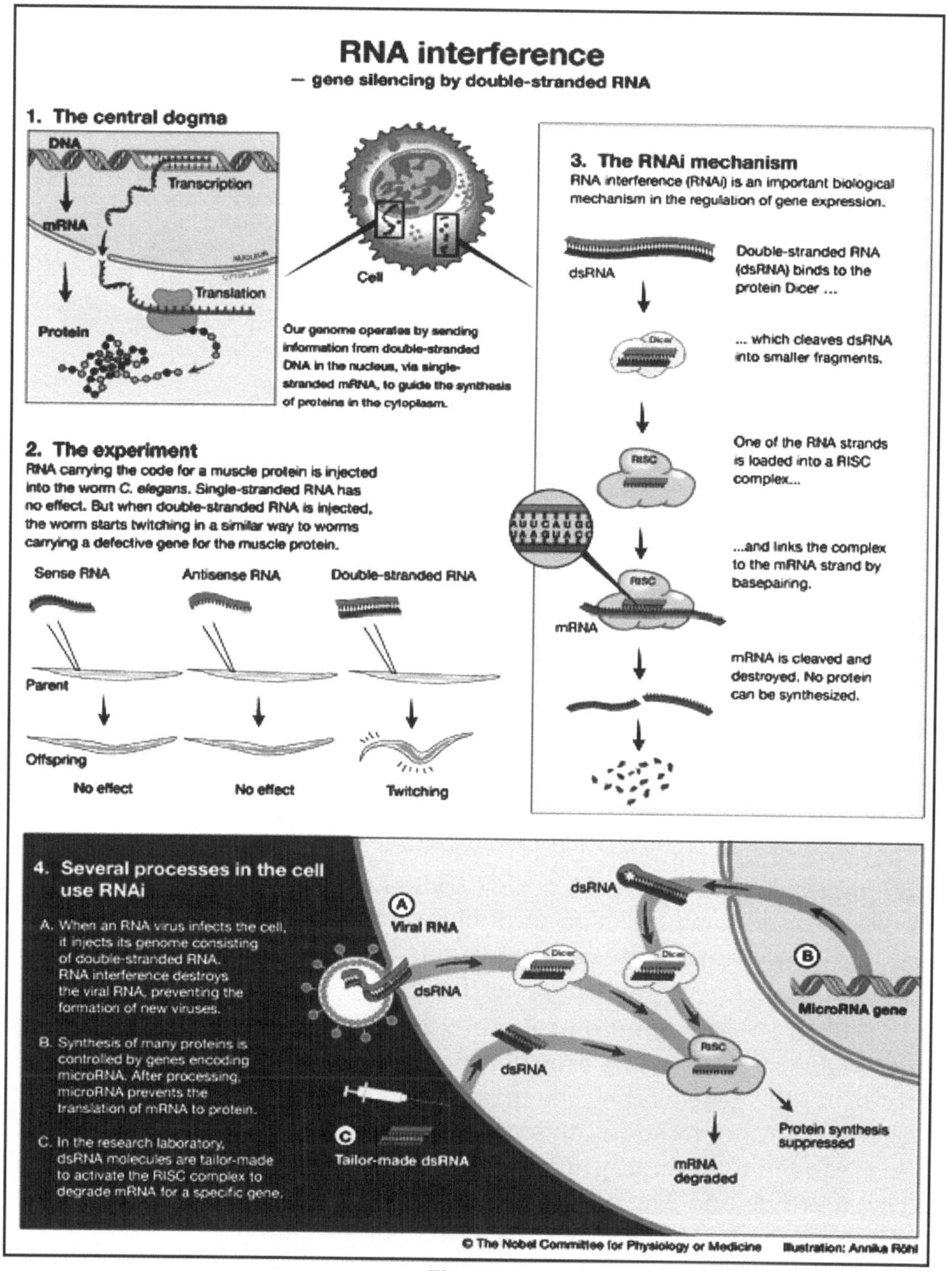

Fig. 7.1

The Discovery of RNA Interference

Andrew Fire and Craig Mello were investigating how gene expression is regulated in the nematode worm *Caenorhabditis elegans* (Fig. 7.2). Injecting mRNA molecules encoding a muscle protein led to no changes in the behaviour of the worms. The genetic code in mRNA is described as being the 'sense' sequence, and injecting 'antisense' RNA, which can pair with the mRNA, also had no effect. But when Fire and Mello injected sense and antisense RNA together, they observed that the worms displayed peculiar, twitching movements. Similar movements were seen in worms that completely lacked a functioning gene for the muscle protein. What had happened?

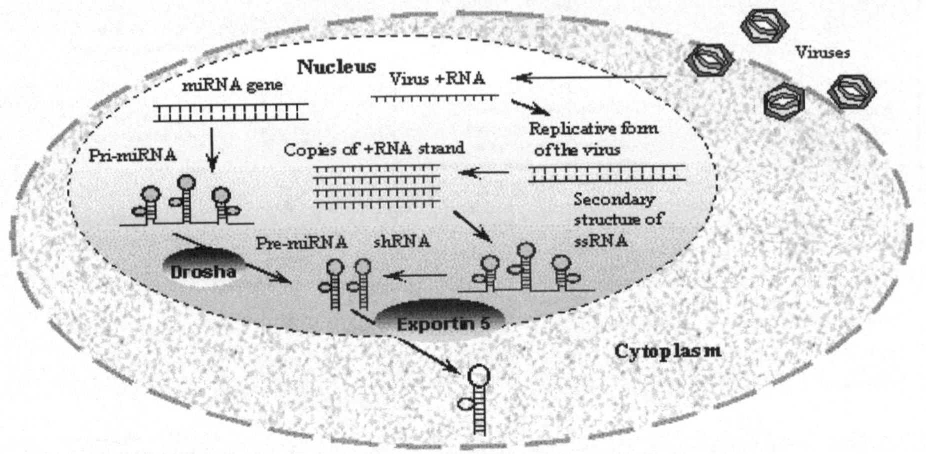

Fig. 7.2

When sense and antisense RNA molecules meet, they bind to each other and form double-stranded RNA. Could it be that such a double-stranded RNA molecule silences the gene carrying the same code as this particular RNA? Fire and Mello tested this hypothesis by injecting double-stranded RNA molecules containing the genetic codes for several other worm proteins. In every experiment, injection of double-stranded RNA carrying a genetic code led to silencing of the gene containing that particular code. The protein encoded by that gene was no longer formed.

After a series of simple but elegant experiments, Fire and Mello deduced that double-stranded RNA can silence genes, that this RNA interference is specific for the gene whose code matches that of the injected RNA molecule, and that RNA interference can spread between cells and even be inherited. It was enough to inject tiny amounts of double-stranded RNA to achieve an effect, and Fire and Mello therefore proposed that RNA interference (now commonly abbreviated to RNAi) is a catalytic process.

Fire and Mello published their findings in the journal *Nature* on February 19, 1998. Their discovery clarified many confusing and contradictory experimental observations and revealed a natural mechanism for controlling the flow of genetic information. This heralded the start of a new research field.

The RNA Interference Machinery is Unraveled

The components of the RNAi machinery were identified during the following years . Double-stranded RNA binds to a protein complex, Dicer, which cleaves it into fragments. Another protein complex, RISC, binds these fragments. One of the RNA strands is eliminated but the other remains bound to the RISC complex and serves as a probe to detect mRNA molecules. When an mRNA molecule can pair with the RNA fragment on RISC, it is bound to the RISC complex, cleaved and degraded. The gene served by this particular mRNA has been silenced.

RNA Interference – A Defense Against Viruses and Jumping Genes

RNA interference is important in the defense against viruses, particularly in lower organisms. Many viruses have a genetic code that contains double-stranded RNA. When such a virus infects a cell, it injects its RNA molecule, which immediately binds to Dicer . The RISC complex is activated, viral RNA is degraded, and the cell survives the infection. In addition to this defense, higher organisms such as man have developed an efficient immune defense involving antibodies, killer cells, and interferons.

Jumping genes, also known as transposons, are DNA sequences that can move around in the genome. They are present in all organisms and can cause damage if they end up in the wrong place. Many transposons operate by copying their DNA to RNA, which is then reverse-transcribed back to DNA and inserted at another site in the genome. Part of this RNA molecule is often double-stranded and can be targeted by RNA interference. In this way, RNA interference protects the genome against transposons.

RNA Interference Regulates Gene Expression

RNA interference is used to regulate gene expression in the cells of humans as well as worms (Fig. 7.4). Hundreds of genes in our genome encode small RNA molecules called microRNAs. They contain pieces of the code of other genes. Such a microRNA molecule can form a double-stranded structure and activate the RNA interference machinery to block protein synthesis. The expression of that particular gene is silenced. We now understand that genetic regulation by microRNAs plays an important role in the development of the organism and the control of cellular functions.

New Opportunities in Biomedical Research, Gene Technology and Health Care

RNA interference opens up exciting possibilities for use in gene technology. Double-stranded RNA molecules have been designed to activate the silencing of specific genes in humans, animals or plants (Fig. 7.4). Such silencing RNA molecules are introduced into the cell and activate the RNA interference machinery to break down mRNA with an identical code.

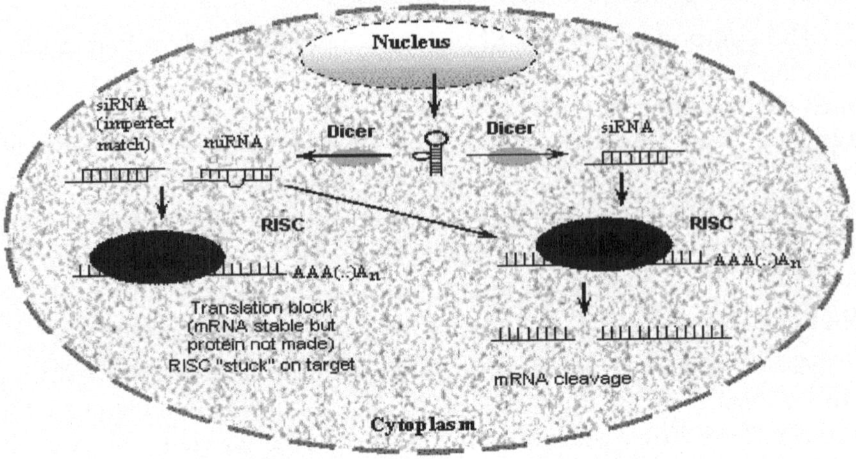

Fig. 7.3

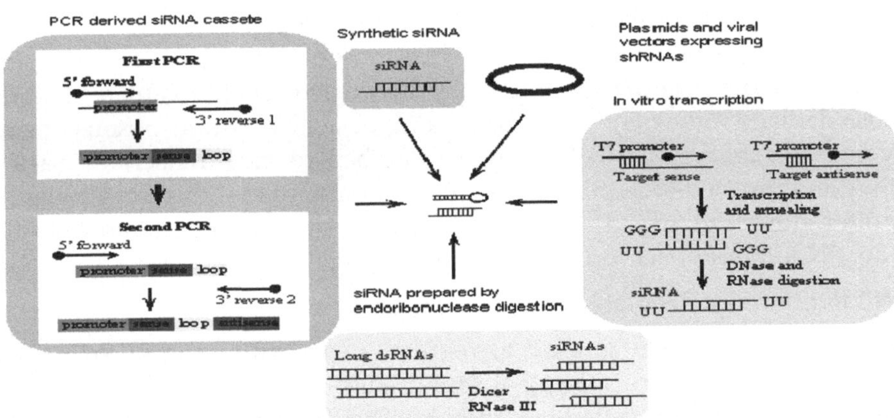

Fig. 7.4

This method has already become an important research tool in biology and biomedicine. In the future, it is hoped that it will be used in many disciplines including clinical medicine and agriculture. Several recent publications show successful gene silencing in human cells and experimental animals. For instance, a gene causing high blood cholesterol levels was recently shown to be silenced by treating animals with silencing RNA. Plans are underway to develop silencing RNA as a treatment for virus infections, cardiovascular diseases, cancer, endocrine disorders and several other conditions.

RNA interference (RNAi) is arguably the hottest topic in science at present. The number of papers published on RNAi has exploded over the last few years and the journal *Science* proclaimed it the biggest scientific breakthrough of 2002. Why is RNAi causing such a fuss? Well, imagine you could identify the role of a gene in a disease by switching it off easily, in the space of just a day, and in almost any organism. Imagine you could then take this tool and treat certain diseases, such as cancer or AIDS, by switching off the causative genes. That's the promise that RNAi offers Around a decade ago, when Richard Jorgensen and colleagues were trying to produce more intensely purple petunias, they had little idea what impact their findings would have on science. They tried to improve the colour by adding another pigment-producing gene to petunias, but to their surprise, this turned them totally white or irregularly coloured. As the normal and –foreign' genes appeared to be turning each other off, they called this process co-suppression.

What was initially thought to be a peculiar effect in petunias was subsequently found to occur in other plants. And curiosity was further aroused when a similar effect was detected in the fungus *Neurospora crassa*. Attempts to enhance orange pigment in the fungus by introducing extra copies of carotenoid pigment genes failed when the orange pigment gene was suppressed in a third of the engineered mould. In some strains, the effect — which was called quelling — was passed on through multiple generations.

At the same time, Guo and Kemphus were investigating the function of the par-1 gene in the nematode worm *Caenorhabditis elegans*. They looked at the effect of blocking the production of the *par-1* protein using a technique called antisense — in which a small synthesized piece of RNA that is complementary to a specific sequence in *par-1* messenger RNA (mRNA) attaches and stops the mRNA from being translated into the protein. Injecting an antisense RNA into the worm gave the expected result: the embryos all died. But they were puzzled when injecting the sense strand (the same sequence as the *par-1* mRNA) — a standard negative control for the experiment — also resulted in embryonic lethality.

Andrew Fire and Craig Mello had observed a similarly confusing result in their studies, and devised an experiment that turned out to be a defining moment in RNAi research. They injected both sense and antisense RNAs into the worms to see if there was an additive effect, but found that this double-stranded RNA (dsRNA) mixture was much more potent than the sum of its parts, silencing the target gene ten times more efficiently than either strand alone. This effect became known as RNA interference.

With the benefit of hindsight, it was clear that co-suppression in plants, quelling in fungi and RNAi in nematodes all shared a common mechanism. Further work showed that this effect was even more widespread, occurring in fruitflies and mammals too. Given the conservation of this mechanism in many organisms and given that this involved RNA, which for decades had been thought of being only the intermediate that allowed DNA to be translated into proteins, scientists rushed to find out what was going on.

DICING AND SILENCING

The precise mechanisms behind RNAi are not yet fully understood, but what was established early on was that the gene-silencing effect occurs after the creation of RNA from DNA (transcription), because dsRNA created to target the introns (which are spliced out of the mRNA) did not activate RNAi—hence the umbrella term of post-transcriptional gene silencing (PTGS) used to describe RNAi, co-suppression and quelling.

The central process of RNAi is the chopping of dsRNA into smaller pieces of a defined length by the appropriately named enzyme Dicer. Dicer chops dsRNA into two classes of smaller RNAs — microRNAs (miRNAs) and small interfering RNAs (siRNAs) — that are around 21-23 nucleotides in length. Although miRNAs also stop protein production (and, as described in another article, the boundaries between siRNAs and miRNAs is becoming blurred), siRNAs are thought to be the main protagonists in RNAi. Dicer delivers these siRNAs to a group of proteins called the RNA-induced silencing complex (RISC), which uses the antisense strand of the siRNA to bind to and degrade the corresponding mRNA, resulting in gene silencing. RNAi is astonishingly efficient, because the RISC is an enzyme and catalyses multiple rounds of RNAi, perhaps hundreds or thousands *in vivo*. It also shows an amazing persistence in some organisms, such as worms, which suggests there could also be an amplification response.

Why RNAi?

It is thought that RNAi, at least in plants, might be an ancient defence mechanism that defends against RNA viruses, transposons and repetitive sequences. But recent work in yeast and the ciliate *Tetrahymena* has shown that RNAi might also influence transcription in the cell nucleus, partly by determining the form of the chromatin in which the DNA is wrapped. So, which genes are transcribed and which remain wrapped up or hidden could be under the control of small RNAs, although how this mechanism works is currently unknown.

Many mysteries of RNAi have yet to unfold, but one thing that is certain is that these small RNAs have revolutinized the way scientists think about how DNA, RNA and proteins are controlled and function. This has caught the imagination of both big pharmaceutical companies, which are using RNAi as a target validation tool, and smaller companies, which are optimizing RNAi methodologies and looking at therapeutic avenues. With some of these companies predicting that the first RNAi-based drugs will begin clinical trials in the next 2-3 years, these might be early days, but they are incredibly exciting ones.

BIOLOGICAL FUNCTIONS OF RNA INTERFERENCE

Endogenous triggers of RNAi pathway include foreign DNA or double-stranded RNA (dsRNA) of viral origin, aberrant transcripts from repetitive sequences in the genome such as transposons, and pre-microRNA (miRNA). In plants, RNAi forms the basis of virus-induced gene silencing (VIGS), suggesting an important role in pathogen resistance. A possible mechanism underlying the regulation of endogenous genes by the RNAi machinery was suggested from studies of *C. elegans*. In mammalian cells long (>30nt) double-stranded RNAs usually cause Interferon response.

A SIMPLIFIED MODEL FOR THE RNAI PATHWAY

A simplified model for the RNAi pathway is based on two steps, each involving ribonuclease enzyme. In the first step, the trigger RNA (either dsRNA or miRNA primary transcript) is processed into an short, interfering RNA (siRNA) by the RNase II enzymes Dicer and Drosha. In the second step, siRNAs are loaded into the effector complex RNA-induced silencing complex (RISC). The siRNA is unwound during RISC assembly and the single-stranded RNA hybridizes with mRNA target. Gene silencing is a result of nucleolytic degradation of the targeted mRNA by the RNase H enzyme Argonaute (Slicer). If the siRNA/mRNA duplex contains mismatches the mRNA is not cleaved. Rather, gene silencing is a result of translational inhibition.

BACKGROUND

RNAi (RNA interference) refers to the introduction of homologous double stranded RNA (dsRNA) to specifically target a gene's product, resulting in null or hypomorphic phenotypes. The use of antisense RNA to interfere with a gene's activity in *C. elegans* was first utilised by Su Guo and Ken Kemphues to study *par-1* ; however, it was reported that control sense RNA also produced a *par-1* mutant phenotype (Cell 81: 611-20, 1995). Subsequently, it was discovered by Fire *et al.* '98 that it is the presence of dsRNA, formed from the annealing of sense and antisense strands present in the *in vitro* RNA preps, that is responsible for producing the interfering activity. Introduction of dsRNA into an adult worm results in the loss of the targeted endogenous mRNA from both the adult and its progeny. This phenomenon has been effectively harnessed to study an ever increasing number of maternal and zygotic genes in *C. elegans*.

The most interesting aspects of RNAi are the following:

- dsRNA, rather than single-stranded antisense RNA, is the interfering agent.
- it is highly specific.
- it is remarkably potent (only a few dsRNA molecules per cell are required for effective interference).
- the interfering activity (and presumably the dsRNA) can cause interference in cells and tissues far removed from the site of introduction

HISTORY AND DISCOVERY

Fig. 7.5

Example petunia plants in which genes for pigmentation are silenced by RNAi. The left plant is wild-type; the right plants contain transgenes that induce suppression of both transgene and endogenous gene expression, giving rise to the unpigmented white areas of the flower.

The discovery of RNAi was preceded first by observations of transcriptional inhibition by antisense RNA expressed in transgenic plants, and more directly by reports of unexpected outcomes in experiments performed by plant scientists in the United States and the Netherlands in the early 1990s. In an attempt to alter flower colors in petunias, researchers introduced additional copies of a gene encoding chalcone synthase, a key enzyme for flower pigmentation into petunia plants of normally pink or violet flower color. The overexpressed gene was expected to result in darker flowers, but instead produced less pigmented, fully or partially white flowers, indicating that the activity of chalcone synthase had been substantially decreased; in fact, both the endogenous genes and the transgenes were downregulated in the white flowers. Soon after, a related event termed *quelling* was noted in the fungus *Neurospora crassa* although it was not immediately recognized as related. Further investigation of the phenomenon in plants indicated that the downregulation was due to post-transcriptional inhibition of gene expression via an increased rate of mRNA degradation. This phenomenon was called *co-suppression of gene expression*, but the molecular mechanism remained unknown.

Not long after, plant virologists working on improving plant resistance to viral diseases observed a similar unexpected phenomenon. While it was known that plants expressing virus-specific proteins showed enhanced tolerance or resistance to viral infection, it was not expected that plants carrying only short, non-coding regions of viral RNA sequences would show similar levels of protection. Researchers believed that viral RNA produced by transgenes could also inhibit viral replication.The reverse experiment, in which short sequences of plant genes were introduced into viruses, showed that the targeted gene was suppressed in an infected plant. This phenomenon was labeled "virus-induced gene silencing" (VIGS), and the set of such phenomena were collectively called *post transcriptional gene silencing*.

After these initial observations in plants, many laboratories around the world searched for the occurrence of this phenomenon in other organisms. Craig C. Mello and Andrew Fire's 1998 *Nature* paper reported a potent gene silencing effect after injecting double stranded RNA into *C. elegans*. In investigating the regulation of muscle protein production, they observed that neither mRNA nor antisense RNA injections had an effect on protein production, but double-stranded RNA successfully silenced the targeted gene. As a result of this work, they coined the term *RNAi*. Fire and Mello's discovery was particularly notable because it represented the first identification of the causative agent for the phenomenon. Fire and Mello were awarded the Nobel Prize in Physiology or Medicine in 2006 for their work.

Designing RNAi Experiments

Several crucial considerations should be beard in mind while designing RNAi experiments. The below examples regard RNAi experiments performed with chemically synthesized siRNA.

1. The first step is to design a suitable siRNA sequence. A growing number of libraries of validated siRNAs directed toward some frequently targeted genes are available. However, if the gene of interest has not been targeted using siRNA before, a novel siRNA must be developed. In mammalian cells RNAi is mediated by 21- to 23-nucleotide siRNAs containing symmetrical two nucleotide 3′ overhangs. Given a siRNA sequence alone, it is not currently possible to predict the degree of gene knockdown produced by a particular siRNA. Nevertheless, several observations have been made that can be taken into account to increase the probability of producing an effective siRNA. The chief variable is the gene target site. Generally, it is recommended that a target site located at least 100-200 nucleotides from the AUG initiation codon is chosen. Targets within 50-100 nucleotides of the termination codon should instead be avoided. The 5′ and 3′ untranslated region (UTR) should also be avoided, since associated regulatory proteins might compromise RNAi. This is just a general recommendation, as some siRNAs targeting the 3′ UTR have also been shown to induce RNAi [McManus MT, Petersen]. Numerous on-line design tools will produce a list of suitable gene target sites. It is important to ensure that the sequence is specific to the target gene by performing a BLAST search in order to avoid cross reaction with unwanted genes. As an example, Biocomputing at the Whitehead Institute for Biomedical Research – a nonprofit independent research and educational institution affiliated with the Massachusetts Institute of Technology – is one of several organizations that has developed a freely available web-based siRNA design tool.

2. The structural characteristics of the siRNA molecules are another crucial aspect to be considered while designing RNAi experiments. SiRNA of 21 nucleotides with 3′-d(TT) or (UU) overhangs are considered the most effective [Elbashir SM, Martinez]. Despite the fact that nucleotide-protein steric interactions contribute to the relationship between siRNA length and activity, the reason for this relationship is not completely elucidated. For optimal siRNA secondary structure, the GC ratio should ideally be between 45 and 55%, and multiple identical nucleotides in series, particularly poly(C) and poly(G), should be avoided to determine any requirements for modification, such as fluorophore labeling to allow for siRNA tracking and quantification of transfection efficiency.
3. To induce RNAi, siRNA must be transfected into the cells of interest. Several transfection reagents exist, the most commonly used being liposomal or amine-based. In some cases electroporation may be used, but cell toxicity can be high with this technique [Benov LC, Antonov PA]. Cell lines show varying responses to different transfection reagents, and it may be necessary to try more than one reagent or approach. Transfection efficiency is optimized by titrating cell density, transfection time, and the ratio of siRNA-to-transfection reagent. The cell passage number and antibiotic use can also affect the efficiency of transfection.
4. Recently, experimental design features have been suggested to guarantee the rigor of RNAi experiments [*Nat Cell Biol* 2003]. Due to the high specificity of RNAi, a siRNA with0 a one-nucleotide sequence mismatch can serve as a negative control. If this approach is used, absence of homology with other targets should be confirmed at the design stage. It is important to remember that mismatched siRNAs could target mutant gene sequences. Therefore loss of functional target gene silencing should be demonstrated to validate this approach. Alternatives include sequences that preset no homology to any known gene. Some investigators have suggested that scrambled siRNA is not sufficiently homologous to the target sequence to function as an adequate control; therefore, they propose a combination of mismatched and scrambled controls [*Nat Cell Biol* 2003]. A more challenging functional control is to demonstrate the "rescue" of the target gene function following artificial overexpression of the target gene. Transfection of a plasmid expressing the gene sequence to which a siRNA is targeted results in production of mRNA that would also be targeted by the siRNA. This problem can be overcome using plasmids containing silent mutations. This approach takes advantage of degeneracy of gene coding, i.e., amino acids are represented by more than one three-nucleotide codon sequence. Rescue is achieved by expression of a protein identical to the native protein from a nucleotide sequence that differs from the native nucleotide sequence to which the siRNA is targeted. Alternatively, siRNAs directed

to the 3′-UTR can be used. Many researchers use more than one siRNA, with each targeted to different areas of the gene sequence. A consistent RNAi response using different siRNAs with a variety of targets within the gene sequence of interest would increase confidence in experimental results. Dose-respons characteristics should be determined and the lowest effective concentration of siRNA be used to avoid nonspecific effects.

5. The effect of RNAi should be quantified at both the mRNA and the protein level. The knockdown of a protein should be probably evaluated after mRNA reduction has been proved: in fact, a reduction in protein levels not accompanied by a decrease in mRNA might indicate that other mechanisms are at work, such as RNAi mediated by microRNA. Northern blot analysis is considered by many to be the gold standard. Real-time reverse transcriptase polymerase chain reaction, incorporating internal controls to quantify "housekeeping" gene transcript levels, can also be used [Mocellin S, Rossi CR]. Protein knockdown can be confirmed by Western blot analysis, immunofluorescence, flow cytometry and phenotypic and/or functional assays. Although RNAi generally occurs within 24 h of transfection, both onset and duration of RNAi depend on the turnover rate of the protein of interest, as well as the rate of dilution and longevity of the siRNAs. The duration of gene silencing can also be modified by factors such as the concentration of serum in the culture medium, which affects cell-cycle rate. It is therefore necessary to determine the time course of any silencing observed under specific conditions using the modalities discussed.

Why does RNAi exist?

RNAi is thought to have evolved about a billion years ago, before plants and animals diverged. The process exists in many living things, including single-celled organisms, plants and human beings.

Current thinking suggests that RNAi evolved as a cellular defense mechanism against invaders such as RNA viruses. When they replicate, RNA viruses temporarily exist in a double-stranded form. This double-stranded intermediate would trigger RNAi and inactivate the virus' genes, preventing an infection.

RNAi may also have evolved to combat the spread of genetic elements called transposons within a cell's DNA. Transposons can wreak havoc by jumping from spot to spot on a genome, sometimes causing mutations that can lead to cancer or other diseases. Like RNA viruses, transposons can take on a double-stranded RNA form that would trigger RNAi to clamp down on the potentially harmful jumping.

How can RNAi be applied to medicine and biomedical research?

Investigators are currently working intensely to understand RNAi's role in normal and diseased cells, and to harness the mechanism for use in medical therapies.

Diseases that can be blocked by knocking down the activity of one or several genes are the most promising targets for RNAi-based therapies. Cancer, for example, is often caused by overactive genes, and quelling their activity could halt the disease. Several pharmaceutical companies are currently testing RNAi-based therapies for various forms of cancer.

Viral infections are also important potential targets for RNAi-based therapies. Reducing the activity of key viral genes would cripple the virus, and numerous studies have already hinted at the promise of RNAi for treating viral infections. In laboratory-grown human cells, investigators have stopped the growth of HIV, polio, hepatitis C and other viruses. RNAi-based therapies against HIV and other viruses are expected to soon enter clinical trials.

The strength of RNAi as a research tool will also have an enormous potential impact on medicine. Knocking down a gene's activity yields a wealth of information about its functions in cellular pathways. But prior to the discovery of RNAi, the process was laborious and could take months.

Now, by harnessing RNAi, investigators can silence selected genes quickly and easily, and can answer questions that were once well beyond their reach. This technique promises to reveal key players in normal and disease processes, and may lead scientists to new drug targets.

Already, RNAi has taught biomedical researchers a few lessons. For years, scientists had been intensely studying how proteins regulate gene activity, focusing most of their attention on proteins called transcription factors. Now RNA, through RNAi and related processes, is recognized as a key partner in the cell's multi-layered approach to gene regulation.

Are there other cellular pathways similar to RNAi?

Not long after RNAi was discovered, scientists uncovered a related process called the microRNA (miRNA) pathway. Both pathways involve double-stranded RNA, but the source of these RNAs differs. Unlike the double-stranded RNA that triggers RNAi, miRNAs are encoded in the genome. Additionally, miRNAs are not completely double-stranded, but rather form hairpin-like structures that contain double-stranded regions. While the miRNA pathway is distinct from RNAi, it borrows extensively from RNAi's tool chest by making use of enzymes such as Dicer.

In contrast to RNAi, the miRNA pathway focuses on regulating the cell's own genes. Scientists believe that humans have more than 200 miRNAs, and they are estimated to regulate as many as a third of our genes. RNA interference: the next genetics revolution?

PRINCIPLES OF RNA INTERFERENCE

RNA interference most likely evolved as a mechanism for cells to eliminate unwanted foreign genes. Foreign genes are often present in cells at high copy numbers, being present as viral genes, transposable elements, or as plasmids introduced experimentally in cell transfection protocols. It has been known for several decades that the level of expression of transgenes usually decreases as the number of copies present in the cell increases and that endogenous homologous genes can also be suppressed by the presence of the transgene (Napoli et al., 1990). Although such gene silencing can occur at the transcriptional level, it is now recognized that a major mechanism of gene suppression occurs post-transcriptionally, and that a major mechanism for this PTGS is RNAi, the selective degradation of mRNAs targeted by siRNAs (Van Blokland et al., 1994). Such PTGS via RNAi can occur very rapidly with proteins for many genes, being decreased within hours, and completely absent within 24 h (Pruss et al., 1997). Based upon these and other findings initially made in studies of plants (Ratcliff et al., 1997), it seems very likely that RNAi evolved as a mechanism to defend plant cells against viral infections.

(a) Post-Transcriptional Gene Silencing and the Discovery of RNA Interference

PTGS and RNAi were discovered in genetic transformation studies of eukaryotic cells, principally plants and worms, wherein it was shown that mRNAs for the encoded transgene alone, or together with mRNAs for homologous endogenous genes are very low or absent despite high levels of transcription (Fire, 1999; Marathe et al., 2000). The ability to manipulate and monitor gene expression in the plant *Arabidopsis thaliana* and the roundworm *Caenorhabditis elegans* (the genomes of both species are now complete) revealed the process of RNAi and allowed the relatively rapid identification of several genes that regulate the RNAi process.

Transgenes insert into the genomes of plants by recombination in an apparently random manner so that the number of inserted copies, their chromosomal location, and their local arrangement within the chromosome vary among transformants. The observation of an inverse correlation between copy number and the level of gene expression suggested that an increased copy number of a particular gene results in silencing of that gene (Assaad et al., 1993). It was initially thought that such gene silencing was due to reduced gene transcription resulting from interactions between closely linked copies that result in the formation of secondary structures that promote methylation and inhibition of transcription (Ye and Signer, 1996). Further studies showed that transcriptional gene silencing (TGS) could also occur in trans, such that one transgene can be silenced by another transgene introduced either by crossing or transformation. It was then proposed that a silencing RNA is produced by one locus that somehow effects the silencing of the other gene by a mechanism involving RNA-mediated inhibition of transcription (Mette et al., 2000). Although some data were consistent with such mechanisms of transcriptional silencing, additional data suggested the involvement of PTGS. The presence of double-stranded RNAs (dsRNAs) and their cleavage into siRNAs of approximately 23 nucleotides was demonstrated, and it was then shown that expression of dsRNA with sequences corresponding to open reading frames in plants results in PTGS (Hamilton and Baulcombe, 1999). Similarly, expression of dsRNAs with sequences complementary to those of endogenous genes results in the selective silencing of those genes in *C. elegans* (Zamore et al., 2000). Collectively, the studies of *A. thaliana* and *C. elegans* showed that both TGS and PTGS can be initiated by the same RNA degradation pathway—TGS occurs when the dsRNA includes promoter sequences, whereas PTGS occurs when the dsRNA includes coding sequences. Although degradation of dsRNA is common to both mechanisms of gene silencing, the results also indicated that dsRNA-mediated TGS and PTGS involve different specific steps.

Although RNAi as a mechanism of PTGS was first discovered in plants and may have evolved as a cellular defense mechanism against foreign DNA and RNA, it is very clear that RNAi is widely employed in most if not all eukaryotic cells as a mechanism to regulate the expression of endogenous genes. In 1998, it was discovered that injection of dsRNA was much more effective for silencing of gene expression in *C. elegans* than was single-stranded antisense RNA (Fire et al., 1998). This experimentally induced PTGS, the first report of the use of RNAi as a tool in biology, was very potent, and remarkably, the PTGS occurred not only in the worms to which the dsRNA was administered, but also in their progeny. It was then demonstrated that the endogenous mRNA was the target of the injected dsRNA by a post-transcriptional mechanism and involving degradation of the targeted mRNA (Montgomery et al., 1998). Surprisingly, it was further shown that the dsRNA is effective at very low concentrations, such that the copy numbers of the targeted mRNA are far greater than the number of dsRNAs present in the cell (Fire et al., 1998; Kennerdell and Carthew, 1998). In addition, the suppression of the protein encoded by the targeted mRNA was found to persist through many rounds of cell division. The latter two observations strongly suggested that cells possess a mechanism for amplifying the RNAi mechanism. Not only can the RNAi process be maintained within cells of a common lineage, but it can also be transferred between cells, as shown in *C. elegans* where injection of dsRNA into the intestine results in silencing of the targeted gene in all cells of the F1 progeny of that worm (Fire et al., 1998). Indeed, dsRNA can enter cells and induce PTGS when worms are soaked in a solution containing the dsRNA or when the worms are fed bacteria expressing dsRNA (Tabara et al., 1998; Timmons and Fire, 1998). Recently, a transmembrane protein called SID-1 was identified as a possible mediator of intercellular transfer of RNAi (Winston et al., 2002).

Subsequently, other organisms were assayed for their capacity to induce RNAi. Evidence for RNAi in Drosophila was first demonstrated by Kennerdell and coworkers (Kennerdell and Carthew, 1998) who showed the involvement of the *frizzled* and *frizzled2* genes in the wingless pathway after introduction of dsRNA into embryos. Again, several techniques were developed in order to use dsRNA in this organism leading to the establishment of cell-free (Tuschl et al., 1999) and cell culture models (Caplen et al., 2000). A system that employed dsRNA as an extended hairpin-loop RNA was developed to induce heritable gene silencing (Kennerdell and Carthew, 2000). The *Drosophila* system has allowed the identification of several endogenous genes that play key roles in the RNAi process. An RNA nuclease activity called RISC (RNA-induced silencing complex) was discovered that is responsible for the degradation of endogenous mRNAs, as well as small nucleotide fragments (~25 nucleotides in length), which could be used as guides by RISC (Hammond et al., 2000). They later characterized RISC as a ribonucleoproteic complex (Hammond et al., 2001). These results were soon extended by showing that RNAi is an ATP-dependent and translation-independent event where the introduced dsRNA is processed into 21-23 nucleotide fragments that guide the cleavage of endogenous transcripts (Zamore et al., 2000). The enzyme responsible for the processing of the dsRNA was later discovered as a RNase III family nuclease named Dicer, a protein with high homology to the *rde-1 C. elegans* gene (Bernstein et al., 2001). To study the functions of RNAi in yeast, Volpe et al. (2002) deleted argonaute, dicer, and RNA-dependent RNA polymerase homologs; deletion resulted in the accumulation of complementary transcripts from centromeric heterochromatic repeats and de-repression of transgenes integrated at the centromere and impairment of centromere function. The authors of the latter study proposed that dsRNA arising from centromeric repeats targets the formation and maintenance of heterochromatin through RNAi.

In mammalian cells, RNAi was first employed as a tool to induce the silencing of the targeted gene (Wianny and Zernicka-Goetz, 2000). This approach was partially successful in mouse embryos (Wianny and Zernicka-Goetz, 2000; Svoboda et al., 2001) and embryonic cell lines (Billy et al., 2001; Yang et al., 2001; Paddison et al., 2002b) where specific gene silencing was achieved. On the other hand, the introduction of dsRNA into mammalian somatic cells presents a major problem because it can induce (in a manner similar to the silencing observed during viral infection) to the activation of the PKR (protein kinase R) and RNAseL pathway, resulting in the inhibition of protein synthesis and induction of apoptosis (Baglioni and Nilsen, 1983; Clarke and Mathews, 1995; Gil and Esteban, 2000). Interestingly, this shows that, in mammalian cells, the mechanisms for RNA interference are not identical to those in lower organisms although RNAi does operate in at least a subset of mammalian cell types, in a Dicer-dependent manner via post-transcriptional mechanisms (Billy et al., 2001; Paddison et al., 2002b). Elbashir et al. (2001a) had the idea of directly introducing 21-23 nucleotide dsRNA (siRNAs) into mouse and human cells to try to avoid the problems associated with the expression of longer dsRNAs. They showed that the siRNA could efficiently trigger silencing in the mammalian cells.

RNAi mechanisms may provide explanations for various biological phenomena that were previously described, but without any understanding of the possible underlying mechanism. For example, it was recently proposed that RNAi mechanisms could explain the controversial process of RNA-mediated memory transfer in planaria (Smalheiser et al., 2001). It will certainly be of interest to investigate possible roles for RNAi in the many different physiological processes that involve modulation of protein levels at a post-transcriptional level.

(b) Easy knockout

As RNAi relies on the sequence-specific interaction between siRNA and mRNA, siRNAs can be tailored to silence almost any gene. siRNAs that have been chemically synthesized or created by *in vitro* transcription systems can induce silencing in several systems, including mammalian cells. Transfected plasmids that produce dsRNA hairpins, called short hairpin RNAs (shRNAs), can also elicit RNAi effects. In the laboratory, the silencing of genes with RNAi seems to be rapid and convenient, and can be used to tackle many genes at the same time. RNAi can be achieved remarkably easily in *C. elegans* — gene silencing occurs by direct feeding of dsRNA feeding with bacteria that expressed dsRNA or even soaking worms in dsRNA, and the effect can also be transmitted to the next generation.

The relative ease with which genes can be silenced using RNAi has caused a minor revolution in molecular biology. Armed with data from genome sequencing projects, gene silencing with RNAi can be used on a breathtaking scale. For example, Julie Ahringer's group at the University of Cambridge has created a library of more than 16,000 cloned dsRNAs (around 86% of the *C. elegans* genome). By feeding these clones to worms, they have determined the function of 1,722 genes, most of which were previously unknown. Gary Ruvkun's group at Harvard Medical School has identified many hundreds of genes involved in fat storage. And Gregory Hannon's group at Cold Spring Harbor are looking to determine the functions of every gene in the human genome. The list of projects in this area is seemingly endless.

APPLICATIONS OF RNA INTERFERENCE TO ESTABLISHING GENE FUNCTION

The most widely used RNAi technology has been in cell culture and in vivo studies aimed at understanding the function of an individual (or multiple) proteins. The kinds of studies described demonstrate the power and flexibility of RNAi for unambiguously establishing (or excluding) a function of individual proteins in various cellular processes. It should also be noted that cells can be transfected with different combinations of multiple siRNAs, each directed against a specific mRNA of interest, to elucidate the specific contributions of the proteins to a biological process involving a multiprotein complex. For example, Wojcik and DeMartino (2002) recently took advantage of the latter feature of RNAi methods to elucidate roles for different subunits of the proteasome in its assembly and function. The power of *C. elegans* and *Drosophila* molecular genetics is providing the opportunity to use genome-wide RNAi to rapidly establish functions of genes in a specific process. For example, Ruvkun and colleagues (Lee et al., 2002c) systematically inactivated 5690 genes in *C. elegans* using RNAi to identify genes that limit lifespan. They identified a mitochondrial leucyl-tRNA synthetase gene and showed that mutations of this gene that impair mitochondrial function increase lifespan, which was associated with decreased ATP levels and oxygen consumption.

(a) Signal Transduction

Intercellular messenger molecules play vital roles in the development and proper functioning of all organisms. Among the most prominent of such signals in mammals are growth factors, cytokines, cell adhesion molecules, neurotransmitters, steroids, and gases such as nitric oxide. Specific receptors located on the cell surface or within the cell transduce responses to the ligand via signaling cascades that are often complex, involving kinases and transcription factors, for example. RNAi methods provide powerful tools for establishing the roles of individual proteins in the signal transduction pathway employed by a specific ligand. Several recent studies have demonstrated the efficacy of siRNA-mediated knockdown of signal transduction proteins and have elucidated roles for those proteins in biological responses of cells. Adaptor proteins of the Shc family transduce signals from a diverse group of growth factors that signal through receptor tyrosine kinases. Liposome-mediated introduction of siRNA against a single isoform of ShcA into HeLa cells was used to selectively reduce levels of that Shc revealing its role in the regulation of cell proliferation (Kisielow et al., 2002). Neurotrophin receptors and integrins (receptors for extracellular matrix molecules such as laminin) are often coupled to a signaling pathway involving phosphatidylinositol 3-kinase and Akt kinase (Gary and Mattson, 2001; Cheng et al., 2003). Decreasing the amount of the 110 β subunit of phosphatidylinositol 3-kinase using siRNAs resulted in a marked decrease in the growth and tissue invasiveness of tumor cells (Czauderna et al., 2003). Small molecule inhibitors have been widely employed to study the functions of various protein kinases in cells. However, most such inhibitors are not specific and affect multiple kinases. RNAi has been successfully employed to unequivocally establish the roles of specific kinases in signal transduction processes. For example, Irie and coworkers (Irie et al., 2002) demonstrated the ability to knockdown levels of specific subtypes of protein kinase C in cultured human and rat cells in a species-specific manner. The existence of an extracellular system for the production of sphingosine-1-phosphate was demonstrated in a study in which siRNAs directed against the sphingosine kinase-1 enzyme were used to inhibit its production and export in cultured endothelial cells (Ancellin et al., 2002).

Calcium plays important roles as an intracellular signal that mediates a variety of responses of cells to environmental stimuli. Mechanisms for regulating levels of calcium in the cytoplasm are complex and involve movements of calcium ions across the plasma membrane, as well as into and out of endoplasmic reticulum and mitochondria. A key role for inositol 1, 4, 5-trisphosphate (IP_3)-mediated release of intracellular calcium in the maturation of mouse oocytes was demonstrated in which siRNAs against the IP_3 receptor-1 were injected into germinal vesicle-intact oocytes (Xu et al., 2003). The siRNAs reduced IP_3 receptor-1 levels by 90% and, following insemination, blocked the intracellular calcium oscillations that play a critical role for the first steps in development. In another study, RNAi-mediated depletion of the endoplasmic reticulum calcium-ATPases resulted in lethality in *C. elegans* (Cho et al., 2000), demonstrating a pivotal role for calcium uptake by this organelle in cell functions and survival.

(b) Cell Cycle Regulation

Because of their fundamental importance for development, tissue homeostasis, and stem cell biology and their centrality to the field of cancer research, genes that regulate the cell cycle have been a prominent focus of studies that employ RNAi. Examples of the kinds of findings obtained using RNAi technologies to knockdown the expression of cell cycle genes are as follows. A requirement of the Mps1 kinase for the spindle assembly checkpoint was established, whereas a role for this kinase in centrosome duplication was ruled out (Stucke et al., 2002). A key role for a novel centrosomal protein called Cep135 in microtubule organization was revealed (Ohta et al., 2002), and a role for centrin-2 in centriole duplication was established (Salisbury et al., 2002). RNAi was used to show that the regulation of cell cycle progression in response to mitogens is controlled by the cyclin-dependent kinase inhibitor p27 (Kip1). Depletion of Plk1 using siRNAs results in activation of cyclin B and inhibits centrosome amplification in hydroxyurea-treated U2OS cells (Liu and Erikson, 2002). RNAi was used to show that the protein PRC1 is a microtubule-associated protein that facilitates bundling of microtubules (Mollinari et al., 2002) and that the processes of centrosome separation and chromosome segregation require the phosphatase Cdc14A in culture human cells (Mailand et al., 2002). Depletion of the origin recognition complex subunit ORC6 using RNAi resulted in cells with decreased DNA replication, multipolar spindles and aberrant mitosis (Prasanth et al., 2002). A novel human protein called Speedy, expressed only during the G_1/S phase of the cell cycle, was shown to enhance cell proliferation by enhancing the activity of Cdk2 (Porter et al., 2002).

(c) Development

The complex and remarkably rapid events that occur during development of the fertilized egg into an adult organism remain largely a mystery. There would appear to be a great potential for RNAi technology to unravel the cellular and molecular events that regulate developmental processes. Methods for silencing single or multiple selected genes in developing embryos in vivo and stem cells in culture (see *Section III. C.*) are beginning to reveal the functions of specific proteins in developmental processes. Nodal is a secreted factor that plays a key role in the formation and patterning of the mesoderm during gastrulation. RNAi was used to demonstrate that the transcriptional corepressor DRAP1 inhibits the transcription factor FoxH1 and thereby regulates signaling by Nodal during mouse embryogenesis (Iratni et al., 2002). Depletion of karyopherins α2 and α3 in cleavage stage porcine embryos revealed different requirements of these two proteins in embryogenesis (Cabot and Prather, 2003). In another study of embryogenesis, siRNAs directed against the mRNAs encoding Oct-3/4 and c-mos resulted in depletion of the encoded proteins, and phenotypes similar to those observed in Oct-3/4 and c-mos knockout mice (Kim et al., 2002). A key role for microtubule-associated protein-2 in the regulation of dendrite outgrowth in developing brain neurons was demonstrated using siRNAs (Krichevsky and Kosik, 2002). The transcription factor myc is known to play a fundamental role in the regulation of cell proliferation. A key role for the novel myc target gene mina53 in the regulation of cell proliferation by myc was demonstrated using RNAi technology (Tsuneoka et al., 2002).

(d) Macromolecular Synthesis and Degradation

Regulated synthesis of nucleic acids, proteins, and lipids, and the turnover of those macromolecules is essential for cell survival and functions. Although biochemical technologies have allowed the identification of various biosynthetic pathways and mechanisms for the degradation of proteins and other macromolecules, the functions of specific proteins in such processes are not well understood. Recent studies have employed RNAi to advance the understanding of the regulation of macromolecular synthesis and degradation. For example, depletion of galactosyltransferase II using siRNAs revealed a critical role for this enzyme in the biosynthesis of the linkage region of glycosaminoglycans (Bai et al., 2001). The regulation of the processing of RNAs transcribed from coding and noncoding regions of the genome is an active area of investigation because of the recent realization of its importance in the regulation of gene expression. Mendell and coworkers (Mendell et al., 2002) used RNAi to show that rent1/Upf1 plays distinct roles in the regulation of splicing and decay of nonsense transcripts. Transfection of cultured HeLa and HepG2 cells with siRNAs directed against the mRNA encoding the acyl-CoA binding protein resulted in cessation of cell proliferation, cell detachment, and death, demonstrating that acyl-CoA binding protein is essential for cell survival (Faergeman and Knudsen, 2002).

(e) Cell Motility

The migration of cells within and among tissues, and extensions of cells such as the axons and dendrites of neurons, is central to the structural and functional organization of all tissues. Although there are a few pharmacological agents that have proven useful in studying cell motility (the actin-depolymerizing agent cytochalasin D and the microtubule-stabilizing agent taxol, for example), a detailed understanding of the molecular regulation of cell motility is lacking. Recent studies have taken advantage of RNAi methods to elucidate roles for specific proteins in regulating cell motility. Depletion of the cytoskeletal linker protein trypanin using siRNAs resulted in a loss of directional cell motility in African trypanosomes that is caused by impaired coordination of the flagellar beating (Hutchings et al., 2002). The growth and guidance of axons in developing neurons is regulated by substrate-associated and soluble ligands encountered by the axonal growth cone. RNAi-mediated depletion of the integrin-interacting protein MIG-15 resulted in a dysregulation of commissural axon navigation in *C. elegans* (Poinat et al., 2002). RNAi has also shown that although actin binding protein 1 is essential for the processes of endocytosis, it is not necessary for lamellipodia formation in human embryonic kidney cells (Mise-Omata et al., 2003). Membrane microdomains called lipid rafts and clathrin-associated domains are increasingly recognized as sites of signal transduction and endocytosis in eukaryotic cells. Proteins critical for the function of the signaling and endocytic functions of these membrane domains are being identified using RNAi approaches. For example, RNAi methods were used to establish an essential role for a J-domain protein called auxilin in clathrin-mediated endocytosis in *C. elegans* (Greener et al., 2001).

(f) Cell Death

In many tissues throughout the body, cells have a finite life span and then undergo apoptosis, a form of programmed cell death in which the cell dies in a well controlled manner and is removed from the tissue without adversely affecting adjacent healthy cells. Apoptosis also plays a key role in sculpting the cellular structure of tissues during embryonic and postnatal development (Baehrecke, 2002). Of course, abnormal cell death is a major problem in a variety of diseases, including neurodegenerative disorders such as Alzheimer's and Parkinson's diseases, and ischemic vascular conditions (Mattson, 2000). Considerable progress is being made in understanding the molecular mechanisms that regulate cell death, with the goal of identifying key targets for therapeutic intervention. Drug development efforts have resulted in several exciting classes of agents that either prevent the death of cells such as neurons, or induce selective death of cancer cells. For example, inhibitors of the pro-apoptotic protein p53 (Duan et al., 2002; Zhu et al., 2002) and caspases (Eldadah and Faden, 2000) are being developed for use in neurodegenerative disorders. RNAi might be used in lieu or in combination with such drugs.

RNAi has recently been employed to establish roles for specific genes in apoptotic and anti-apoptotic pathways. For example, a critical role for p73δ in p53-mediated apoptosis was demonstrated by showing that depletion of p73δ using siRNA prevents cell death (Kartasheva et al., 2002). Depletion of the catalytic subunit of DNA-dependent protein kinase using siRNAs increased the sensitivity of human fibroblasts to radiation-induced death because of an impaired ability to sense and repair the DNA damaged by the radiation (Peng et al., 2002). RNAi was used to establish a role for the calcium-binding protein calreticulin in necrotic cell death in *C. elegans* (Xu et al., 2001). Many cells express one or more inhibitor-of-apoptosis proteins (IAPs) that can prevent apoptosis by directly binding to and inhibiting caspases. RNAi was used to identify the serine protease Omi/HtrA2 as a mammalian XIAP-binding protein that sensitizes cells to apoptosis (Martins et al., 2002). In a study of cell death in neurons, RNAi was used to show that myocyte enhancer factor 2A is required for activity-dependent cell survival (Gaudilliere et al., 2002). In another study, RNAi was used to deplete cells of apoptosis-inducing factor (AIF), thereby preventing apoptosis (Wang et al., 2002).

Associations between expression of a gene and a particular biological process are often taken as evidence for a major role for the protein encoded by that gene in that biological process. However, correlations do not establish cause-effect relationships. A well known example of this fact is found in the record of studies of the transcription factor NF-κB. Because NF-κB was shown to be activated in several different types of cells during the process of apoptosis, it was assumed that NF-κB functioned in the cell death process. However, subsequent studies in which NF-κB activity was selectively blocked revealed that this transcription factor actually induced the expression of anti-apoptotic proteins and that cells died more readily when NF-κB function was blocked (Mattson and Camandola, 2001). Thus, in addition to revealing the function of a specific protein, RNAi can also be used to establish that a protein is not involved in a particular process

(g) Viral Invasion/Replication

It is believed that endogenous RNAi mechanisms evolved, at least in part, to protect cells against infectious pathogens such as viruses. For example, by producing siRNAs directed against genes required for viral replication, the infected cells prevented propagation of the virus (Lindenbach and Rice, 2002). The development of RNAi technology has verified the importance of RNAi mechanisms in viral invasion and is revealing the underlying molecular interactions. Treatment of various types of cultured cells with siRNAs directed against both viral and cellular targets has revealed specific roles for the targeted proteins in the processes of viral invasion or replication. When cells were treated with siRNAs directed against the HIV-1 tat or reverse transcriptase genes, or against the NF-κB p65 subunit of the host cells, the expression of these viral and cellular proteins were decreased and HIV-1 replication was inhibited, demonstrating the ability of RNA interference to elucidate the biological roles of cellular and viral regulatory factors involved in the control of HIV-1 gene expression (Surabhi and Gaynor, 2002). When human and mouse cells were pretreated with siRNAs to the poliovirus genome, the replication of the virus in those cells was dramatically reduced (Gitlin et al., 2002). In another study it was shown that siRNAs can efficiently silence both cellular lamin AC and hepatitis C virus RNAs in Huh-7 hepatoma cell lines resulting in an 80-fold decrease in HCV RNA within 4 days (Randall et al., 2003). The latter study further showed that the same siRNAs could be used to almost completely eliminate the virus from cells with an established infection. The expression of the human papilloma virus E6 and E7 genes was silenced resulting in the accumulation of cellular p53 protein, transactivation of the cell cycle control p21 gene and reduced cell growth (Jiang and Milner, 2002). A final example of the use of RNAi in the discovery of mechanisms of viral infection is a study of hepatitis delta virus (HDV) which uses a host-encoded RNA-editing machinery to express two essential proteins from the same coding sequence (Wong and Lazinski, 2002). The authors employed siRNAs to deplete either a small or long form, or both forms, of an adenosine deaminase that acts on RNA (ADAR)1. They found that editing during viral replication was only inhibited when both forms of the enzyme were depleted, demonstrating a cooperative interaction between the short and long forms of ADAR1 in viral replication.

THERAPEUTIC APPLICATIONS OF RNA INTERFERENCE

The most obvious clinical uses of RNAi are for diseases in which selective depletion of one or a few specific proteins would be expected to slow or halt the disease process in the affected cells. Ideally this would be accomplished with no or tolerable side effects. Although there are candidate gene targets for many different diseases, we will focus on four different types of diseases that are very common and for which RNAi approaches are currently being tested in preclinical studies.

(a) Cancer

There are two general abnormalities in cancer cells— they exhibit dysregulation of the cell cycle resulting in uncontrolled growth and they are resistant to death as a result of abnormalities in one or more proteins that mediate apoptosis (Nam and Parang, 2003). The goals for RNAi approaches for cancer therapy are therefore to knock out the expression of a cell cycle gene and/or an anti-apoptotic gene in the cancer cells thereby stopping tumor growth and killing the cancer cells. To selectively eliminate cancer cells without damaging normal cells, the RNAi would be targeted to a gene specifically involved in the growth or survival of the cancer cell, or the siRNAs would be selectively delivered into the cancer cells.

For many years antisense oligodeoxynucleotide technology was pursued in preclinical studies of cancer therapies but with discouraging results overall (Jansen and Zangemeister-Wittke, 2002). Recent studies have clearly demonstrated advantages of RNAi methods for the growth suppression and killing of cancer cells. In one study, siRNA was shown to be greater than an order of magnitude more potent than antisense DNA in suppressing gene expression in human hepatoma and pancreatic cancer cell lines (Aoki et al., 2003). In another study four different myeloid leukemia cell lines (HL-60, U937, THP-1, and K562) were transfected with dsRNA duplexes corresponding to the endogenous c-raf and bcl-2 genes (Cioca et al., 2003). Levels of Raf-1 and Bcl-2 proteins were markedly decreased in each of the transfected cell lines; combined RNAi for c-raf and bcl-2 induced apoptosis in HL-60, U937, and THP-1 cells and increased their sensitivity to the DNA-damaging agent etoposide. Activation of tumor necrosis factor (TNF) receptors and related death receptors can induce death of some cancer cells, but may simultaneously activate pathways that promote cell survival; one protein that inhibits the TNF cell death pathway is called FLIP (FLICE-like inhibitory protein). When FLIP expression was suppressed in cancer cells using siRNAs, the cells were more sensitive to being killed when death receptors were activated (Siegmund et al., 2002).

Viral vectors have also been used to express siRNAs and inhibit cancer cell growth and tumorogenicity. For example, a retroviral vector was used to specifically and stably inhibit expression of the oncogenic K-RAS(V12) allele in human tumor cells (Brummelkamp et al., 2002b). Depletion of K-RAS(V12) resulted in loss of anchorage-independent growth and tumorigenicity. In addition to blocking the expression of normal genes that are required for cancer cell growth and survival, RNAi can be used to target specific cancer-causing mutations. For example, dsRNA was employed to target the M-BCR/ABL fusion site to kill leukemic cells with such a rearrangement (Wilda et al., 2002). Leukemic cells without BCR/ABL rearrangement were not killed by M-BCR/ABL-dsRNA. Several other studies have demonstrated efficacy of liposome-mediated or viral vector-mediated transfection of cancer cells in suppressing their growth and/or inducing their death (Zhang et al., 2002a). The next step in the development of RNAi technology for cancer therapy will be to establish methods for targeting tumor cells in vivo. Another approach might be to target genes that promote angiogenesis. Tumor cells require a rich supply of blood and achieve this by stimulating the process of angiogenesis; it may therefore be possible to inhibit tumor growth by targeting the vascular endothelial cells involved in angiogenesis. As evidence, it was shown that depletion of the crk adaptor protein using RNAi inhibited the migration of cultured vascular endothelial cells (Nagashima et al., 2002).

(b) Infectious Diseases

Diseases caused by viruses and bacteria continue to be major causes of death worldwide and are an increasing concern because of the emergence of resistant strains and the potential use of infectious pathogens by terrorists (Tan et al., 2000; Franz and Zajtchuk, 2002). Currently, HIV infection has reached epidemic proportions in many African countries and also continues to be a major cause of morbidity and death among homosexuals and intravenous drug users. Other prominent infectious diseases include influenza, hepatitis, Lyme disease, and West Nile virus. Many deaths also result from bacterial infections, with pneumonia and sepsis being prominent examples. The ability of RNAi to inhibit the replication or cellular uptake of viruses and other infectious agents has been clearly demonstrated in cell culture studies and, therefore, holds promise for the treatment of human patients. The ability of HIV-1 to infect cells and replicate can be severely compromised by targeting of viral genes using siRNAs. Examples include the suppression of HIV-1 replication in human cells transfected with siRNA directed against tat and the rev gene (Capodici et al., 2002; Jacque et al., 2002; Lee et al., 2002a; Novina et al., 2002). Transfection of human cells with siRNAs directed against different genes in the poliovirus genome resulted in resistance of the cells to infection with poliovirus (Gitlin et al., 2002). The ability of siRNAs targeting the gene encoding the death receptor Fas to protect mice from liver failure and fibrosis in two models of autoimmune hepatitis was tested by Song and colleagues (Song et al., 2003). Intravenous injection of Fas siRNA specifically reduced Fas protein levels in the livers of mice during a 10-day period. Fas siRNA treatment abrogated hepatocyte necrosis and inflammatory infiltration and markedly reduced serum concentrations of transaminases demonstrating a clear hepatoprotective effect of the siRNA therapy.

(c) Cardiovascular and Cerebrovascular Diseases

Cardiovascular disease is the leading cause of death in the United States and many other industrialized countries. It most commonly results from the progressive occlusion of arteries in a process called atherosclerosis, which can ultimately culminate in a myocardial infarction or stroke. Atherosclerosis involves damage to vascular endothelial cells, local production of inflammatory cytokines, and the recruitment of macrophages to the site forming foam cells; in addition, apoptosis of foam cells and vascular smooth muscle cells occurs (Geng and Libby, 2002). The severe ischemia that occurs in heart or brain cells during a myocardial infarction or stroke results in the death of cardiac muscle cells or neurons. Although some of the cells die rapidly by necrosis, many other cells die more slowly by apoptosis; data from animal studies suggest that such cardiac myocytes and brain neurons that die by apoptosis can be saved (Mattson et al., 2000; Zhao and Vinten-Johansen, 2002).

It may be possible to use RNAi technology to intervene in the process of atherosclerosis or to reduce the damage to heart tissue and brain cells that patients suffer following a myocardial infarction or stroke. A key step in the process of atherosclerosis is the up-regulation of cell adhesion molecules in vascular endothelial cells, which play an essential role in the recruitment of macrophages to the site of endothelial damage. The production of cell adhesion molecules can be selectively suppressed in cultured cells (Jarad et al., 2002). In another study relevant to the pathogenesis of atherosclerosis, it was shown that mevastatin, an inhibitor of cholesterol synthesis, suppresses cell proliferation by inhibiting cyclin-dependent kinase-2 (Ukomadu and Dutta, 2003).

(d) Neurodegenerative Disorders

Alzheimer's disease, Parkinson's disease, Huntington's disease, and amyotrophic lateral sclerosis are examples of relatively common age-related neurodegenerative disorders that are increasing as average life expectancy increases. Each disorder is characterized by the dysfunction and death of specific populations of neurons: hippocampal and cortical neurons involved in learning and memory processes in Alzheimer's disease, dopamine-producing neurons in the substantia nigra that control body movements in Parkinson's disease, and spinal cord motor neurons in amyotrophic lateral sclerosis. Specific genetic mutations are responsible for a small percentage of cases of Alzheimer's and Parkinson's disease and amyotrophic lateral sclerosis (Hardy, 2001), whereas all cases of Huntington's disease result from mutations (polyglutamine expansions) in the huntingtin protein (Rubinsztein, 2002). Studies of patients, and of animal and cell culture models of each disease, have revealed shared biochemical cascades that result in neuronal death. Those cascades include increased oxidative stress, dysregulation of cellular calcium homeostasis and apoptosis (Mattson, 2000). There have therefore been two different strategies for preventative and therapeutic interventions in neurodegenerative disorders. One strategy is to block the disease-specific events that are believed to initiate the neurodegenerative process, whereas the second strategy targets downstream events in the neurodegenerative cascade. For example, an abnormality in the proteolytic processing of the amyloid precursor protein is believed to be a key early event in Alzheimer's disease pathogenesis, and two enzymes called β- and γ-secretases that are responsible for cleaving of amyloid precursor protein to generate the neurotoxic amyloid β-peptide are being targeted for drug development. RNAi has recently been used to identify additional proteins, such as APH-1, that are critical for production of amyloid β-peptide (Lee et al., 2002b). Downstream targets include proteins involved in the production of reactive oxygen species, in the regulation of calcium homeostasis, and in the process of apoptosis (Mattson, 2000, 2003).

Recent studies have shown that cultured neurons can be efficiently transfected with siRNAs and that the targeted genes are effectively silenced. In one study it was shown that cultured neurons can be depleted of the p75 neurotrophin receptor, a protein in the TNF receptor family that has been implicated in neuronal apoptosis in certain settings (Higuchi et al., 2003). Pro-apoptotic members of the Bcl-2 family (Colussi et al., 2000) and caspases (Quinn et al., 2000) have been effectively targeted and neuronal death prevented, using RNAi methods. Caplen and colleagues (Caplen et al., 2002) performed studies aimed at determining whether RNAi could be used to target the pathogenic process in inherited neurodegenerative disorders caused by polyglutamine expansions. They used *Drosophila* and human tissue culture models of spinobulbar muscular atrophy, a disease caused by CAG expansions in the gene encoding the androgen receptor. They assessed the abilities of different siRNAs to selectively inhibit expression of transcripts that included a truncated human androgen receptor gene containing different CAG repeat lengths (16-112 repeats). They found that RNA duplexes containing CAG repeat tracts only induced gene-specific inhibition when flanking androgen receptor sequences were included. Sequence-specific small dsRNAs of 22 nucleotides rescued the toxicity and caspase-3 activation induced by plasmids expressing a transcript encoding an expanded polyglutamine tract. Thus, it is possible, at least in cell culture, to selectively silence a transcript associated with an important group of genetic diseases by RNAi.

Several aspects of neuronal cell biology provide opportunities for novel uses of RNA. Neurons possess complex morphologies with long axons and dendrites, and synapses that are often located at considerable distances from the cell body (for example, the presynaptic terminals of the axons of the lower motor neurons that innervate muscles in the foot in humans can be more than a meter from their cell bodies in the spinal cord). Recent findings suggest that the neurodegenerative cascades that occur in different neurodegenerative disorders may be activated first in synapses. Indeed, it has been shown that apoptotic biochemical cascades can be activated in synapses causing their degeneration (Mattson et al., 1998). Accordingly, pharmacological agents (p53 and caspase inhibitors; Glazner et al., 2000; Gilman et al., 2003) and antisense treatments (Par-4 antisense; Duan et al., 1999) that target apoptotic cascades have been shown to protect synapses in cell culture models of neurodegenerative disorders. RNAi technology would seem to be an ideal approach to target synaptic proteins involved in the pathogenesis of neurodegenerative disorders.

THE FUTURE OF RNA INTERFERENCE IN BIOLOGY AND MEDICINE

Even at this early stage of understanding the molecular mechanisms of RNAi and in the development of methods for the use of RNAi technology for selective gene silencing, it is clear that RNAi will be a widely used tool for establishing the functions of genes. The ability to selectively deplete a single protein of interest in cultured cells using siRNAs, and plasmids and viral vectors, is now established. Improvements on the currently available protocols for RNAi are being made, and the methods are being applied by thousands of investigators in diverse fields. With the advent of these methods has come an explosion of studies that have employed RNAi. Indeed, although there were only nine publications listed on Medline in the years 1987 through 1998 inclusive, there are 631 listed from 1999 to the time of writing of this article. The current status of RNAi as an experimental tool is such that many investigators are now aware of the technology, but most have not yet implemented it in their own studies. The development of RNAi kits by several companies will facilitate the implementation of RNAi methods by essentially any investigator, regardless of their knowledge of RNAi mechanisms. However, major hurdles remain to be crossed, including the application of RNAi methods to in vivo studies. Once it becomes possible to reliably target a specific gene and deplete the protein encoded by that gene from one or all cell types in an organism, a wealth of information will flow from studies of processes ranging from embryogenesis to the function of organ systems.

As for uses of RNAi in medicine, its potential remains to be established. The application of gene therapy approaches for the treatment of specific diseases has progressed much more slowly than initially anticipated. There are, of course, many potential gene targets for therapeutic intervention using RNAi (Fig. 7.4). Studies that employ RNAi to counteract a disease process in vivo are emerging. For example, RNAi that targeted the Fas gene (Song et al., 2003) or the hepatitis C virus genome (Wilson et al., 2003) protected mice from hepatitis. One might expect that the next demonstrations of successful treatment of disease in mice will come from models of cancer and neurodegenerative disorders. Because of the potential of RNAi for therapeutic intervention, major efforts should be placed on preclinical studies using this technology.

RNA INTERFERENCE (RNAi) – IN PLANTS

Methods to Induce RNAi in Plants

One of the biggest challenges in RNAi research is the delivery of the active molecules that will trigger the RNAi pathway in plants. In this system, a number of methods for delivery of dsRNA or siRNA into different cells and tissue include transformation with dsRNAforming vectors for selected gene(s) by an *Agrobacterium* mediated transformations [19, 35], delivery cognate dsRNA of *uidA* GUS (β-glucuronidase) and TaGLP2a: GFP (green fluorescent protein) reporter genes into single epidermal cells of maize, barley and wheat by particle bombardment [36], introducing a *Tobacco rattle virus* (TRV)-based vector in tomato plants by infiltration [37], delivery of dsRNA into tobacco suspension cells by cationic oligopeptide polyarginine-siRNA complex; infecting plants with viral vectors that produce dsRNA [38] and delivery of siRNA into cultured plant cells of rice, cotton and slash pine for gene silencing by nanosense pulsed laser-induced stress wave (LISW) [40]. Among these the most reliable and commonly used approaches for delivery of dsRNA to plants cells are agroinfiltration,micro-bombardment and VIGS. These are discussed in the following sections.

Agroinfiltration

Agroinfiltration is a powerful method to study processes connected with RNAi. The injection of *Agrobacterium* carrying similar DNA constructs into the intracellular spaces of leaves for triggering RNA silencing is known as agroinoculation or agroinfiltration [41]. In most cases agroinfiltration is used to initiate systemic silencing or to monitor the effect of suppressor genes. In plants, cytoplasmic RNAi can be induced efficiently by agroinfiltration, similar to a strategy for transient expression of T-DNA vectors after delivery by *Agrobacterium tumefaciens*. The transiently expressed DNA encodes either an ss- or dsRNA, which is typically a hairpin (hp) RNA. The infiltration of hairpin constructs are especially effective, because their dsRNA can be processed directly to siRNAs, while the constructs expressing ssRNA can also be useful to induce silencing [42-45] and for dissecting the mechanism of gene silencing, especially concerned with its suppressors, systemic silencing signal and also for simple protein purification [42-45]. Besides, they provide a rapid, versatile and convenient way for achieving a very high level of gene expression in a distinct and defined zone.

Micro-Bombardment

In this method, a linear or circular template is transferred into the nucleus by micro-bombardment. Synthetic siRNAs are delivered into plants by biolistic pressure to cause silencing of GFP expression. Bombarding cells with particles coated with dsRNA, siRNA or DNA that encode hairpin constructs as well as sense or antisense RNA, activate the RNAi pathway.

The silencing effect of RNAi is occasionally detected as early as a day after bombardment, and it continues up to 3 to 4 days of post bombardment. Systemic spread of the silencing occurred 2 weeks later to manifest in the vascular tissues of the non-bombarded leaves of *Nicotiana benthamiana* that were closest to the bombarded ones. After one month or so, the loss of GFP expression was seen in non-vascular tissues as well. RNA blot hybridization with systemic leaves indicated that the biolistically delivered siRNAs induced due to *de novo* formation of siRNAs, which accumulated to cause systemic silencing [29].

Virus Induced Gene Silencing (VIGS)

Modified viruses as RNA silencing triggers are used as a mean for inducing RNA in plants. Different RNA and DNA viruses have been modified to serve as vectors for gene expression [46,47]. Some viruses, such as *Tobacco mosaic virus* (TMV), *Potato virus X* (PVX) and TRV, can be used for both protein expression and gene silencing [48-51]. All RNA virus-derived expression vectors will not be useful as silencing vectors because many have potent anti-silencing proteins such as TEV (*Tobacco etch virus*), that directly interfere with host silencing machinery [48,52]. Similarly, DNA viruses have not been used extensively as expression vectors due to their size constraints for movement [53]. However, a non-mobile Maize streak Virus (MSV)-derived vector has been successfully used for long-term production of protein in maize cell cultures [48]. Using viral vectors to silence endogenous plant genes requires cloning homologous gene fragments into the virus without compromising viral replication and movement. This was first demonstrated in RNA viruses by inserting sequences into TMV [54], and then for DNA viruses by replacing the coat protein gene with a homologous sequence [53]. These reports used visible markers for gene silencing phytoene desaturase(*PDS)* and chalcone synthase (*CHS*), providing a measure of the tissue specificity of silencing as these have been involved in carotenoid metabolic pathway. The *PDS* gene acts on the antenna complex of the thylakoid membranes, and protects the chlorophyll from photooxidation. By silencing this gene, a drastic decrease in leaf carotene content resulted into the appearance of photobleaching symptom [55,56]. Similarly, over expression of *CHS* gene causes an albino phenotype instead of producing the anticipated deep orange color [57]. As a result, their action as a phenotypic marker helps in easy understanding of the mechanism of gene silencing. Most viruses are plus-strand RNA viruses or satellites, whereas *Tomato golden mosaic virus* (TGMV) and *Cabbage leaf curl virus* (CaLCuV) are DNA viruses. Though RNA viruses replicate in the cytoplasm DNA viruses replicate in plant nuclei using the host DNA replication machinery.

Both types of viruses induce diffusible, homology- dependent systemic silencing of endogenous genes. However, the extent of silencing spread and the severity of viral symptoms can vary significantly in different host plants and host/virus combinations. With the variety of viruses and the diversity of infection patterns, transmission vectors, and plant defenses it is not surprising that viruses differ with respect to silencing [58]. Because the continuing development of virus-based silencing vectors can extend VIGS to economically important plants, it is useful to consider some of the characteristics of successful VIGS vectors.

RNAi in Plant Disease Management

Despite substantial advances in plant disease management strategies, our global food supply is still threatened by a multitude of pathogens and pests. This changed scenario warrants us to respond more efficiently and effectively to this problem. The situation demands judicious blending of conventional, unconventional and frontier technologies. In this sense, RNAi technology has emerged as one of the most potential and promising strategies for enhancing the building of resistance in plants to combat various fungal, bacterial, viral and nematode diseases causing huge losses in important agricultural crops. The nature of this biological phenomenon has been evaluated in a number of host-pathogen systems and effectively used to silence the action of pathogen. Many of the examples listed below illustrate the possibilities for commercial exploitation of this inherent biological mechanism to generate disease-resistant plants in the future by taking advantage of this approach.

1. Management of Plant Pathogenic Fungi

RNA-mediated gene silencing (RNA silencing) is used as a reverse tool for gene targeting in fungi. Homologybased gene silencing induced by transgenes (co-suppression), antisense, or dsRNA has been demonstrated in many plant pathogenic fungi, including *Cladosporium fulvum* [59], *Magnaporthae oryzae* [60-62], *Venturia inaequalis* [63], *Neurospora crassa* [64], *Aspergillus nidulans* [65], and *Fusarium graminearum* [9] whether it is suitable for large scale mutagenesis in fungal pathogens remains to be tested. Hypermorphic mechanism of RNA interference implies that this technique can also be applicable to all those plant pathogenic fungi, which are polyploid and polykaryotic in nature, and also offers a solution to the problem where frequent lack of multiple marker genes in fungi is experienced. Simultaneous silencing of several unrelated genes by introducing a single chimeric construct has been demonstrated in case of *Venturia inaequalis* [63]. *HCf*-1, a gene that codes for a hydrophobin of the tomato pathogen *C. fulvum* [66], was co-suppressed by ectopic integration of homologous transgenes. Transformation of *Cladosporium fulvum* with DNA containing a truncated copy of the hydrophobin gene *HCf*-1 caused co-suppression of hydrophobin synthesis in 30% of the transformants. The co-suppressed isolates had a hydrophilic phenotype, lower levels of *HCf*-1 mRNA than wild type and contain multiple copies of the plasmid integrated as tandem repeats at ectopic sites in the genome. The transcription rate of *HCf*-1 in the co-suppressed isolates was higher in the untransformed strains, which suggested that silencing acted at the post transcriptional level. This was due to ectopic integration of the transgene next to promoters which initiate transcription to form antisense RNA and that this in turn determines down-regulation of *HCf*-1. But gene silencing was not associated with DNA cytosine methylation [59]. Similarly, the silencing of *cgl*1 and *cgl*2 genes using the *cgl*2 hairpin construct in *Cladosporium fulvum* has also been reported [67], though the effect was possibly restricted to highly homolougous genes (exons of *cgl* 1 and *cgl* 2 are 87% identical). However, the less homologus *cgl* 3 (53% overall identity to *cgl* 2) was not affected as the target specificity always depends upon the actual sequence alignment and more over, short regions of high density that led to unwanted off-targets effects. Such a strategy could be exploited for protecting the consumable products of vegetables and fruits crops from the post-harvest diseases caused by different plant pathogens in future. Hairpin vector technology resulted in simultaneous high frequency silencing of a green fluorescent protein (*GFP*) transgene and an endogenous trihydroxynaphthalene\ reductase gene (*THN*) in *Venturia inaequalis* [63] *GFP* transgene, acting as easily detectable visible marker while the trihydroxynaphthalene reductase gene (*THN*) playing role in melanin biosynthesis. High frequency gene silencing was achieved using hairpin constructs for the *GFP* or the *THN* genes transferred by *Agrobacterium* (71 and 61%, respectively). *THN*-silenced transformants exhibited a distinctive light brown phenotype and maintained the ability to infect apple. Silencing of both genes with this construct occurred at a frequency of 51% of all the transformants. All 125 colonies silenced for the GFP gene were also silenced for THN [63]. Similarly, multiple gene silencing has been achieved in *Cryptococcus neoformans* using chimeric hairpin constructs [39] and in plants using partial sense constructs [68]. The first effort towards the systematic silencing of *Magnaporthe grisea*, a causal organism of rice blast was carried by using the enhanced green florescent protein gene as a model [60]. To assess the ability of RNA species to induce silencing in fungus, plasmid construct expressing sense, antisense and hairpin RNA were introduced into an e*GFP*-expressing transformants. The fluorescence of *eGFP* in the transformants was silenced much more efficiently by hairpin RNA of *eGFP* than by other RNA species. In the silenced transformants, the accumulation of *eGFP* mRNA was drastically reduced. But not methylation of coding or promoter region was involved. The small interfering RNA molecules of 19-23 nucleotides were observed in both sense and antisense strands of *eGFP* gene [60]. Later on a protocol for silencing the *mpg*1 and polyketide synthase-like genes was also developed [9]. *Mpg*1 gene is a hydrophobin gene which is essential for pathogenicity as it act as a cellular relay for adhesion and trigger for the development of appressorium [69]. Their work on this host-pathogen system revealed that they were successfully able to silence the above mentioned genes at varying degrees by pSilent-1-based vectors in 70-90% of the resulting transformants. Ten to fifteen percent of the silenced transformants exhibited almost "null phenotype". This vector was also efficiently applicable to silence a *GFP* reporter in another ascomycete fungus *Colletotrichum lagenarium* [9]. A novel high through put approach for gene function analysis using RNAi, which provides an alternative to the gene knock-out by homologous recombination was also described [Q. B. Nguyen, N. Kadotani]. The authors developed an RNA silencing vector, pSilent-Dual1 (pSD1) that carries two convergent dual promoters, the *Aspergillus nidulans* tryptophan promoter (PtrpC) and the *A. nidulans* glyceraldehyde-3- phosphate dehydrogenase promoter (Pgpd). Both promoters have been used to drive constitutive gene expression in a large number of filamentous fungi. A multicloning site (MCS) has been inserted between two promoters. The greatest merit of the pSD1 system over others, such as hpRNA or intron spliced hair-pin RNA (ihpRNA) silencing system is that it allows a single step cloning for generation of an RNAi construct. To facilitate efficient screening for silenced transformants, *gfp* gene was incorporated the into pSD1 system. It allows expression of a chimeric RNA and assessment of gene silencing efficiency by utilizing a recipient strain that produces GFP and therefore, fluoresces green when using epifluorescence microscopy. A main bottleneck of this system is its lower silencing efficiency compared with hpRNA or ihpRNA-expressing RNA-silencing vectors. Formation of dsRNA in the pSD1 system requires physical annealing of two different RNA molecules in the target cells while that in the hpRNA systems is achieved by self-folding of inverted repeats within RNA molecule. The difference in dsRNA formation between the systems can be a major cause of the different silencing efficiencies. The authors generated a series of knock-down mutants of almost all known calcium related genes in the genome of *M. oryzae* and examined for phenotypical defects. Gene knock-down requires relatively short stretches of sequence information. This is a major advantage for phytopathogens for which there is little sequence information available. As RNAi works at the mRNA level, its efficacy is not compromised by the presence of non-transformed nuclei or multicopy genes due to aneuploidy [R. J. Weld]. RNAi causes only a partial reduction, but not a complete loss of, in gene expression.Partial gene suppression is considered a main drawback of RNAi. However, it could be a merit where the effect of an essential gene on a phenotype is of interest. Gene knock-down offers a more convenient and effective tool, especially in combination with an inducible promoter that allows gene expression to be diminished at specific stages during development [K.M. Plummer]. Another disadvantage of gene knock-down is, as it requires only a short sequence, that genes other than those targeted might be silenced. This causes unexpected changes in gene expression patterns (off-target effects). Testing for the possibility of off-target effects is simpler for phytopathogen species for which complete genome sequence data are available but remains elusive for those phytopathogens whose genomes have not been sequenced [K.M. Plummer]. In another study, RNA interference (RNAi) strategy was used to specifically knockdown 59 individual rice genes encoding putative LRR-RLKs, and a novel rice blast resistance-related gene (designated as OsBRR1) was identified by screening T0 RNAi population using a weakly virulent isolate of *Magnaporthe oryzae*, Ken 54-04. Wild-type plants (*Oryza sativa* L. cv. 'Nipponbare') showed intermediate resistance to Ken 54-04, while OsBRR1 suppression plants were susceptible to Ken 54-04 . Furthermore, OsBRR1-overexpressing plants exhibited enhanced resistance to some virulent isolates. OsBRR1 expression was low in leaves and undetectable in roots under normal growth conditions, while its transcript was significantly induced in leaves infected with the blast fungus (Ken 54-04) and was moderately affected by ABA, JA and SA treatment. Overexpression or RNAi suppression of OsBRR1did not cause visible developmental changes in rice plants.

2. Management of Plant Pathogenic Bacteria

One of the striking examples of bacterial disease management where RNAi showed a remarkable type of gene Biotechnology and Plant Disease Control-Role of RNA Interference regulation has been documented [12]. They developed a crown gall disease management strategy that targets the process of tumourogensis (gall formation) by initiating\ RNAi of the *iaaM* and *ipt* oncogenes. Expression of these genes is a prerequisite for wild type tumor formation. Transgenic *Arabidopsis thaliana* and *Lycopersicon esculentum* transformed with RNAi constructs, targeting *iaaM* and *ipt* gene(s) showed resistance to crown gall disease. Transgenic plants generated through this technology contained a modified version of these two bacterial gene(s) required to cause the disease and was the first report to manage a major bacterial disease through RNAi. The extra genes recognize and effectively shut down the expression of the corresponding bacterial gene during infection, thus preventing the spread of infection. The incoming bacteria could not make the hormones needed to cause tumors and plants deficient in silencing were hyper-susceptible to *A. tumefaciens* [28]. Successful infection relied on a potent anti-silencing state established in tumors whereby siRNA synthesis is specifically inhibited. The procedure can be exploited to develop broadspectrum resistance in ornamental and horticultural plants which are susceptible to crown gall tumorigenesis. This approach can be advocated for the effective management of those pathogens which multiply very rapidly and results in tumor formation such as *Albugo candida, Synchytrium endobioticum, Erwinia amylovora* etc. The natsiRNA (nat-siRNAATGB2) was strongly induced in *Arabidopsis* upon infection by *Pseudomonas syringae pv tomato* and down-regulates a PPRL gene that encodes a negative regulator of the RPS2 disease resistance pathway. As a result, the induction of nat-siRNAATGB2 increases the RPS2-mediated race-specific resistance against *P. syringae* pv *tomato* in *Arabidopsis* [Katiyar-Agarwal]. Recently, the accumulation of a new class of sRNA, 30 to 40 nucleotides in length, termed long-siRNAs (lsiRNAs), was found associated with *P. syringae* infection. One of these lsiRNAs, AtlsiRNA-1, contributes to plant bacterial resistance by silencing AtRAP, a negative regulator of plant defense [Katiyar-Agarwal S. Katiyar-Agarwal]. A *Pseudomonas* bacterial flagellin derived peptide is found to induce the accumulation of miR393 in *Arabidopsis*. miR393 negatively regulates mRNAs of F-box auxin receptors, resulting in increased resistance to the bacterium (*P. syringae*), and the overexpression of miR393 was shown to reduce the plant's bacterial titer by 5-fold [Katiyar-Agarwal S. Katiyar-Agarwal].

3. Management of Plant Pathogenic Viruses

Antiviral RNAi technology has been used for viral disease management in human cell lines [C. D. Novina, M. F Murray]. Such silencing mechanisms (RNAi) can also be exploited to protect and manage viral infections in plants [C. D. Novina, M. F Murray]. The effectiveness of the technology in generating virus resistant plants was first reported to PVY in potato, harbouring vectors for simultaneous expression of both sense and antisense transcripts of the helper-component *proteinase* (*HC-Pro*) gene [P. M. Waterhouse E.J. Chapman,]. The *P1/HC-Pro* suppressors from the potyvirus inhabited silencing at a step down stream of dsRNA processing, possibly by preventing the unwinding of duplex siRNAs, or the incorporation into RISC or both [A.I. Prokhnevsky M. Pooggin]. The utilization of RANi technology has resulted in inducing immunity reaction against several other viruses in different plant-virus systems . In phyto-pathogenic DNA viruses like geminiviruses non-coding intergenic region of *Mungbean yellow mosaic India virus* (MYMIV) was expressed as hairpin construct under the control of the 35S promoter and used as biolistically to inoculate MYMIV-infected black gram plants and showed a complete recovery from infection, which lasted until senescence [P.V. Shivaprasad]. RNAi mediated silencing of geminiviruses using transient protoplast assay where protoplasts were co-transferred with a siRNA designed to replicase (Rep)-coding sequence of *African cassava mosaic virus* (ACMV) and the genomic DNA of ACMV resulted in 99% reduction in *Rep* transcripts and 66% reduction in viral DNA [R. Vanitharani, P. Chellappan ,]. It was observed that siRNA was able to silence a closely related strain of ACMV but not a more distantly related virus. More than 40 viral suppressors have been identified in plant viruses[86]. Results from some of the well-studied virus suppressors indicated that suppressors interfere with systemic signaling for silencing [44]. During last few years, the *p69* encoded by *Turnip yellow mosaic virus* has been identified as silencing suppressors that prevented host RDR dependent secondary dsRNA synthesis [J. Chen, W. X. Li, D. Xie]. *P*14 protein encoded by aureus viruses suppressed both virus and transgene-induced silencing by sequestering both long dsRNA and siRNA without size specificity [Z. Merai, Z. Kerenyi]. Multiple suppressors have been reported in *Citrus tristeza virus* where *p*20 and coat protein (*CP*) play important role in suppression of silencing signal and *p*23 inhibited intracellular silencing [27]. Multiple viral components, viral RNAs and putative RNA replicase proteins were reported for a silencing or suppression of *Red clover necrotic mosaic virus* [89]. In this case, the RNA silencing machinery deprived of DICER-like enzymes by the viral replication complexes appears to be the cause of the suppression. *Pns*10 encoded by *Rice dwarf virus* suppressed local and systemic S-PTGS but not IR-PTGS suggesting that *Pns10* also targets an upstream step of dsRNA formation in the silencing pathway [X. Cao, P. Zhou, X. Zhang Q. W.]. A 273-bp (base pair) sequence of the *Arabidopsis* miR159 a pre-miRNA transcript expressing amiRNAs was used against the viral suppressor genes *P*69 and *HC-Pro* to provide resistance against *Turnip yellow mosaic virus* and *Turnip mosaic virus* infection, respectively [Niu, S. S. Lin, J. Qu]. In addition, a dimeric construct harboring two unique amiRNAs against both viral suppressors conferred resistance against these two viruses in inoculated *Arabidopsis* plants. Similarly, a different amiRNA vector was used to target the 2 b viral suppressor of the *Cucumber mosaic virus* (CMV), a suppressor that interacted with and blocked the slicer activity of *AGO*1 had also shown to confer resistance to CMV infection in transgenic tobacco [J. Ye and R. X. Fang,]. A strong correlation between virus resistance and the expression level of the 2 b-specific amiRNA was shown for individual plant lines. It is evident from above-mentioned reports that the RNA components, such as single strand template RNA, dsRNA and/or siRNA of the silencing pathways are the preferred targets of most viral suppressors. However, plant viruses\ are known to have evolved a counter-silencing mechanism by encoding proteins that can overcome such resistance [A. Díaz-Pendón and S. W. Ding]. These suppressors of gene silencing are often involved in viral pathogenicity, mediate synergism among plant viruses and result in the induction of more severe disease. Simultaneous silencing of such diverse plant viruses can be achieved by designing hairpin structures that can target a distinct virus in a single construct . Contrarily, the RNAi system may cause an increase in the severity of viral pathogenesis and/or encode proteins, which can inactivate essential genes in the RNAi machinery [S. M. Elbashir, W. Lendeckel] that helps them in their replication in the host genome . Transgenic rice plants expressing DNA encoding ORF IV of Rice tungro bacilliform virus (RTBV), both in sense and in anti-sense orientation, resulting in the formation of dsRNA, were generated. Specific degradation of the transgene transcripts and the accumulation of small RNA were observed in transgenic plants. In

RTBV-ODs2 line, RTBV DNA levels gradually rose from an initial low to almost 60% of that of the control at 40 days after inoculation [H. Tyagi, S. Rajasubramaniam]. For the effective control of PRSV and Papaya leaf-distortion mosaic virus (PLDMV), an untranslatable chimeric construct containing truncated PRSV YK CP and PLDMV P-TW-WF CP genes has been transferred into papaya (*Carica papaya* cv. 'Thailand') by *Agrobacterium*-mediated transformation via embryogenic tissues derived from immature zygotic embryos of papaya [Y.J. Kung, T.A. Yu, C.H. Huang]. Based on sequence profile of silencing suppressor protein, HcPro, it was that PRSV-HcPro acts as a suppressor of RNA silencing through micro RNA binding in a dose dependent manner. In planta expression of PRSV-HcPro affects developmental biology of plants, suggesting the interference of suppressor protein in micro RNA-directed regulatory pathways of plants. Besides facilitating the establishment of PRSV, it showed strong positive synergism with other heterologous viruses as well [S.K. Mangrauthia, P. Singh].

4. Management of Plant Parasitic Nematodes

Several major plant parasitic nematodes such as the rootknot (*Meloidogyne* spp.) and cyst (*Heterodera* spp.) along with other minor nematodes cause significant damage to important agricultural crops such as legumes, vegetables and cereals in most parts of the world. Therefore, a natural, eco-friendly defense strategy that delivers a cost-effective control of plant parasitic nematodes is needed urgently which is difficult to achieve through conventional approaches. However, the origin of RNAi technology from classical *C. elegans* studies has shown Biotechnology and Plant Disease Control-Role of RNA Interference the ways and means to explore the possibilities of this mechanism for protecting plants from nematode damage.

In this context, two approaches have been advocated *i.e.*, (1) relies on targeting plant genes that are involved with the infection process; and (2) targets the essential genes within the nematode. RNAi can be induced in *C. elegans* by feeding it dsRNA, hence it was reasoned that expressing hpRNAs containing sequences of vital nematode genes in the host plant might deliver dsRNA to a feeding nematode to incapacitate or kill it. After the demonstration of gene silencing using siRNA duplexes in the nematode , the use of RNAi has rapidly emerged as the technique for plant nematologists to put their efforts, especially for nematode management in agriculture. RNAi-mediated suppression of a gene plays an indispensable role in hampering the nematode development and may adversely affect the progression of pathogenesis in direct or indirect ways. There are accumulating evidences for the efficacy of RNAi in plant parasitic nematode management and a wide range of genes have been targeted for silencing in cyst and rootknot nematode species. RNAi in the context of phyto-parasitic nematodes was used as early as the beginning of this century, when stimulation of oral ingestion by second-stage juveniles of cyst nematodes *H. glycines, G. pallida* [E. Urwin, C. J. Lilley] and rootknot nematode *M. incognita* was achieved by using octopamine [M. Bakhetia, W. Charlton,]. Later on, resorcinol- and serotonininducing dsRNA uptake by second stage juvenile of *M. incognita* was found to be more effective than octopimine [M.N. Rosso, M.P. Dubrana]. The genes targeted by RNAi to date are expressedin a range of different tissues and cell types. The ingested dsRNA can silence genes in the intestine [J. Shingles, C. J. Lilley], female reproductive system [C.J. Lilley, S.A. Goodchild], sperm [Q. Chen, S. Rehman,], and both subventral and dorsal oesophageal glands [R.M. Steeves, T.C. Todd]. Uptake of dsRNA from the gut is a proven route to systemic RNAi in *C. elegans*. The systemic nature of RNAi in plant parasitic nematodes following ingestion of dsRNA suggests that they share similar uptake and dispersal pathways. However, RNAi of a *chitin synthase* gene expressed in the eggs of *Meloidogyne artiella* was achieved by soaking intact eggs contained within their gelatinous matrix in a solution containing dsRNA [G. Huang, R. Allen, E.L. Davis,]. The enzyme plays a key role in the synthesis of the chitinous layer in the eggshell. Depletion of its transcript by RNAi led to a reduction in stainable chitin in eggshells and a delay in hatching of juveniles from treated eggs. Similarly, RNAi targeting for *cysteine proteinase* transcripts did not reduce parasitic population of established nematodes on plants but result into the alteration of their sexual fate in favour of males at 14 days after invasion . On the other hand *H. glycines* exposed to dsRNA corresponding to a protein with homology to C-type lectins did not affect sexual fate, but 41% fewer nematodes were recovered from the plants. But treatment with dsRNA corresponding to the major sperm protein (MSP) had no effect on nematode development or sexual fate 14 days after treatment. In Biotechnology and Plant Disease Control-Role of RNA Interference addition to this, reduction in transcript abundance for targeted mRNAs in the infective juvenile and for MSP transcripts when males reached sexual maturity and sperm are produced was observed . In further extension of such types of experiments showed efficient FITC uptake by soaking *M. incognita*, 90-95% of individuals swallowed the dye when the target was a dual oxidase (an enzyme comprised with a peroxidase domain EF-hands and NADPH oxidase domain and potentially involved in extracellular matrix development). The effect of RNAi was observed when root knot nematode (RKN) juveniles were fed on dual oxidase-derived dsRNA, the reduction in the number and size of established females at 14 and 35 days post- infection with an overall reduction of 70% in egg production was observed . RNAi has also been induced for a *chitin synthase* gene that is expressed in the eggshells of *M. artiella* after soaking its developing eggs in a dsRNA . *Heterodera schachtii* induces syncytial feeding structures in the roots of host plants, and this requires the up-regulation of *Suc* transporter genes to facilitate increased nutrient flow to the developing structure. Targeting these genes and downregulating them with RNA silencing resulted in a significant reduction of female nematode development [E. Fanelli, M. Di Vito, J.T. Jones]. Indeed, tobacco plants transformed with hpRNA constructs against two such root-knot nematode genes have shown such an effect: the target mRNAs in the plant parasitic nematodes were dramatically reduced, and the plants showed effective resistance against the parasite [J. Fairbairn, A.S. Cavalloro]. In another study mRNA abundances of targeted nematode genes were specifically reduced in nematodes feeding on plants expressing corresponding RNAi constructs. Furthermore, this host-induced RNAi of all four nematode parasitism genes led to a reduction in the\ number of mature nematode females. Although no complete resistance was observed, the reduction of developing females ranged from 23% to 64% in different RNAi lines S. Sindhu, T R. Maier, M. G. Mitchum,]. These observations demonstrate the relevance of the targeted parasitism genes during the nematode life cycle and more importantly, suggest that a viable level of resistance in crop plants may be accomplished in the future by using RNAi technology against cyst nematodes.

PATHOGENS TARGETED BY RNAi

RNA Silencing-mediated Resistance Against RNA, DNA Viruses, and Viroids

Currently, most of the successful resistance mediated by RNA silencing has been reported against RNA viruses as most being described on the above 'approaches to induce RNAi' section.

In comparison to successful resistance against RNA viruses, effective resistance against DNA viruses has been rarely obtained. DNA viruses, such as geminiviruses, a family of plant DNA viruses that possess a circular and single-stranded DNA genome, seem less susceptible to RNA silencing. Fortunately, Seemanpillai reported that the expression of a transgene driven by a geminiviral promoter could be silenced by infection with the homologous genimivirus. This process has been correlated with another RNA silencing mechanism, TGS or the RdDM pathway [A. Fitzgerald, J. A. Van Kha and K. M. Plummer], implying that the geminivirus genome may also be targeted by an RNA silencing mechanism. In fact, inoculation of blackgram (*Vigna mungo*) leaves, via bombardment with a hpRNA construct containing the promoter sequence of geminivirus *Vigna mungo* yellow mosaic virus (VMYMV) under the control of the 35 S promoter, showed that most of the plants completely recovered from the VMYMV infection [M. Goldoni, G. Azzalin], suggesting that the RNA silencing strategy is also effective in engineering resistance to DNA viruses.

Interestingly, a recent report showed that the geminivirus Bean golden mosaic virus (BGMV) can also be suppressed by the expression of a hpRNA transgene derived from a replicase coding sequence (AC1) [D.M. Hammond and N.P. Keller], suggesting that a geminivirus can be targeted by both PTGS and TGS mechanisms [T. M. Hammond G. C. Segers J. C. Abbott].

A viroid is one type of plant RNA pathogen with a highly structured circular ssRNA, which does not encode any proteins and is dependent on host proteins for replication. This stable structure serves as the dsRNA substrate for the host Dicer-like enzyme. As expected, it was found that abundant siRNAs were detected in viroid-infected host plants in previous studies [11, 69-71]. The secondary structure was shown to restrict the accessibility of the siRNA-RISC complex, which makes viroids resistant to siRNA-RISC cleavage [H. Nakayashiki and Q. B. Nguyen]. While the PSTVd-derived hpRNA transgene displayed wild-type symptoms similar to viroid infection in one report [H. Peng, Q. Zhang], another showed that the PSTVd genome can be targeted for degradation by the transgenic expression of a PSTVd-derived hpRNA, and this resistance is associated with a high accumulation of hpRNA-siRNAs [S. Katiyar-Agarwal], suggesting that this RNA silencing strategy may be applicable to engineer resistance to viroid pathogens.

RNA Silencing-mediated Resistance to Plant Fungal Pathogens

Unlike plant viral pathogens, which replicate and propagate inside of the infected plant cells, interactions between some plant fungal pathogens and their corresponding host occurs via a highly specialized cell called a haustorium, which is surrounded by the extrahaustorial matrix bordered by plant and fungal membranes on either side. This represents the interface for signal exchange as well as nutrient uptake [Katiyar-Agarwal]. This close contact of the interaction partners might also facilitate the uptake of dsRNA or siRNA from the host plant cells into the fungal pathogens to create RNA silencing-mediated resistance. Proof of concept for this host-induced gene silencing (HIGS) of fungal genes was recently obtained for the barley powdery mildew *Blumeria graminis*, a biotrophic fungal pathogen [L. Navarro, P. Dunoyer]. Via transgenic expression of the dsRNA directed against *B. graminis* target transcripts in barley, a significant reduction of disease symptoms of a *B. graminis* infection was observed, whereas transgenic control that had lost the hairpin RNAi cassette was as susceptible as wild-type control plants [L. Navarro, P. Dunoyer], suggesting trafficking of dsRNA or siRNA from host plants into *B. graminis*. This may lead to an RNA silencing-based crop protection strategy against fungal pathogens.

RNA Silencing-mediated Resistance to Plant Nematodes and Insects

Previous studies report several trials of directly injecting or orally administering exogenous dsRNA into insects to reduce target genes expression [L. Gitlin ,V. Bitko and S. Barik, J.M. Jacque] and the reduced development of rootknot nematodes, as well as *Lepidoptera* and *Coleoptera* insects, feeding on transgenic plants that carry RNAi constructs against target genes in these pests [C.D. Novina, M.F Murray, E. Ullu, A. Djikeng]. The uptake of dsRNA or siRNA into these animals occurs by sucking or chewing on plant material, followed by resorption in the (mid) gut system, which may make this method a lasting and cost-effective method of RNA silencing-mediated resistance to insects. A successful example of the control of an insect pest in the field via the RNA silencing-mediated transgenic method is targeting of the cotton bollworm gene, CYP6AE14. This gene is highly expressed in the midgut and is responsible for larval growth and cotton bollworm tolerance to cotton gossypol. The larval growth was obviously retarded, and the CYP6AE14 transcript was reduced in the midgut when cotton bollworm larvae were fed with CYP6AE14-derived hpRNA transgenic cotton, indicating that siRNAs expressed by CYP6AE14-hpRNA are active in triggering PTGS-mediated cleavage in the pest body [P.M. Waterhouse, M. W. Graham and M. B. Wang]. However, we do not know whether the siRNAs are processed by plant RNA silencing machinery before spreading into midgut cells or if they are processed directly by pest RNA silencing machinery in midgut cells. Undoubtedly, the uptake of either dsRNA or siRNA or both implied that HIGS-mediated resistance might be a general approach to the application of pest control.

STRATEGIES FOR IMPROVING THE NUTRITIONAL VALUE OF FOOD CROPS

Although efforts have been made to improve crop yield by traditional plant breeding and genetic engineering techniques, the focus has now shifted to improve the nutritional value of plants. Some major diseases such as coronary disease and cancer can be prevented by supplementing, for example, essential amino acids, fatty acids, minerals and vitamins in our diet (Key *et al.*, 2002). Plant food rich in these essential nutrients could improve human health and life expectancy. RNAi technology offers advanced and appropriate means to fulfill these requirements.

Different strategies of RNAi technology have been successfully used in various food crops. The technology has been used to produce crops with improved levels of essential amino acids such as lysine in maize and rice. Along the same line, the level of the seed storage protein glutelin has been successfully reduced in rice. Fatty acid (such as stearic acid and oleic acid) content has been enhanced in cottonseed oil using RNAi. Starch content in maize and wheat has been manipulated to meet the dietary requirement of patients with gastrointestinal diseases. The levels of metabolites such as flavonoids and carotenoids have been elevated in tomatoes, thereby reducing the risk of coronary heart disease, certain kinds of cancers and vision-related problems. It has also been possible to successfully develop cottonseed as a rich source of protein by reducing the content of toxic terpenoid-gossypol. RNAi can be exploited for making seedless fruits or berries. A reduced level of caffeine content has been shown in coffee seeds using this technology, which can be beneficial to patients with hypertension.

Rice: Rice is one of the major staple food crops; it is consumed by more than half of the world's population. RNAi technology has been used to develop rice plants with reduced level of glutelin content, a major seed storage protein accounting for 60% of the total endosperm protein in rice. It is encoded by two gene families, GluA and GluB (Kusaba *et al.*, 2003). Iida *et al.* (1993) developed a mutant line with low glutelin content (LGC-1) where the content of prolamin, another seed storage protein, was found to increase. However, prolamin accumulates in protein body I whereas glutelin is found in protein body II. As protein body I is hardly digested in the human body, LGC-1 can be conveniently used as a low protein rice. This is useful for patients with kidney disorders who require a low protein intake. Kusaba and his team (2003) have revealed the mechanism of reduction of glutelin content in LGC-1 to be mediated by GluB hairpin RNA.

Wheat: Wheat is another essential food crop consumed by more than 35% of the world's population and is widely cultivated. Transgenic wheat with an increased amylose content has been generated using RNAi. Starch consists of two polymers, amylose and amylopectin; amylose cannot be easily digested, contributing to a higher value of resistant starch (RS). Amylopectin is synthesized by a complex pathway involving several isoforms of starch synthase, starch branching enzymes (SBE), and starch debranching enzymes. In monocots, SBE consists of SBEI and two forms of SBE II: SBEIIa and SBE IIb. It is found that RS contributes to some of the benefits ascribed to dietary fibre in wholegrain cereal foods. Regina *et al.* (2006) produced a high amylose (more than 70%) phenotype wheat by silencing the expression of SBE IIa and SBE IIb genes. They also showed that its consumption raised the content of RS in rats, thus proving it to be beneficial as a dietary supplement.

Maize: Maize constitutes a staple food in many regions of the world. In maize, zeins storage proteins are present in abundance; these hold importance due to their nutritional value, and have been classified into 4 subfamilies: α, γ and zeins (Ueda & Messing, 1993). Zeins are encoded by single or low copy gene loci with the exception of alpha zeins. Genomic studies have characterized the alpha zeins to be subdivided into 19 and 22 kD zein subfamilies (Segal *et al.*, 2003). The encoding of a few hydrophobic amino acids in alpha zein proteins is responsible for the imbalance in seed nutritional content. The opaque2 (o2) mutation inhibits the transcription of 22 kD alpha zein component, which is thus greatly reduced in the endosperm. However, this mutation also produces disadvantage by altering one or more other genes, affecting the seeds in other ways. Segal *et al.* (2003) have used RNAi technology to obtain a dominant o2 phenotype where the stable and heritable expression of the recombinant sequence produced a specific reduction in 22 kD alpha zein protein. At the same time it also maintained the higher level of lysine and reduced level of leucine, alanine and glutamine. Lysine synthesis is strongly regulated by a feedback inhibition loop in which lysine inhibits the activity of dihydrodipicolinate synthase (DHPS), the first enzyme in the pathway specifically committed to lysine biosynthesis. In addition to this, excess lysine is catabolised by a pathway that is initiated by two enzymes, namely, lysine-ketoglutarate reductase and saccharopine dehydrogenase. Therefore, this amino acid cannot be accumulated in seeds beyond a certain level. However, it has been reported that by suppressing lysine catabolism a significant amount of lysine can be accumulated using RNAi technology (Houmard *et al.*, 2007). Scientists achieved this by targeting the expression of these two enzymes, lysine-ketoglutarate reductase and saccharopine dehydrogenase, in the endosperm of maize seeds.

Barley: Barley is one of the most nutritional cereals, containing most of the vital nutrients such as metals like zinc, copper and phosphorous, as well as other nutrients like calcium and iron, nitrous compounds, fat and starch.

Barley yellow dwarf virus (BYDV) and cereal yellow dwarf virus (CYDV) together cause cereal diseases in over 50 countries. BYDV causes average losses of about 15% in barley, 17% in wheat, and 25% in oats (Lister and Ranieri, 1995). Varieties of barley plant have been developed using RNAi technology that are resistant to barley yellow dwarf virus (BYDV). Wang *et al.* (2000) have used hpRNA containing the polymerase gene sequences of BYDV-PAV (a species of virus) to transform barley and found that one third of these independently transformed plants were extremely resistant to BYDV-PAV. These BYDV-immune barley plants have a great potential to be deployed in field to reduce the losses in barley crops and increase the overall yield. Recently, Regina *et al.* (2010) have used the RNAi strategy of silencing SBE IIa and SBE IIb genes, as in the case of wheat, to increase amylose content in seeds of barley.

Tomato: Tomatoes and tomato-derived products are a rich dietary source of carotenoids and flavonoids. Increased lycopene (a carotene) imparts to the fruit a more appealing colour and has a nutritional value as an antioxidant, and flavonoids are hydrophilic antioxidants. Both carotenoids and flavonoids in the diet are important to reduce the risk of heart disease and certain cancers. Reports have shown that attempts to elevate both the carotenoid and flavonoid content at the same time have not been successful. Davuluri *et al.* (2005) suppressed an endogenous photomorphogenesis regulatory gene DE-ETIOLATED1 (DET1) using fruit-specific promoters and RNAi technology. DET1 is a regulatory gene which represses several signaling pathways controlled by light. Thus, RNAi can be judiciously used to manipulate the expression of a plant regulatory gene influencing the production of phytonutrients generated from independent biosynthetic pathways.

It has been shown that RNAi can be a novel approach to obtain parthenocarpic tomato fruits by engineering the flavonoid pathway. Using this technique, Schijlen *et al.* (2007) have down-regulated the flavonoid biosynthesis pathway by suppressing the expression of CHS (chalcone synthase), the first gene in the pathway. They demonstrated that all transgenic lines with reduced flavonoid content developed parthenocarpic fruits. Although no correlation between flavonoids and parthenocarpic fruit development has been reported, it is well known that flavonoids are essential for pollen development and pollen tube formation. From these observations, scientists have speculated that the phenomenon of defective pollen tube formation leading to seedless variety is linked to the suppression of the CHS gene.

Potato and *Sweet potato:* The potato (*Solanum tuberosum*) has been a major human staple food for 8,000 years, and after wheat, maize and rice it is the fourth most important crop.

The carotenoids that potatoes accumulate in the greatest amounts are zeaxanthin xanthophylls. Zeaxanthin is an immediate biochemical derivative of beta-carotene. As the molecular basis of carotenoid biosynthesis has become more deeply understood (Cunningham and Gantt, 1998), it is now clear that beta-carotene hydroxylase (bch) is the enzyme responsible for converting beta-carotene to zeaxanthin. Van Eck *et al.* (2007) used RNAi-mediated silencing of the beta carotene hydroxylase (bch) gene to enhance the content of beta-carotene, a precursor of vitamin A, in potatoes. The results indicate that elevated levels of beta-carotene can be produced by this strategy, which may permit development of provitamin A enriched potatoes. Their report also demonstrated that silencing of the bch gene can increase the content of not only beta carotene but lutein, another carotenoid. These transformed potatoes may serve as a source of vitamin A.

Sweet potato (*Ipomoea batatas*) is an important food crop which is required by various industries as a raw material. A new sweet potato variety that contains high amylose or low amylose would be beneficial to different industries. Transgenic amylose-free sweet potato plants were produced by inhibiting the expression of granule-bound starch synthaseI (GBSS1), the key enzyme in the starch biosynthesis, through RNA interference (Otani *et al.*, 2007). Shimada *et al.* (2006) obtained transgenic sweet potato plants that produced a starch with higher amylose content by exploiting an RNAi technique to target the starch branching enzyme II (SBEII). Thus, RNAi is an effective method to manipulate gene expression in the starch metabolic pathway.

Brassica: Brassica napus (canola) seeds are a rich source of seed storage proteins, as well as valuable oil and oil-related products. Sinapine (sinapoylcholine) is the most abundant anti-nutritional phenolic compound in seeds of cruciferous species and therefore is a target for elimination in canola (*Brassica napus*) seeds. Sinapine causes an unpleasant flavor in the meat and milk of animals fed on canola/*B. napus* (Pearson *et al.*, 1980), and excessive consumption of sinapine may cause serious growth and reproductive problems (Pearson *et al.*, 1980).

Bhinu *et al.* (2009) have used an RNAi technology in canola for improving the seed quality by down-regulating two genes: ferulic acid 5-hydroxylase (FAH) and sinapoylglucose:choline sinapoyltransferase (SCT). The transgenic lines showed up to 90% reduction of sinapine content and a higher level of choline in the seeds. Plants with both low sinapine and higher choline levels would provide better quality canola seeds that would add value to the meal and animal feed industry. Using RNAi approach, Wei *et al.* (2009) reported higher levels of lutein, -carotene and zeaxanthin by constitutive silencing of regulatory gene DE-ETIOLATED 1 (DET 1).

Cotton: Cotton (*Gossypium hirsutum*) is primarily grown for fibre production for more than 7,000 years. It is the most important cash crop in Asian and African countries, and the world's sixth largest source of vegetable oil. Cottonseed oil is typically composed of about 26% palmitic acid (C16:0), 15% oleic acid (C18:1) and 58% linoleic acid (C18:2). A high level of palmitic acid is nutritionally undesirable as it raises the level of low-density lipoprotein (LDL) cholesterol. Furthermore, cholesterol-raising properties are enhanced due to the hydrogenation process. This is done to achieve the very high stability required in deep-frying food service applications. This process also results in the production of trans-fatty acids, which are now recognized as having cholesterol-raising properties (Liu *et al.*, 2002).

As a result of these factors, there is a need to develop oils which are low in palmitic acid and rich in either oleic acid (C18:1) or stearic acid (C18:0). RNA interference has been successfully used to generate modified fatty acid content in cottonseeds. The ghSAD-1 and ghFAD 2-1 genes in cotton encode stearoyl-ACPΔ9 desaturase and Δ12 desaturase, respectively. Liu *et al.* (2002) reported the use of hpRNA gene silencing constructs to achieve the seed-specific silencing of both ghSAD-1 and ghFAD 2-1 resulting in development of high stearic (upto 40%) and oleic acid (upto 77%) content in cottonseed oils.

CONCLUSION

RNAi is now commonly used in biological and biomedical research to study the effect of blocking expression of a given gene. As the effect is rarely complete, it is generally termed a "knock-down" to distinguish it from the "knock-out" achieved by deletion of the gene. Although significant advances have been made as compared to previous methods, RNAi has its own limitations. Not every sequence works, most researchers reporting a success rate of about one in three. Moreover, although the effects are generally believed to be highly sequence-specific, some doubts remain as to whether or not some of the observed effects are "off target." Some residual activation of the interferon system has been reported, as well as degradation of closely related, but non-identical, mRNAs. Nevertheless, RNAi remains the most promising functional genomics tool recently developed. DNA microarray technology has now enabled the level of expression of every gene in the genome to be determined under any condition [34, 35].

This has led to a huge accumulation of data on genes whose expression is significantly altered in several diseases. To take an example, large databases have been established of genes that are pathologically regulated in cancer. In some cases this has resulted in the identification of key genes involved in tumor development and provided important new therapeutic targets. However, in most cases the pattern of gene expression is far too complex to allow for identification of the relatively small number of misexpressed genes that are involved in causing or maintaining the disease rather than the much larger number that are innocent bystanders. The ability of RNAi to provide relatively easy ablation of gene expression has opened up the possibility of using collections of siRNAs to analyse the significance of hundreds or thousands of different genes whose expression is known to be upregulated in a disease, given an appropriate tissue culture model of that disease. Perhaps more important still is the possibility of using genome-wide collections of siRNAs, whether synthetic or in viral vectors, as screening tools. Two main avenues of research can rely upon RNAi libraries. First, in a high-throughput manner each gene in the genome is knocked-down one at a time and the cells or organism scored for a desired outcome, such as death of a cultured cancer cell but not a normal cell. Due to the very large numbers of assays required to screen all 35-50,000 genes in the human genome, this approach is highly labor-intensive and time consuming. The other approach is to use large pools of RNAi viral vectors and apply a selective pressure that only cells with the desired change in behavior can survive. The identity of the genes knocked-down in the surviving cells can then be identified by sequencing the RNA interference vectors that they carry. Both approaches show consider-able promise in identifying novel genes that may make important therapeutic targets for inhibition either by conventional drug discovery methods or, more intriguingly, by RNA interference itself.

The nutritional value of human vegetable foods is one of the focuses of plant breeding in agriculture and plays an increasing role in prevention of various human diseases associated with malnutrition. Tremendous efforts have been invested in improving the nutritional value of human plant foods and livestock feeds over the past years. RNAi and miRNA technologies of gene silencing are newly developed genomics tools that have great advantages over antisense and co-suppression due to their higher silencing efficiency and shortened time period for screening for the targeted plants. These technologies are particularly useful in conjunction with the practice of gene or pathway discoveries through nutritional genomics, trancriptomics, proteomics, and metabolomics in plants to improve human health. Tissue or organ-specific RNAi vectors have recently been proven to be useful for targeted gene silencing in specific plant tissues and organs with minimal interference with the normal plant life cycle. New-generation RNAi vectors, the miRNA vectors have been developed with high silencing accuracy and fewer side effects in plants. Genetic engineering of highly nutritional food crops requires both gene silencing and counter-silencing technologies. Developing vectors that can suppress the RNAi pathway but overexpress transgenes in a tissue-specific manner will revolutionize this field. Such vectors could be based on various viral RNA silencing suppressors and their derivatives. Future directions will focus on developing finely tuned RNAi-based gene silencing vectors that are able to operate in a temporally and spatially controlled manner.

REFERENCES

1. Key, T.J., Allen, N.E., Spencer, E.A. and Travis, R.C. 2002. The Effect of Diet on Risk of Cancer. *The Lancet* 360: 861-868.
2. Kusaba, M. 2004. RNA Interference in Crop Plants. *Current Opinion in Biotechnology* 15: 139-143.
3. Kusaba, M., Miyahara, K., Lida, S., Fukuoka, H., Takario, T., Sassa, H., Nishimura, M. and Nishio, T. 2003. Low Glutenin Content 1: A Dominant Mutation that Suppresses the Glutenin Multigenefamily via RNA Silencing in Rice. *Plant Cell* 15: 1455-1467.
4. Regina, A., Bird, A., Topping, D., Bowden, S., Freeman, J., Barsby, T., Kosar-Hashemi, B., Li, Z., Rahman.
5. Regina, A., Kosar-Hashemi, B., Ling, S., Li, Z., Rahman, S. and Morell, M. 2010. Control of Starch Branching in Barley Defined Through Differential RNAi Suppression of Starch Branching Enzyme IIa and IIb. *Journal of Experimental Botany* 61(5): 1469-1482.
6. Ueda, T. and Messing, J. 1993. Manipulation of Amino Acid Balance in Maize Seeds. *Genetic Engineering* 15: 109-130.
7. Segal, G., Song, R. and Messing, J. 2003. A New Opaque Variant of Maize by a Single Dominant RNA-Interference-Inducing Transgene. *Genetics* 165: 387-397.
8. Schijlen, E.G., de Vos, W.M., Martens, C.H.R., Martens, S., Jonker, H.H., Rosin, F.M., Molthoff, J.W., Tikunov, Y.M., Angenent, G.C., van Tunen, A.J. and Bovy, A.G. 2007. RNA Interference Silencing of Chalcone Synthase, the First Step in the Flavonoid Biosynthesis Pathway, Leads to Parthenocarpic Tomato Fruits. *Plant Physiology* 144: 1520-1530.
9. Otani, M., Hamada, T., Katayama, K., Kitahara, K., Kim, S. H., Takahata, Y., Suganuma, T. and Shimada, T. 2007. Inhibition of the Gene Expression for Granule-bound Starchsynthase I by RNA Interference in Sweet Potato Plants. *Plant Cell Reports* 26: 1801-1807.
10. Cunningham, F.X. and Gantt, E. 1998. Genes and Enzymes of Carotenoid Biosynthesis in Plants. *Annual Review of Plant Physiology and Plant Molecular Biology* 49: 557-583.
11. Pearson, A.W., Butler, E.J. and Fenwick, R.G. 1980. Rapeseed Meal and Egg Taint: The Role of Sinapine. *Journal of Science Food Agriculture* 31: 898-904.
12. Wei, S., Li, X., Gruber, M.Y., Li, R., Zhou, R., Zebarjadi, A., Hannoufa, A. 2009. RNAi-mediated Suppression of DET1 Alters the Levels of Carotenoids and Sinapate Esters in Seeds of *Brassica napus*. *Journal of Agricultural Food and Chemistry* 57: 5326-5333.

13. Bhinu, V.S., Schafer, U.A., Li, R., Huang, J. and Hannoufa, A. 2009. Targeted Modulation of Sinapine Biosynthesis Pathway for Seed Quality Improvement in *Brassica napus*. *Transgenic Research* 18: 31-44.

14. Liu, Q., Singh, S.P. and Green, A.G. 2002. High-Stearic and High-Oleic Cottonseed Oils Produced by Hairpin RNA-Mediated Post-Transcriptional Gene Silencing. *Plant Physiology* 129: 1732-1743.

15. Abbas-Terki T, Blanco-Bose W, Deglon N, Pralong W, and Aebischer P (2002) Lentiviral-mediated RNA Interference. Hum Gene Ther 13: 2197-2201.

16. Ancellin N, Colmont C, Su J, Li Q, Mittereder N, Chae SS, Stefansson S, Liau G, and Hla T (2002) Extracellular Export of Sphingosine Kinase-1 Enzyme. Sphingosine 1-phosphate Generation and the Induction of Angiogenic Vascular Maturation. J Biol Chem 277: 6667-6675.

17. Aoki Y, Cioca D, Oidaira H, Kamiya J, and Kiyosawa K (2003) RNA Interference may be more Potent than Antisense RNA in Human Cancer Cell Lines. Clin Exp Pharmacol Physiol 30: 96-102.

18. Assaad FF, Tucker KL, and Signer ER (1993) Epigenetic Repeat-induced Gene Silencing (RIGS) in Arabidopsis. Plant Mol Biol 22: 1067-1085.

19. *Baehrecke EH (2002) How death shapes life during development. Nat Rev Mol Cell Biol 3: 779-787.*

20. Baglioni C and Nilsen TW (1983) Mechanisms of Antiviral Action of Interferon. Interferon 5: 23-42.

21. Bai X, Zhou D, Brown JR, Crawford BE, Hennet T, and Esko JD (2001) Biosynthesis of the Linkage Region of Glycosaminoglycans: Cloning and Activity of Galactosyltransferase II, the Sixth Member of the Beta 1, 3-galactosyltransferase Family (beta 3GalT6). J Biol Chem 276: 48189-48195.

22. Bernstein E, Caudy AA, Hammond SM, and Hannon GJ (2001) Role for a Bidentate Ribonuclease in the Initiation Step of RNA Interference. Nature (Lond) 409: 363-366.

23. Billy E, Brondani V, Zhang H, Muller U, and Filipowicz W (2001) Specific Interference with Gene Expression Induced by Long, Double-stranded RNA in Mouse Embryonal Teratocarcinoma Cell Lines. Proc Natl Acad Sci USA 98: 14428-14433.

24. Cabot RA and Prather RS (2003) Cleavage Stage Porcine Embryos may have Differing Developmental Requirements for Karyopherins alpha2 and alpha3. Mol Reprod Dev 64: 292-301.

25. Caplen NJ, Fleenor J, Fire A, and Morgan RA (2000) dsRNA-mediated Gene Silencing in Cultured Drosophila Cells: A Tissue Culture Model for the Analysis of RNA Interference. Gene (Amst) 252: 95-105.

26. Caplen NJ, Taylor JP, Statham VS, Tanaka F, Fire A, and Morgan RA (2002) Rescue of Polyglutamine-mediated Cytotoxicity by Double-stranded RNA-mediated RNA Interference. Hum Mol Genet 11: 175-184.

27. Capodici J, Kariko K, and Weissman D (2002) Inhibition of HIV-1 Infection by Small Interfering RNA-mediated RNA Interference. J Immunol 169: 5196-5201.

28. Caudy AA, Myers M, Hannon GJ, and Hammond SM (2002) Fragile X-related Protein and VIG Associate with the RNA Interference Machinery. Genes Dev 16: 2491-2496.

29. Cheng A, Wang S, Yang D, Xiao R, and Mattson MP (2003) Calmodulin Mediates Brain-derived Neurotrophic Factor Cell Survival Signaling Upstream of Akt Kinase in Embryonic Neocortical Neurons. J Biol Chem 278: 7591-7599.

30. Cho JH, Bandyopadhyay J, Lee J, Park CS, and Ahnn J (2000) Two Isoforms of Sarco/Endoplasmic Reticulum Calcium ATPase (SERCA) are Essential in Caenorhabditis Elegans. Gene (Amst) 261: 211-219.

31. Czauderna F, Fechtner M, Aygun H, Arnold W, Klippel A, Giese K, and Kaufmann J (2003) Functional Studies of the PI(3)-kinase Signalling Pathway Employing Synthetic and Expressed siRNA. Nucleic Acids Res 31: 670-682.

32. Dalmay T, Hamilton A, Rudd S, Angell S, and Baulcombe DC (2000) An RNA-dependent RNA Polymerase Gene in Arabidopsis is Required for Posttranscriptional Gene Silencing Mediated by a Transgene but not by a Virus. Cell 101: 543-553.

33. Duan W, Rangnekar V, and Mattson MP (1999) Par-4 Production in Synaptic Compartments Following Apoptotic and Excitotoxic Insults: Evidence for a Pivotal Role.

34. Duan W, Zhu X, Ladenheim B, Yu QS, Guo Z, Oyler J, Cutler RG, Cadet JL, Greig NH, and Mattson MP (2002) p. 53 Inhibitors Preserve Dopamine Neurons and Motor Function in Experimental Parkinsonism. Ann Neurol 52: 597-606.

35. Kennerdell JR and Carthew RW (1998) Use of dsRNA-mediated Genetic Interference to Demonstrate that Frizzled and Frizzled 2 Act in the Wingless Pathway. Cell 95: 1017-1026.

36. Kennerdell JR and Carthew RW (2000) Heritable Gene Silencing in Drosophila Using Double-stranded RNA. Nat Biotechnol 18: 896-898.

37. Jiang M and Milner J (2002) Selective Silencing of Viral Gene Expression in HPV-positive Human Cervical Carcinoma Cells Treated with siRNA, a Primer of RNA Interference. Oncogene 21: 6041-6048.

38. Ketting RF, Fischer SE, Bernstein E, Sijen T, Hannon GJ, and Plasterk RH (2001) Dicer Functions in RNA Interference and in Synthesis of Small RNA Involved in Developmental Timing in C. Elegans. Genes Dev 15: 2654-2659.

39. Kim MH, Yuan X, Okumura S, and Ishikawa F (2002) Successful Inactivation of Endogenous Oct-3/4 and c-mos Genes in Mouse Preimplantation Embryos and Oocytes Using Short Interfering RNAs. Biochem Biophys Res Commun 296: 1372-1377.

40. Kisielow M, Kleiner S, Nagasawa M, Faisal A, and Nagamine Y (2002) Isoform-specific Knockdown and Expression of Adaptor Protein ShcA Using Small Interfering RNA. Biochem J 363: 1-5.

41. Lee NS, Dohjima T, Bauer G, Li H, Li MJ, Ehsani A, Salvaterra P, and Rossi J (2002a) Expression of Small Interfering RNAs Targeted Against HIV-1 rev Transcripts in Human Cells. Nat Biotechnol 20: 500-505.

42. Lee SF, Shah S, Li H, Yu C, Han W, and Yu G (2002b) Mammalian APH-1 Interacts with Presenilin and Nicastrin and is Required for Intramembrane Proteolysis of Amyloid-beta Precursor Protein and Notch. J Biol Chem 277: 45013-45019.

43. Lee SS, Lee RY, Fraser AG, Kamath RS, Ahringer J, and Ruvkun G (2002c) A Systematic RNAi Screen Identifies a Critical Role for Mitochondria in C. Elegans Longevity. Nat Genet 33: 40-48.

44. Elbashir SM, Martinez J, Patkaniowska A, Lendeckel W, and Tuschl T (2001b) Functional Anatomy of siRNAs for Mediating Efficient RNAi in Drosophila Melanogaster Embryo Lysate. EMBO (Eur Mol Biol Organ) J 20: 6877-6888.

45. Gilman CP, Chan SL, Guo Z, Zhu X, Greig NH, and Mattson MP (2003) p. 53 is Present in Synapses where it Mediates Mitochondrial Dysfunction and Synaptic Degeneration in Response to DNA Damage and Oxidative and Excitotoxic Insults. Neuromolecular Med 3: 159-172.

46. Gitlin L, Karelsky S, and Andino R (2002) Short interfering RNA Confers Intracellular Antiviral Immunity in Human Cells. Nature (Lond) 418: 430-434.

47. Glazner GW, Chan SL, Lu C, and Mattson MP (2000) Caspase-mediated Degradation of AMPA Receptor Subunits: A Mechanism for Preventing Excitotoxic Necrosis and Ensuring Apoptosis. J Neurosci 20: 3641-3649.

48. Greener T, Grant B, Zhang Y, Wu X, Greene LE, Hirsh D, and Eisenberg E (2001) Caenorhabditis Elegans Auxilin: A J-domain Protein Essential for Clathrin-mediated Endocytosis *in vivo*. Nat Cell Biol 3: 215-219.

49. Hamilton AJ and Baulcombe DC (1999) A Species of Small Antisense RNA in Post-transcriptional Gene Silencing in Plants. Science (Wash DC) 286: 950-952.

50. Hammond SM, Bernstein E, Beach D, and Hannon GJ (2000) An RNA-directed Nuclease Mediates Post-transcriptional Gene Silencing in Drosophila Cells. Nature (Lond) 404: 293-296.

51. Hammond SM, Boettcher S, Caudy AA, Kobayashi R, and Hannon GJ (2001) Argonaute2, a Link Between Genetic and Biochemical Analyses of RNAi. Science (Wash DC) 293: 1146-1150.

52. Banerjee D and Slack F (2002) Control of Developmental Timing by Small Temporal RNAs: A Paradigm for RNA-mediated Regulation of Gene Expression. Bioessays 24: 119-129.

53. Barton GM and Medzhitov R (2002) Delivery of Small Interfering RNA into Primary Cells. Proc Natl Acad Sci USA 99. 14943-14945.

54. Elbashir SM, Harborth J, Lendeckel W, Yalcin A, Weber K, and Tuschl T (2001a) Duplexes of 21-nucleotide RNAs Mediate RNA Interference in Cultured Mammalian Cells. Nature (Lond) 411: 494-498.

55. Faergeman NJ and Knudsen J (2002) Acyl-CoA Binding Protein is an Essential Protein in Mammalian Cell Lines. Biochem J 368: 679-682.

56. Fire A, Xu S, Montgomery MK, Kostas SA, Driver SE, and Mello CC (1998) Potent and Specific Genetic Interference by Double-stranded RNA in Caenorhabditis Elegans. Nature (Lond) 391: 806-811.

57. Franz DR and Zajtchuk R (2002) Biological Terrorism: Understanding the Threat, Preparation and Medical Response. Dis Mon 48: 493-564.

58. Gary DS and Mattson MP (2001) Integrin Signaling via the PI3-kinase-Akt Pathway Increases Neuronal Resistance to Glutamate-induced Apoptosis. J Neurochem 76: 1485-1496.

59. Hutchings NR, Donelson JE, and Hill KL (2002) Trypanin is a Cytoskeletal Linker Protein and is Required for Cell Motility in African Trypanosomes. J Cell Biol 156: 867-877.

60. Iratni R, Yan YT, Chen C, Ding J, Zhang Y, Price SM, Reinberg D, and Shen MM (2002) Inhibition of Excess Nodal Signaling during Mouse Gastrulation by the Transcriptional Corepressor DRAP1. Science (Wash DC) 298: 1996-1999.

61. Irie N, Sakai N, Ueyama T, Kajimoto T, Shirai Y, and Saito N (2002) Subtype- and Species-specific Knockdown of PKC Using Short Interfering RNA. Biochem Biophys Res Commun 298: 738-743.

62. Liu X and Erikson RL (2002) Activation of Cdc2/cyclin B and Inhibition of Centrosome Amplification in Cells Depleted of Plk1 by siRNA. Proc Natl Acad Sci USA 99: 8672-8676.

63. Marathe R, Anandalakshmi R, Smith TH, Pruss GJ, and Vance VB (2000) RNA Viruses as Inducers, Suppressors and Targets of Post-transcriptional Gene Silencing. Plant Mol Biol 43: 295-306.

64. Ohta T, Essner R, Ryu JH, Palazzo RE, Uetake Y, and Kuriyama R (2002) Characterization of Cep135, a Novel Coiled-coil Centrosomal Protein Involved in Microtubule Organization in Mammalian Cells. J Cell Biol 156: 87-99.

65. Paddison PJ, Caudy AA, Bernstein E, Hannon GJ, and Conklin DS (2002a) Short Hairpin RNAs (shRNAs) Induce Sequence-specific Silencing in Mammalian Cells. Genes Dev 16: 948-958.

66. Nagashima K, Endo A, Ogita H, Kawana A, Yamagishi A, Kitabatake A, Matsuda M, and Mochizuki N (2002) Adaptor Protein Crk is Required for Ephrin-B1-induced Membrane Ruffling and Focal Complex Assembly of Human Aortic Endothelial Cells. Mol Biol Cell 13: 4231-4242.

67. Nam NH and Parang K (2003) Current Targets for Anticancer Drug Discovery. Curr Drug Targets 4: 159-179.

68. Napoli C, Lemieux C, and Jorgensen R (1990) Introduction of a Chimeric Chalcone Synthase Gene into Petunia Results in Reversible Co-suppression of Homologous Genes in Trans. Plant Cell 2: 279-289.

69. Peng Y, Zhang Q, Nagasawa H, Okayasu R, Liber HL, and Bedford JS (2002) Silencing Expression of the Catalytic Subunit of DNA-dependent Protein Kinase by Small Interfering RNA Sensitizes Human Cells for Radiation-induced Chromosome Damage, Cell Killing and Mutation. Cancer Res 62: 6400-6404.

70. Poinat P, De Arcangelis A, Sookhareea S, Zhu X, Hedgecock EM, Labouesse M, and Georges-Labouesse E (2002) A Conserved Interaction Between Beta1 Integrin/PAT-3 and Nck-interacting Kinase/MIG-15 that Mediates Commissural Axon Navigation in C. Elegans. Curr Biol 12: 622-631.

71. Porter LA, Dellinger RW, Tynan JA, Barnes EA, Kong M, Lenormand JL, and Donoghue DJ (2002) Human Speedy: A Novel Cell Cycle Regulator that Enhances Proliferation Through Activation of Cdk2. J Cell Biol 157: 357-366.

72. Prasanth SG, Prasanth KV, and Stillman B (2002) Orc6 Involved in DNA Replication, Chromosome Segregation and Cytokinesis. Science (Wash DC) 297: 1026-1031.

73. Pruss G, Ge X, Shi XM, Carrnington JC, and Vance VB (1997) Plant Viral Synergism: The Potyviral Genome Encodes a Broad-range Pathogenicity Enhancer that Transactivates Replication of Heterologous Viruses. Plant Cell 9: 1749-1759.

74. Randall G, Grakoui A, and Rice CM (2003) Clearance of Replicating Hepatitis C Virus Replicon RNAs in Cell Culture by Small Interfering RNAs. Proc Natl Acad Sci USA 100: 235-240.

75. Ratcliff F, Harrison BD, and Baulcombe DC (1997) A Similarity Between Viral Defense and Gene Silencing in Plants. Science (Wash DC) 276: 1558-1560.

76. Smalheiser NR, Manev H, and Costa E (2001) RNAi and Brain Function: was McConnell on the Right Track? Trends Neurosci 24: 216-218.

77. Stucke VM, Sillje HH, Arnaud L, and Nigg EA (2002) Human Mps1 Kinase is Required for the Spindle Assembly Checkpoint but not for Centrosome Duplication. EMBO (Eur Mol Biol Organ) J 21: 1723-1732.

78. Sui G, Soohoo C, Affar el B, Gay F, Shi Y, Forrester WC, Shi Y (2002) A DNA Vector-based RNAi Technology to Suppress Gene Expression in Mammalian.

79. Tabara H, Sarkissian M, Kelly WG, Fleenor J, Grishok A, Timmons L, Fire A, and Mello CC (1999) The Rde-1 gene, RNA Interference and Transposon Silencing in C. Elegans. Cell 99: 123-132.

80. Timmons L and Fire A (1998) Specific Interference by Ingested dsRNA. Nature (Lond) 395: 854.

81. Tiscornia G, Singer O, Ikawa M, and Verma IM (2003) A General Method for Gene Knockdown in Mice by Using Lentiviral Vectors Expressing Small Interfering RNA. Proc Natl Acad Sci USA 100: 1844-1848.

82. Tsuneoka M, Koda Y, Soejima M, Teye K, and Kimura H (2002) A Novel Myc Target Gene, Mina53, that is Involved in Cell Proliferation. J Biol Chem 277: 35450-35459.

83. Van Blokland R, Van Der Geest N, Mol JMN, and Kooter JM (1994) Transgene-mediated Expression of Chalcone Synthase Expression in Petunia Hybrida Results from an Increase in RNA turnover. Plant J 6: 861-877.

84. Wianny F and Zernicka-Goetz M (2000) Specific Interference with Gene Function by Double-stranded RNA in Early Mouse Development. Nat Cell Biol 2: 70-75.

85. Wilda M, Fuchs U, Wossmann W, and Borkgardt A (2002) Killing of Leukemic Cells with a BCR/ABL Fusion Gene by RNA Interference (RNAi). Oncogene 21: 5716-5724.

86. Wilson JA, Jayasena S, Khvorova A, Sabatinos S, Rodrigue-Gervais IG, Arya S, Sarangi F, Harris-Brandts M, Beaulieu S, and Richardson CD (2003) RNA Interference Blocks Gene Expression and RNA Synthesis from Hepatitis C Replicons Propagated in Human Liver Cells. Proc Natl Acad Sci USA 100: 2783-2788.

87. Xu K, Tavernarakis N, and Driscoll M (2001) Necrotic Cell Death in C. Elegans Requires the Function of Calreticulin and Regulators of Ca(2+) Release from the Endoplasmic Reticulum. Neuron 31: 957-971.

88. Xu Z, Williams CJ, Kopf GS, and Schultz RM (2003) Maturation-associated Increase in IP(3) Receptor Type 1: Role in Conferring Increased IP(3) Sensitivity and Ca(2+) Oscillatory Behaviour in Mouse Eggs. Dev Biol 254: 163-171.

89. Zhang D, Li F, Weidner D, Mnjoyan ZH, and Fujise K (2002a) Physical and Functional Interaction Between Myeloid Cell Leukemia 1 Protein (MCL1) and Fortilin. The Potential Role of MCL1 as a Fortilin Chaperone. J Biol Chem 277: 37430-37438.

90. Zhang H, Kolb FA, Brondani V, Billy E, and Filipowicz W (2002b) Human Dicer Preferentially Cleaves dsRNAs at Their Termini without a Requirement for ATP. EMBO (Eur Mol Biol Organ) J 21: 5875-5885.

91. Zhu X, Yu QS, Cutler RG, Culmsee CW, Holloway HW, Lahiri DK, Mattson MP, and Greig NH (2002) Novel p53 Inactivators with Neuroprotective Action: Syntheses and Pharmacological Evaluation of 2-imino-2, 3, 4, 5, 6, 7-hexahydrobenzothiazole and 2-imino-2, 3, 4, 5, 6, 7-hexahydrobenzoxazole derivatives. J Med Chem 45: 5090-5097.

92. Ishizuka A, Siomi MC, and Siomi H (2002) A Drosophila Fragile X Protein Interacts with Components of RNAi and Ribosomal Proteins. Genes Dev 16: 2497-2508.

93. Siegmund D, Hadwiger P, Pfizenmaier K, Vornlocher HP, and Wajant H (2002) Selective Inhibition of FLICE-like Inhibitory Protein Expression with Small Interfering RNA Oligonucleotides is Sufficient to Sensitize Tumor Cells for TRAIL-induced Apoptosis. Mol Med 8: 725-732.

94. Papaefthimiou I, Hamilton A, Denti M, Baulcombe D, Tsagris M, Tabler M: Replicating Potato Spindle Tuber Viroid RNA is Accompanied by Short RNA Fragments that are Characteristic of Post-transcriptional Gene Silencing.

95. A. Fitzgerald, J. A. Van Kha and K. M. Plummer, "Simultaneous Silencing of Multiple Genes in the Apple Scab Fungus *Venturia inaequalis*, by Expression of RNA with Chimeric Inverted Repeats," *Fungal Genetics and Biology*, Vol. 41, 2004, pp. 963-971.

96. M. Goldoni, G. Azzalin, G. Macino and C. Cogoni, "Efficient Gene Silencing by Expression of Double Stranded RNA in *Neurospora crassa*," *Fungal Genetics and Biology*, Vol. 41, 2004, pp. 1016-1024.

97. T.M. Hammond and N. P. Keller, "RNA Silencing in *Aspergillus nidulans* is Independent of RNA-Dependent RNA polymerase," *Genetics*, Vol. 169, 2005, pp. 607-617.
98. P. Spanu, "HCf-1, a Hydrophobin from the Tomato PathoGen *Cladosporium fulvum*," Gene, Vol. 93, 1997, pp. 89-96.
99. G.C. Segers, W. Hamada, R.P. Oliver and P.D. Spanu, "Isolation and Characteristaion of Five Different Hydrophobin-Encoding cDNA from the Fungal Tomato Pathogen *Cladosporium fulvum*," *Molecular and General Genetics*, Vol. 261, 1999.
100. N.J. Talbot, M.J. Kershaw, G.E. Wakley, O.M.H. de Vries, J.G.H. Wessels and J.E. Hamer, "MPG1 Encodes a Fungal Hydrophobin Involved in Surface Interactions during Infection-Related Development of *Magnaporthe grisea*," *Plant Cell*, Vol. 8, 1996, pp. 985-999.
101. Q. B. Nguyen, H. Nakayashiki, S. Kasahara, Y. Tosa, S. Mayama and H. Nakayashiki, "Systematic Functional Analysis of Calcium-Signalling Proteins in the Genome of the Rice-Blast Fungus, *Magnaporthe oryzae*, Using a High-Throughput RNA-Silencing System," *Molecular Microbiology*, Vol. 68, 2008, pp. 1348-1365.
102. R.J. Weld, K.M. Plummer, M.A. Carpenter, and H.J. Ridgway, "Approaches to Functional Genomics in Filamentous Fungi," *Cell Research*, Vol. 16, 2006, pp. 31-44.
103. H. Nakayashiki and Q. B. Nguyen, "RNA Interference: Roles in Fungal Biology," *Current Opinion in Microbiology*, Vol. 11, 2008, pp. 1-9.
104. H. Peng, Q. Zhang, Y. Li, C. Lei, Y. Zhai, X. Sun, D. Sun, Y. Sun and T. Lu, "A Putative Leucine-Rich Repeat Receptor Kinase, OsBRR1, is Involved in Rice Blast Resistance," *Planta*, Vol. 230, 2009, pp. 377-385.
105. S. Katiyar-Agarwal, R. Morgan, D. Dahlbeck, O. Borsani, J.A. Villegas, J. Zhu, B.J. Staskawicz and H. Jin, "A Pathogen-Inducible Endogenous siRNA in Plant Immunity," *Proceedings of the National Academy of Sciences of the USA*, Vol. 103, 2006, pp. 47-52.
106. S. Katiyar-Agarwal S. Katiyar-Agarwal, S. Gao, A. Vivian-Smith and H. Jin, "A Novel Class of Bacteria-Induced Small RNAs in Arabidopsis," *Genes and Development*, Vol. 21, 2007, pp. 3123-3134.
107. Katiyar-Agarwal, L. Navarro, P. Dunoyer, F. Jay, B. Arnold, N. Dharmasini, M. Estelle, O. Vionnet and J. D. Jones, "A Plant miRNA Contributes to Antibacterial Resistance by Repressing Auxin Signaling," *Science*, Vol. 312, 2006, pp. 436-439.
108. V. Bitko and S. Barik, "Phenotypic Silencing of Cytoplasmic Genes with Sequence Specific Double Stranded Short Interfering RNA and Its Applications in the Reverse Genetics of Wild Type Negative Strand RNA Virus," *BMC Microbiology*, Vol. 1, 2001, pp. 34-44.
109. L. Gitlin, S. Karelsky, and R. Andino, "Short Interference Confers Intracellular Antiviral Immunity in Human Cells," *Nature*, Vol. 4, 2002, pp. 418-430.
110. L. Gitlin ,V. Bitko and S. Barik ,J.M. Jacque, K. Triques and M. Stevenson, "Modulation of HIV-1 Replication by RNA Interference," *Nature*, Vol. 418, 2002, pp. 435-438.
111. C.D. Novina, M. F Murray, D.M. Dykxhoorn, P.J. Beresford, J. Riess, S.K. Lee, R.G. Collman, J. Lieberman, P. Shanker and P.A. Sharp, "siRNA-Directed Inhibition of HIV-1 Infection," *Nature Mediterranean*, Vol. 8, 2002, pp. 681-686.
112. C.D. Novina, M.F Murray, E. Ullu, A. Djikeng, H. Shi, and C. Tschudi, "RNA Interference: Advances and Questions," *Philosophical Transactions of the Royal Society of London British Biological Science*, Vol. 29, 2002, pp. 65-70.

113. P. M. Waterhouse, M. W. Graham and M. B. Wang, "Virus Resistance and Gene Silencing in Plants can be Induced by Simultaneous Expression of Sense and Antisense RNA," *Proceedings of the National Academy of Sciences of the USA*, Vol. 95, 1998, pp. 13959-13964.

114. E.J. Chapman, A.I. Prokhnevsky, K. Gopinath, V.V. Dolja and J.C. Carrington, "Viral RNA Silencing Suppressors Inhibit the micro-RNA Pathway at an Interphase Step," *Genes and Developmen*t, Vol. 18, 2004, pp. 1179- 1186.

115. M. Pooggin, P.V. Shivaprasad, K. Veluthambi and T. Hohn, "RNAi Targetting of DNA Viruses," *Nature Bio*Biotechnology and Plant Disease Control-Role of RNA Interference.

116. R. Vanitharani, P. Chellappan and C.M. Fauquet, "Short Interfering RNA-Mediated Interference of Gene Expression and Viral DNA Accumulation in Cultured Plant Cells," *Proceedings of the National Academy of Sciences of the USA*, Vol. 100, 2003, pp. 9632-9636.

117. V. Ruiz-Ferrer and O. Voinnet, "Viral Suppression of RNA Silencing: 2b Wins the Golden Fleece by Defeating Argonaute," *Bioassays*, Vol. 29, 2007, pp. 319-323.

118. J. Chen, W.X. Li, D. Xie, J.R. Peng, and S.W. Ding, "Viral Virulence Protein Suppresses RNA Silencing- Mediated Defense but Upregulates the Role of microRNA in Host Gene Regulation," *Plant Cell*, Vol. 16, No. 5, 2004, pp. 1302-1313.

119. Z. Merai, Z. Kerenyi, A. Molnar, E. Barta, A. Valcozi, G. Bistray, Z. Havelda, J. Burgyan and D. Silhavy, "Aureusvirus P14 is an Efficient RNA Silencing Suppressor that Binds Double Stranded RNAs without Size Specificity," *Journal of Virology*, Vol. 79, 2005, pp. 7217- 7226.

120. A. Takeda, M. Tsukuda, H. Mizumoto, K. Okamoto, M. Kaido, K. Mise and T. Okuno, "A Plant RNA Virus Suppressor RNA Silencing through RNA Replication," *The EMBO Journal*, Vol. 24, 2005 pp. 3147-3157.

121. X. Cao, P. Zhou, X. Zhang, S. Zhu, X. Zhong, Q. Xiao, B. Ding and Y. Li, "Identification of an RNA Silencing Suppressors from a Plant Double Stranded RNA Virus," *Journal of Virology*, Vol. 79, 2005, pp. 13018-13027.

122. X. Cao, P. Zhou, X. Zhang Q.W. Niu, S. S. Lin, J.L. Reyes, K.C. Chen, H. W. Wu, S.D. Yeh and N.H. Chua, "Expression of Artificial microRNAs in Transgenic *Arabidopsis thaliana* Confers Virus Resistance," *Nature Biotechnology*, Vol. 24, 2006, pp. 1420-1428.

123. J. Qu, J. Ye and R.X. Fang, "Artificial microRNA-Mediated Virus Resistance in Plants," *Journal of Virology*, Vol. 81, 2007, pp. 6690-6699.

124. J.A. Díaz-Pendón and S. W. Ding, "Direct and Indirect Roles of Viral Suppressors of RNA Silencing in Pathogenesis," *Annual Review of Phytopathology*, Vol. 46, 2008, pp. 303-326.

125. S.M. Elbashir, W. Lendeckel, and T. Tuschl, "RNA Interference is Mediated by 21 and 22-Nucleotide RNAs," *Genes and Development*, Vol. 15, 2001, pp. 188-200.

126. H. Tyagi, S. Rajasubramaniam, M.V. Rajam and I. Dasgupta, "RNA Interference in Rice against Rice Tungro Bacilliform Virus Results in Its Decreased Accumulation in Inoculated Rice Plants," *Transgenic Research*, Vol. 17, 2008, pp. 897-904.

127. Y.J. Kung, T.A. Yu, C.H. Huang, H.C. Wang, S.L. Wang and S.D. Yeh, "Generation of Hermaphrodite Transgenic Papaya Lines with Virus Resistance via Transformation of Somatic Embryos Derived from Adventitious Roots of *in vitro* shoots," *Transgenic Research*, 2009, in press.

128. S.K. Mangrauthia, P. Singh and S. Praveen, "Genomics of Helper Component Proteinase Reveals Effective Strategy for Papaya Ringspot Virus Resistance," *Molecular/Biotechnology*, Vol. 44, 2010, pp. 22-29.

129. I.B. Fofana, A. Sangare, R. Collier, C. Taylor and C. M. Fauquet, "A Geminivirus-Induced Gene Silencing System for Gene Function Validation in Cassava," *Plant Molecular Biology*, Vol. 56, 2004, pp. 613-624.

130. S. Holzberg, P. Brosio, C. Gross and G.P. Pogue, "Barley Stripe Mosaic Virus-Induced Gene Silencing in a Monocot Plant," *Plant Journal*, Vol. 30, 2002, pp. 315.

131. S.R. Scofield, L. Huang, A.S. Brandt and B.S. Gill, "Development of a Virus-Induced Gene Silencing System for Hexaploid Wheat and Its Use in Functional Analysis of the Lr21-Mediated Leaf Rust Resistance Pathway," *Plant Physiology*, Vol. 138, 2005, pp. 2165-2173.

132. C. Cakir and M. Tör, "Factors Influencing Barley Stripe Mosaic Virus-Mediated Gene Silencing in Wheat," *Physiological and Molecular Plant Pathology*, Vol. 74, 2010, pp. 246-253.

133. C. Zhang and S. A. Ghabrial, "Development of Bean Pod Mottle Virus-Based Vectors for Stable Protein Expression and Sequence-Specific Virus-Induced Gene Silencing in Soybean," *Virology*, Vol. 344, 2006, pp. 401-411.

134. C. Zhang, C. Yang, S.A. Whitham and J.H. Hill "Development and Use of an Efficient DNA-Based Viral Gene Silencing Vector for Soybean," *Molecular Plant Microbe Interaction*, Vol. 22, 2009, pp. 123-131.

135. C. Zhang, J. D. Bradshaw, S.A. Whitham and J.H. Hill "The Development of an Efficient Multi-Purpose BPMV Viral Vector Set for Foreign Gene Expression and RNA Silencing," *Plant Physiology*, 2010, in press.

136. X.S. Ding, W.L. Schneider, S.R. Chaluvadi, R.M. Rouf Mian and R.S. Nelson, "Characterization of a Brome Mosaic Virus Strain and Its Use as a Vector for Gene Silencing in Monocotyledonous Hosts," *Molecular Plant Microbe Interaction*, Vol. 19, 2006, pp. 1229-1239.

137. G.D. Constantin, B.N. Krath, S.A. MacFarlane, M. Nicolaisen, I.E. Johansen and O.S. Lund, "Virus- Induced Gene Silencing as a Tool for Functional Genomics in a Legume Species," *Plant Journal*, Vol. 40, 2004, pp. 622-631.

138. M. Naylor, J. Reeves, J.I. Cooper, M.L. Edwards and H. Wang, "Construction and Properties of a Gene Silencing Vector Based on Poplar Mosaic Virus (Genus *Carlavirus*)," *Journal of Virology Methods*, Vol. 124, 2005, pp. 27-36.

139. M.T. Ruiz, O. Voinnet and D.C. Baulcombe, "Initiation and Maintenance of Virus-Induced Gene Silencing," *Plant Cell*, Vol. 10, 1998, pp. 937-946.

140. O. Faivre-Rampant, E. M. Gilroy, K. Hrubikova, I. Hein, S. Millam, G.J. Loake, P. Birch, M. Taylor and C. Lacomme, "Potato Virus X-Induced Gene Silencing in Leaves and Tubers of Potato," *Plant Physiology*, Vol. 134, 2004, pp. 1308-1316.

141. V.V. Gossele, I.I. Fache, F. Meulewaeter, M. Cornelissen and M. Metzlaff, "SVISS-a Novel Transient Gene Silencing System for Gene Function Discovery and Validation in Tobacco," *The Plant Journal*, Vol. 32, 2002, pp. Biotechnology and Plant Disease Control-Role of RNA Interference .68 859- 866.

142. F. Ratcliff, A. M. Martin-Hernandez and D. C. Baulcombe, "Tobacco Rattle Virus as a Vector for Analysis of gene Functions by Silencing," *Plant Journal*, Vol. 25, 2001, pp. 237-245.

143. G. Brigneti, A.M. Martin-Hernandez, H. Jin, J. Chen, D.C. Baulcombe, B. Baker, and J. D. Jones, "Virus-Induced Gene Silencing in *Solanum* Species," *The Plant Journal*, Vol. 39, 2004, pp. 264-272.

144. E. Chung, E. Seong, Y.C. Kim, E.J. Chung, S.K. Oh, S. Lee, J.M. Park, Y. H. Joung and D. Choi, "A Method of High Frequency Virus Induced Gene Silencing in Chili Pepper *Capsicum annuum* L. cv. *Bukang*)," *Molecular\ Cell*, Vol. 17, 2004, pp. 377-380.

145. L.C. Hileman, S. Drea, G. Martino, A. Litt and V.F. Irish, "Virus Induced Gene Silencing is an Effective Tool for Assaying Gene Function in the Basal Eudicot Species *Papaver somniferum* (Opium Poppy)," *The Plant Journal*, Vol. 44, 2005, pp. 334-341.

146. B. Gould and E. M. Kramer, "Virus-Induced Gene Silencing as a Tool for Functional Analyses in the Emerging Model Plant *Aquilegia* (columbine, *Ranunculaceae*)," *BMC Plant Methods*, Vol. 12, 2007, pp. 6.

147. H. Hou and W. Qiu, "A Novel Co-Delivery System Consisting of a Tomato Bushy Stunt Virus and a Defective Interfering RNA for Studying Gene Silencing," *Journal of Virology Methods*, Vol. 111, 2003, pp. 37-42.

148. C. Peele, C.V. Jordan, N. Muangsan, M. Turnage, E. Egelkrout, P. Eagle, L. Hanley-Bowdoin and D. Robertson, "Silencing of a Meristematic Gene Using Geminivirus-Derived Vectors," *Plant Journal*, Vol. 27, 2001, pp. 357-366.

149. X. Tao and X. Zhou, "A Modified Viral Satellite DNA that Suppresses Gene Expression in Plants," *The Plant Journal*, Vol. 38, 2004, pp. 850-860.

150. M.R. Godge, A. Purkayastha, I. Dasgupta and P.P. Kumar, "Virus-Induced Gene Silencing for Functional Analysis of Selected Genes," *Plant Cell Reporter*, Vol. 27, 2008, pp. 209-219.

151. P.E. Urwin, C.J. Lilley and H.J. Atkinson, "Ingestion of Double-Stranded RNA by Pre-Parasitic Juvenile Cyst Nematodes Leads to RNA Interference," *Molecular Plant-Microbe Interactions*, Vol. 15, 2002, pp. 747-752.

152. M. Bakhetia, W. Charlton, H.J. Atkinson and M.J. McPherson, "RNA Interference of Dual Oxidase in the Plant Nematode *Meloidogyne incognita*," *Molecular Plant-Microbe Interaction*, Vol. 18, 2005, pp. 1099-1106.

153. M.N. Rosso, M.P. Dubrana, N. Cimbolini, S. Jaubert and P. Abad, "Application of RNA Interference to Root-Knot Nematode Genes Encoding Esophageal Gland Proteins," *Molecular Plant-Microbe Interactions*, Vol. 18, 2005, pp. 615-620.

154. J. Shingles, C.J. Lilley, H.J. Atkinson and P.E. Urwin,"*Meloidogyne incognita*: Molecular and Biochemical Characterization of a Cathepsin L Cysteine Proteinase and the Effect on Parasitism Following RNAi," *Experimental Parasitology*, Vol. 115, 2007, pp. 114-120.

155. C.J. Lilley, S.A. Goodchild, H.J. Atkinson and P.E. Urwin, "Cloning and Characterization of a *Heterodera glycines* Mino peptidase cDNA," *International Journal of Parasitology*, Vol. 35, 2005, pp. 1577-1585.

156. R.M. Steeves, T.C. Todd, J.S. Essig and H.N. Trick, "Transgenic Soybeans Expressing siRNAs Specific to a Major Sperm Protein Gene Suppress *Heterodera glycines* Reproduction," *Functional Plant Biology*, Vol. 33, 2006, pp. 991-999.

157. Q. Chen, S. Rehman, G. Smant and J.T. Jones, "Functional Analysis of Pathogenicity Proteins of the Potato Cyst Nematode *Globodera rostochiensis* Using RNAi," *Molecular Plant-Microbe Interactions*, Vol. 18, 2005, pp. 621-625.

158. G. Huang, R. Allen, E.L. Davis, T.J. Baum and R.S. Hussey, "Engineering Broad Root-Knot Resistance in Transgenic Plants by RNAi Silencing of a Conserved and Essential Root-Knot Nematode Parasitism Gene," *Proceedings of the National Academy of Sciences of the USA*, Vol. 103, 2006, pp. 4302-14306.

159. E. Fanelli, M. Di Vito, J.T. Jones and C. De Giorgi, "Analysis of Chitin Synthase Function in a Plant Parasitic Nematode, *Meloidogyne artiellia*, Using RNAi," *Gene*, Vol. 349, 2005, pp. 87-95.

160. Y. Hoffman, C. Aflalo, A. Zarka, J. Gutman, T.Y. James, and S. Boussiba, "Isolation and Characterization of a Novel Chytrid Species (phylum Blastocladiomycota), Parasitic on the Green Alga *Haematococcus*," Mycological Research, Vol. 112, 2008, pp. 70-81.

161. D.J. Fairbairn, A.S. Cavalloro, M. Bernard, J. Mahalinga- Iyer, M.W. Graham and J.R. Botella, "Host-Delivered RNAi: An Effective Strategy to Silence Genes in Plant Parasite Nematodes," *Planta*, Vol. 226, 2007, pp. 1525-1533.

162. S. Sindhu, T.R. Maier, M.G. Mitchum, R.S. Hussey, E.L. Davis and T.J. Baum "Effective and Specific in Planta RNAi in Cyst Nematodes: Expression Interference of Four Parasitism Genes Reduces Parasitic Success," *Journal of Experimental Botany*, Vol. 60, 2009, pp. 315-324.

163. Jacque JM, Triques K, and Stevenson M (2002) Modulation of HIV-1 Replication by RNA Interference. Nature (Lond) 418: 435-438.

164. Jansen B and Zangemeister-Wittke U (2002) Antisense Therapy for Cancer–the Time of Truth. Lancet Oncol 3: 672-683.

165. Jarad G, Wang B, Khan S, DeVore J, Miao H, Wu K, Nishimura SL, Wible BA, Konieczkowski M, Sedor JR, and Schelling JR (2002) Fas Activation Induces Renal Tubular Epithelial Cell beta 8 Integrin Expression and Function in the Absence of Apoptosis. J Biol Chem 277: 47826-47833.

166. Kartasheva NN, Contente A, Lenz-Stoppler C, Roth J, and Dobbelstein M (2002) p53 Induces the Expression of its Antagonist p73 Delta N, Establishing an Autoregulatory Feedback Loop. Oncogene 21: 4715-4727.

167. Tabara H, Sarkissian M, Kelly WG, Fleenor J, Grishok A, Timmons L, Fire A, Mello CC: The rde-1 Gene, RNA Interference, and Transposon Silencing in C. Elegans. Cell 1999, 99:123-127. PubMed Abstract I Publisher Full Text Winston WM, Molodowitch C, Hunter CP: Systemic RNAi in C. elegans Requires the Putative Transmembrane Protein SID-1.

168. Elbashir SM, Lendeckel W, Tuschl T: RNA Interference is Mediated by 21- and 22-nucleotide RNAs. *Genes Dev* 2001, 15:188-194.

169. Donze O, Picard D: RNA Interference in Mammalian Cells Using siRNAs Synthesized with T7 RNA Polymerase. *Nucleic Acids Res* 2002, 30: e46-52.

170. Paddison PJ, Caudy AA, Hannon GJ: Stable Suppression of Gene Expression by RNAi in Mammalian Cells. *Proc Natl Acad Sci USA* 2002, 99: 1443-1448.

171. Bogenhagen DF, Sakonju S, Brown DD: A Control Region in the Center of the 5S RNA Gene Directs Specific Initiation of Transcription: II. The 3′ Border of the Region. *Cell* 1980, 19: 27-31

172. Elbashir SM, Martinez J, Patkaniowska A, Lendeckel W, Tuschl T: Functional Anatomy of siRNAs for Mediating Efficient RNAi in Drosophila Melanogaster Embryo Lysate. *EMBO J* 2001, 20: 6877-6882.

173. Yang S, Tutton S, Pierce E, Yoon K: Specific Double-stranded RNA Interference in Undifferentiated Mouse Embryonic Stem Cells. *Mol Cell Biol* 2001, 21: 7807-7812.

174. Brummelkamp TR, Bernards R, Agami R: A System for Stable Expression of Short Interfering RNAs in Mammalian Cells. *Science* 2002, 296: 550-554.

175. Shen C, Buck AK, Liu X, Winkler M, Reske SN: Gene Silencing by Adenovirus-delivered siRNA. *FEBS Lett* 2003, 539: 111-115.

176. Stewart SA, Dykxhoorn DM, Palliser D, Mizuno H, Yu EY, An DS, Sabatini DM, Chen IS, Hahn WC, Sharp PA, Weinberg RA, Novina CD: Lentivirus-delivered Stable Gene Silencing by RNAi in Primary Cells. *RNA* 2003, 9: 493-498.

177. Brummelkamp TR, Bernards R, Agami R: Stable Suppression of Tumorigenicity by Virus-mediated RNA Interference. *Cancer Cell* 2002, 2: 243-247.

178. Devroe E, Silver PA: Retrovirus-delivered siRNA. *BMC Biotechnol* 2002, 2: 15-21.

179. Barton GM, Medzhitov R: Retroviral Delivery of Small Interfering RNA into Primary Cells. *Proc Natl Acad Sci USA* 2002, 99: 14943-14948.

180. McManus MT, Petersen CP, Haines BB, Chen J, Sharp PA: Gene Silencing Using Micro-RNA Designed Hairpins. *RNA* 2002, 8: 842-849.

181. Elbashir SM, Martinez J, Patkaniowska A, Lendeckel W, Tuschl T: Functional Anatomy of siRNAs for Mediating Efficient RNAi in Drosophila Melanogaster Embryo Lysate. *EMBO J* 2001, 20: 6877-6882.

182. Benov LC, Antonov PA, Ribarov SR: Oxidative Damage of the Membrane Lipids After Electroporation. *Gen Physiol Biophys* 1994, 13: 85-91. PubMed Abstract.

183. Whither RNAi ? *Nat Cell Biol* 2003, 5: 489-492.

184. Mocellin S, Rossi CR, Pilati PL, Nitti D, Marincola F: Quantitative Real-time PCR: A Powerful Ally in Cancer Research. *Trends Mol Med* 2003, 9: 189-195.

185. Mocellin S, Wang E, Panelli M, Pilati PL, Marincola F: DNA Array-based Gene Profiling in Tumor Immunology. *Clin Cancer Res* 2004, 15: 4597-4605.

186. Mocellin S, Provenzano M, Rossi CR, Pilati PL, Nitti D, Lise M: DNA Array-based Gene Profiling: from Surgical Specimen to the Molecular Portrait of Cancer. *Ann Surg* 2004, in Press.

187. Hammond, S.M., Caudy, A.A. & Hannon, G.J. Post-transcriptional Gene Silencing by Double-stranded RNA. *Nature Rev. Genet.* 2, 110-119 (2001).

188. Seemanpillai M, Dry I, Randles J, Rezaian A: Transcriptional Silencing of Geminiviral Promoter-driven Transgenes Following Homologous Virus Infection. *Mol Plant Microbe Interact* 2003, 16: 429-438.

189. Pooggin M, Shivaprasad PV, Veluthambi K, Hohn T: RNAi Targeting of DNA Virus in Plants. *Nat Biotechnol* 2003, 21: 131-132.

190. Aragao FJ, Faria JC: First Transgenic Geminivirus-resistant Plant in the Field. *Nat Biotechnol* 2009, 27: 1086-1088.

191. Buchmann RC, Asad S, Wolf JN, Mohannath G, Bisaro DM: Geminivirus AL2 and L2 Proteins Suppress Transcriptional Gene Silencing and Cause Genome-wide Reductions in Cytosine Methylation. *J Virol* 2009, 83: 5005-5013.

192. Rodriguez-Negrete EA, Carrillo-Tripp J, Rivera-Bustamante RF: RNA Silencing Against Geminivirus: Complementary Action of Posttran scriptional Gene Silencing and Transcriptional Gene Silencing in Host Recovery. *J Virol* 2009, 83: 1332-1340.

193. Zhang Z, Chen H, Huang X, Xia R, Zhao Q, Lai J, Teng K, Li Y, Liang L, Du Q, Zhou X, Guo H, Xie Q: BSCTV C2 Attenuates the Degradation of SAMDC1 to Suppress DNA Methylation-mediated Gene Silencing in Arabidopsis. *Plant Cell* 2011, 23: 273-288.

194. Itaya A, Folimonov A, Matsuda Y, Nelson RS, Ding B: Potato Spindle Tuber Viroid as Inducer of RNA Silencing in Infected Tomato. *Mol Plant Microbe Interact* 2001, 14: 1332-1334. *Nucleic Acids Res* 2001, 29: 2395-2400.

195. Denti MA, Boutla A, Tsagris M, Tabler M: Short interfering RNAs Specific for Potato Spindle Tuber Viroid are Found in the Cytoplasm but not in the Nucleus. *Plant J* 2004, 37: 762-769.

Pages: 174-195

BIODIVERSITY, BIOTECHNOLOGY AND ENVIRONMENTAL CONSERVATION

Edited by: Dr. Pawan Kumar 'Bharti'; Mr. Govinda Bhandari

ISBN: 978-93-5056-750-0

Edition: 2015

Published by: Discovery Publishing House Pvt. Ltd., New Delhi (India)

CHAPTER 8

Trichoderma
A Gift of God to Mankind for Managing Plant Diseases and Promoting Sustainability

Sanjeev Kumar and **Archana Rani***

ABSTRACT

Trichoderma is a genus of asexually reproducing fungi that is present in all types of soils. *Trichoderma* species have been recognized as antagonists of soil-borne and foliage pathogens and as efficient decomposers of cellulosic waste materials. Root colonization by *Trichoderma* spp. also frequently enhances root growth and development, crop productivity, resistance to abiotic stresses and the uptake and use of nutrients. *Trichoderma* can be applied directly to target area i.e. to seeds or seedlings and a single application using an existing delivery system (seed treatment, biopriming, furrow treatment) can significantly reduce crop losses. A number of successful products based on different species of Trichoderma have been commercialized in India and elsewhere. Whatever the limitations these Trichoderma products may have, it can be addressed by

Department of Plant Pathology, Jawahar Lal Nehru Krishi Vishwavidyalaya, Jabalpur - 482 004 (MP), (India).

* Department of Agricultural Biotechnology and Molecular Biology, RAU, Pusa, Samastipur, (Bihar), (India).

enhancing biocontrol through manipulation of the environment, accurate strain identification by molecular approach, using mixtures of beneficial organisms, physiological and genetic enhancement of biocontrol mechanisms, and manipulation of formulations. In some instances, other alternative methods that alone do not provide adequate protection may be integrated with application of biocontrol agents to provide additive or synergistic effects. This book chapter tries to present the approaches adopted by researcher all over the world.

Key words: Biological control, Disease management, Commercialization, Mode of action.

INTRODUCTION

Plant diseases have been concerned with mankind since agriculture began and played a crucial role in the destruction of natural resources and contributing 13 to 20 per cent losses in crop production worldwide (Kumar., 2014). In particular, soil-borne pathogens cause important losses, fungi being the most aggressive. The distribution of several phytopathogenic fungi, such as *Pythium*, *Phytophthora*, *Botrytis*, *Rhizoctonia* and *Fusarium* have widely spread during the last few years due to change the introduced in farming with detrimental effects on crops of economic importance. In addition, not only growing crops but also stored fruits prey to fungal infection (Chet *et al.*, 1997).

Chemical control of plant diseases can be impressive but this is comparatively a short term measure and additionally, the accumulation of harmful chemical residues sometimes causes serious ecological problems. In recent years, the increasing use of potentially hazardous chemicals in agriculture has been resulted in growing concern of both environment and public health properties. Moreover use of such chemicals entails a substantial cost to the nation and developing country like India can not afford it. By contrast, the use of microorganisms that antagonize plant pathogens (Biological control) is risk free when it results enhancement of resident antagonist. Antagonist of phytopathogenic fungi has been used to control plant diseases, and 90 % of such applications have been carried out with different strains of the fungus Trichoderma. The most common BCAs of the Trichoderma genus are strains of *T. viride*, *T. virens* and above all *T. harzianum*, which is a species of aggregate that includes different strains used as BCAs of phytopathogenic and viral vector fungi. (Grondona *et.al* 1997).

What is *Trichoderma* ?

Trichoderma is a genus of asexually reproducing fungi that are often the most frequently isolated soil fungi; nearly all temperate and tropical soils contain 101–103 culturable propagules per gram. These fungi also colonize woody and herbaceous plant materials, in which the sexual TELEOMORPH (genus *Hypocrea*) has most often been found. However, many strains, including most biocontrol strains, have no known sexual stage. In nature, the asexual forms of the fungi persist as clonal, often HETEROKARYOTIC, individuals and populations that probably evolve independently in the asexual stage .They show a high level of genetic diversity, and can be used to produce a wide range of products of commercial and ecological interest. They are prolific producers of extracellular proteins, and are best known for their ability to produce enzymes that degrade cellulose and chitin — although they also produce other useful enzymes (Harman & Kubicek., 1998).

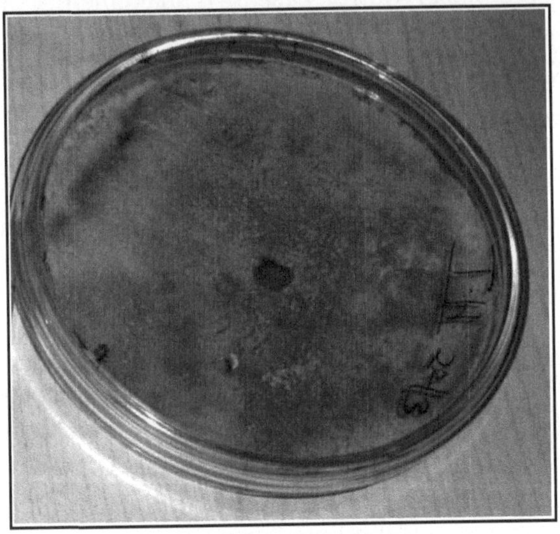

Trichoderma harzianum

For instance, different strains produce more than 100 different metabolites that have known antibiotic activities (Sivasithamparam & Ghisalberti.,1998). *Trichoderma* species have long been recognized as agents for the control of plant disease and for their ability to increase plant growth and development, high reproductive capacity, ability to survive under very unfavorable conditions, efficiency in the utilization of nutrients, capacity to modify the rhizosphere, strong aggressiveness against phytopathogenic fungi and efficacy in promoting plant growth and defense mechanisms. They are becoming widely used in agriculture, and the most useful strains show a property that is known as 'rhizosphere competence'— that is, the ability to colonize and grow in association with plant roots. These properties have made Trichoderma a ubiquitous genus present in any habitat and at high population densities (*Chet et.al* 1997). Trichoderma is more efficient in acidic than alkaline soils. Trichoderma BCAs control ascomycetous, deuteromycetous and basidiomycetous fungi, which are mainly soil borne but also air borne pathogens (Monte., 2001).

Discovery of *Trichoderma*

The genus *Trichoderma* was first proposed as a genus over two hundred years ago by Persoon (1794) in Germany. He showed microscopically similar fungi described as appearing like mealy powder enclosed by a hairy covering. The four species were proposed by Persoon i.e. *T. viride, T. nigroscens, T. aureum* and *T. roseum*. However, the *Trichoderma* is presently considered as *Trichoderma* Pers. Ex. Fr. In India, it was first time isolated by Thakur and Norris during the year 1928 from Madras. The potential value of the genus *Trichoderma* as bioagents was first reported by Weindling in 1932.

Taxonomical Position of *Trichoderma*

Position	Asexual Stage (Conidia)	Sexual Stage (Ascospore)
Kingdomi	Fungi	Fungi
Phylum	Ascomycota Ascomycota Ascomycota	Ascomycotina
Sub-divison	Deuteromycotina	Ascomycotina
Class	Hyphomycetes	Pyrenomycetes
Order	Monilliales	Sphariales
Family	Moniliaceae	Hypocrease
Genus	Trichoderma	Hypocrea

Biodiversity and Phylogeny of *Trichoderma*

The first description of a fungus named *Trichoderma* dates back to 1794 (Persoon., 1794), and in 1865, a link to the sexual state of a *Hypocrea* species was suggested (Tulasne and Tulasne., 1865). However, the different species assigned to the genus *Trichoderma/Hypocrea* were difficult to distinguish morphologically. It was even proposed to reduce taxonomy to only a single species, *Trichoderma viride*. Hence, it took until 1969 that development of a concept for identification was initiated (Rifai., 1969; Samuels., 2006). Thereafter, numerous new species of *Trichoderma/Hypocrea* were discovered, and by 2012, the genus already comprised more than 100 phylogenetically defined species. In some cases, especially in earlier reports, misidentifications of certain species occurred, for example with the name *Trichoderma harzianum* which has been used for many different species (Kullnig *et al.*, 2001). In recent years, safe identification of new species was significantly facilitated by development of an oligonucleotide barcode (TrichOKEY) and a customized similarity search tool (TrichoBLAST), (Druzhinina et al. 2005; Kopchinskiy *et al.* 2005). A further useful tool for characterization of newly isolated *Trichoderma* species (but also recombinant strains) are phenotype microarrays, which allow for investigation of carbon utilization patters for 96 carbon sources (Bochner *et al.*, 2001; Druzhinina *et al.*, 2006). Several species could be characterized with well-defined isoenzyme patterns during cellulose-acetate electrophoresis, suggesting that this method can be used for the analysis of biochemical diversity. between and within particular species of the genus Trichoderma (Kredics *et al.*, 2012).The continued efforts to elucidate diversity and geographical occurrence of *Trichoderma/Hypocrea* resulted in detailed documentations of the genus in Europe and worldwide (Samuels *et al.*. 2002a; Chaverri and Samuels., 2003; Jaklitsch., 2009). At present, the International Sub commission on *Trichoderma/Hypocrea* lists 104 species, which have been characterized at the molecular level. Species of the genus produce a broad array of pigments from bright greenish-yellow to reddish in color, although some are also colorless. Similarly, conidial pigmentation varies from colorless to various green shades and sometimes also gray or brown.

Characteristics of *Trichoderma* spp.

Trichoderma spp. are ubiquitous colonizers of cellulosic materials and can thus often be found wherever decaying plant material is available (Kubicek *et a,l.* 2008; Jaklitsch., 2009) as well as in the rhizosphere of plants, where they can induce systemic resistance against pathogens (Harman., 2000). Despite the early suggested link between *Trichoderma* and *Hypocrea* (Tulasne and Tulasne., 1865), this anamorph–teleomorph relationship was only confirmed more than 100 years later for *Trichoderma reesei* and *Hypocrea jecorina* (Kuhls *et al.*, 1996). Nevertheless, *T. reesei* was then termed a clonal, asexual derivative of *H. jecorina* because all attempts to cross the available strains of this species had failed. It took more than a decade until a sexual cycle was reported in any *Trichoderma* species (Seidl *et al.*, 2009), and a detailed study on molecular evolution of this species led to the discovery of a described sympatric agamospecies *Trichoderma parareesei* (Druzhinina *et al.*, 2010).

Especially because of the industrial importance of *T. reesei*, the availability of a sexual cycle was a landmark discovery and now paves the way for elucidation of sexual development also in other members of the genus. *Trichoderma* spp. are highly successful colonizers of their habitats, which is reflected both by their efficient utilization of the substrate at hand as well as their secretion capacity for antibiotic, metabolites and enzymes. They are able to deal with such different environments as the rich and diversified habitat of a tropical rain forest as well as with the dark and sterile setting of a biotechnological fermentor or shake flask. Under all these conditions, they respond to their environment by regulation of growth, conidiation, enzyme production, and hence adjust their lifestyle to current conditions, which can be exploited for the benefit of mankind. One of these environmental factors is the presence or absence of light. *Trichoderma* has a long tradition of research toward the effect of light on its physiology and development, which already started in 1957 and largely paralleled that of *Phycomyces blakesleeanus* (Schmoll *et al.*, 2010). Besides effects on growth, reproduction, and secondary metabolite biosynthesis, which are common light responses in fungi, also a surprising influence of light on cellulase gene expression has been found (Schmoll *et al.*, 2005). This link between light response and metabolic processes was further substantiated by a study on carbon source utilization using phenotype microarrays in light and darkness (Friedl *et al.*, 2008). Studies on the molecular basis of these light effects revealed that interconnections between the signaling pathways of light response, heterotrimeric G-proteins, the cAMP-pathway, sulfur metabolism, and oxidative stress are operative in *Trichoderma* (Schmoll *et al.*, 2010).

In recent years, research with *Trichoderma* has been facilitated significantly by sequencing of the genomes of three strains representing the most important applications of this genus: The genome sequence of *T. reesei*, the industrial workhorse (Martinez et al. 2008;), surprisingly revealed that, despite its importance in industrial cellulase production, its genome comprises the fewest amount of genes encoding cellulolytic and hemicellulolytic enzymes. Analysis and annotation of the genomes of *Trichoderma atroviride* and *Trichoderma virens*, two important biocontrol species is still in progress. Interestingly, the genomes of *T. atroviride* and *T. virens* are significantly larger than that of *T. reesei*, and they comprise roughly 2000 genes more than does *T. reesei*. It will be interesting to learn the significance of this considerable difference in genome sizes in the physiology of these fungi. These milestones in research with *Trichoderma* enabled detailed studies, which provided intriguing insights into their lifestyle, physiology, and the underlying mechanisms at the molecular level (Brunner *et al.*, 2008; Schmoll., 2008; Seidl *et al.*, 2009).

Trichoderma species- Opportunistic, Avirulent, Plant Symbionts

Trichoderma spp. have evolved as opportunistic plant symbionts, as they can proliferate, compete and survive in soil and other complex ecosystems. They are also capable of colonizing roots and, in fact, increase in numbers when there are abundant healthy roots in the ecosystem. As they colonize plant roots they invade the superficial layers of the root, but do not penetrate further, at least in part because they elicit plant defence reactions. Therefore, although *Trichoderma* spp. probably have an intrinsic ability to attack plants, they are usually avirulent. The plant defence reactions can become systemic and protect the entire plant from a range of pathogens and diseases, even when *Trichoderma* spp. grow only on the roots. This root colonization also increases the growth of roots and of the entire plant, thereby increasing plant productivity and the yields of reproductive organs. They also help plants to overcome abiotic stresses, and improve nutrient uptake. These findings indicate that *Trichoderma* spp. have developed a symbiotic rather than a parasitic relationship with plants.

Secret of Success of *Trichoderma* as BCAs

The success of *Trichoderma* strains as BCAs is due to their:

- High reproductive capacity.
- Ability to survive under very unfavorable conditions.
- Efficiency in the utilization of nutrient.
- Capacity to modify the rhizosphere
- Strong aggressiveness against phyto pathogenic fungi
- And efficiency in promoting plant growth and defense mechanisms.

Benefits of *Trichoderma*

Disease Control: *Trichoderma* is a potent biocontrol agent and used extensively for soil born diseases. It has been used successfully against pathogenic fungi belonging to various genera, viz. *Fusarium, Phytopthara, Scelerotia etc.*

Plant Growth Promoter: Trichoderma strains solubilize phosphates and micronutrients. The application of Trichoderma strains with plants increases the number of deep roots, thereby increasing the plant's ability to resist drought.

Biochemical Elicitors of Disease: *Trichoderma* strains are known to induce resistance in plants. Three classes of compounds that are produced by *Trichoderma* and induce resistance in plants are now known. These compounds induce ethylene production, hypersensitive responses and other defense related reactions in plant cultivars.

Transgenic Plants: Introduction of endochitinase gene from *Trichoderma* into plants such as tobacco and potato plants has increased their resistance to fungal growth. Selected transgenic lines are highly tolerant to foliar pathogens such as *Alternaria alternata, A. solani,* and *Botrytis cirerea* as well as to the soil-borne pathogen, *Rhizectonia* spp.

Bioremediation: Trichoderma strains play an important role in the bioremediation of soil that are contaminated with pesticides and herbicides. They have the ability to degrade a wide range of insecticides: organochlorines, organophosphates and carbonates.

Foods and textiles: *Trichoderma* spp. are highly efficient producers of many extracellular enzymes. They are used commercially for production of cellulases and other enzymes that degrade complex polysaccharides. They are frequently used in the food and textile industries for these purposes. For example, cellulases from these fungi are used in "biostoning" of denim fabrics to give rise to the soft, whitened fabric—stone-washed denim. The enzymes are also used in poultry feed to increase the digestibility of hemicelluloses from barley or other crops.

Plant growth promotion: For many years, the ability of these fungi to increase the rate of plant growth and development, including, especially, their ability to cause the production of more robust roots has been known. The mechanisms for these abilities are only just now becoming known.Some of these abilities are likely to be quite profound. Recently, we have found that one strain increases the numbers of even deep roots (at as much as a meter below the soil surface). These deep roots cause crops, such as corn, and ornamental plants, such as turfgrass, to become more resistant to drought. Perhaps even more importantly, our recent research indicates that corn whose roots are colonized by *Trichoderma* strain T-22 require about 40% less nitrogen fertilizer than corn whose roots lack the fungus. Since nitrogen fertilizer use is likely to be curtailed by federal mandate to minimize damage to estuaries and other oceanic environment, the use of this organism may provide a method for farmers to retain high agricultural productivity while still meeting new regulations likely to be imposed.

Modes of Action of *Trichoderma*

The following are the modes of biocontrol action of *Trichoderma*:

Mycoparasitism

Trichoderma spp. parasitize a range of other fungi. The events leading to mycoparasitism are complex, and take place as follows: first, *Trichoderma* strains detect other fungi and grow tropically towards them (Chet *et.al.*, 1981). Once the fungi come into contact, *Trichoderma* spp. attach to the host and can coil around it and form APPRESSORIA on the host surface. Attachment is mediated by the binding of carbohydrates in the *Trichoderma* cell wall to lectins on the target fungus. Once in contact, the *Trichoderma* produce several fungitoxic cell-wall-degrading enzymes , and probably also peptaibol antibiotics (Benhamou and Chet., 1997)). The combined activities of these compounds result in parasitism of the target fungus and dissolution of the cell walls. At the sites of the appressoria, holes can be produced in the target fungus, and direct entry of *Trichoderma* hyphae into the lumen of the target fungus occurs. There are at least 20–30 known genes, proteins and other metabolites that are directly involved in this interaction, which is typical of the complex systems that are used by these fungi in their interactions with other organisms.

Antibiosis

Antibiosis occurs during interactions involving low molecular weight diffusible compounds or antibiotics produced by *Trichoderma* strains that inhibit the growth of other microorganisms. *Trichoderma* known for its mycoparasitic activity against several fungal plant pathogens is aided by the production of different chitinases, ß-1, 3-glucanases and proteases and cellulase. These extra cellular enzymes such as ß-1, 3-glucanase, chitinase and cellulase are effective in disrupting the mycelium of plant pathogenic fungi (Samuels *et al.*, 2002). Production of volatile compounds was not detected on the four isolates of *T. harzianum* that were tested *in vitro* against *R. solani* (Cumagun *et al.*, 1997b). Coconut smell is typical of *T viride* isolates (Rifai., 1969), suggesting the presence of volatile compounds that are inhibitory to pathogen growth (Dennis and Webster., 1971). The isolation and over expression of tri5 (trichodiene synthase) gene in *T. brevicompactum* Tb41tri5 transformant increased the trichodermin production and fungal activity against *Aspergillus fumigates* and Fusarium spp. (Tijerino *et al.*, 2011).The greater efficacy of antibiotic engineered biocontrol strains raises the scope of designating effective biocontrol strains against various crop diseases.

Competitive Saprophytic Ability

Competition for substrates is the most important factor for fungi as is competition for light in the case of evolution of plants (Garrett., 1956). Competition is the phenomenon in which the pathogen and the introduced *Trichoderma* compete for the availability of space and nutrients. *Trichoderma* is capable of degrading straw with mycoparasitic ability against several plant pathogenic fungi. Cumagun *et al.*, (2009) found that the higher the amount of inoculum of *T. harzianum* strain no 94-016, the higher percent colonization of rice straw in the soil. Further tests were carried out to compare the decomposition of rice straw on the surface and buried in the soil and the effect of moisture on soil decomposition. The depth of rice straw and moisture content are factors identified as significant in affecting crop residue decomposition. Buried rice straw inoculated with *T. harzianum* strain no 94-016 with watering on a daily basis provided better decomposition (Cumagun *et al.*, (2009). Knowledge gained from this study could help better understand and design field application of the beneficial microorganisms for disease management.

Induced Resistance

Induced systemic resistance is believed to be one of the most important mechanisms of biocontrol effects of *Trichoderma* (Harman *et al.*, 2006). A variety of strains of *T. virens*, *T. asperellum*, *T. atroviride* and *T. harzianum* induce metabolic changes in plants that increase resistance to a wide range of plant-pathogenic microorganisms and viruses. (Table 8.1). Moreover, this response seems to be broadly effective for many plants; for example,*T harzianum* strain T-22 induces resistance in plants as diverse as tomatoes and maize, which indicates that there is little or no plant specificity. When spores or other propagative structures are added to soil and come into contact with plant roots, they germinate and grow on root surfaces, and at least some infect the outer few root cells. They produce at least three classes of substance that elicit plant defence responses that prevent further infection of roots by plant pathogens.

Table 8.1: Evidence for, and Effectiveness of, Induced Resistance in Plants by *Trichoderma* species

Species and Strain	Plant	Pathogens	Evidence or Effects	Time after Application	Efficacy	References
T. harzianum T-1 & T22; T *virens* T31	Cucumber	*Green mottle mosaic virus*	Protection of leaves when Trichoderma strains were present only on roots	7 days	Disease induced reduction in growth eliminated	Lo *et, al* 2000
T. harzianum T-22	Tomato	*Alternaria solani*	Protection of leaves when T-22 was present only on roots	3 months	Up to 80% reduction in early blight from natural field infection	Seamon, 2003
Trichoderma GT3-2	Cucumber	*C. orbiculare p. syringae pv. lachrymans*	Protection of leaves when *Trichoderma* strains were present only on roots; induction of lignification and superoxide generation	1 day	59% and 52% protection from disease caused by *C. orbicularepv.* lachrymans present only on roots; or *P. syringae*, respectively	Koike 2001
T. harzianum	Pepper	*Phytophthora capsici*	Protection of stems when *Trichoderma* strains were present only on roots	9 days	~40% reduction in lesion length	Ahmed *et.al* 2000

These elicitors include peptides, proteins and low-molecular weight compounds. In some cases, the resistance is localized — as seems to be the case with *T. virens* on cotton — but in most plant–*Trichoderma* systems, the resistance is systemic. At least for a short period of time, increased expression of defence-related genes occurs throughout the plant. This process can be transitory, but strongly potentiates the expression of defence-related proteins when plants are challenged by pathogens at sites distant from the location of the *Trichoderma* strain. These results indicate that the initial reactions, which include production of pathogenesis-related proteins, have features in common with SAR. At least for the interaction between *T. asperellum* and cucumber, a longer-term response includes low levels of expression of pathogenesis-related proteins before pathogen infection. This response therefore has elements in common with ISR.

Enhancement of Biocontrol Ability of *Trichoderma*

There are constraints in using *Trichoderma* as biocontrol agents. *Trichoderma* colonizes in the spermosphere effectively but they do not survive well in the rhizosphere (Deacon, 1994). The same author observed that *Trichoderma* spp. are active only in some types of soil and season thus achieving only transitory localized dominance of the rhizosphere. For this reason, another constraint is the quiescent and inactive nature of *Trichoderma* spores in the soil and because of this, *Trichoderma* cannot be added as spores (Vidhyasekaran., 2004). Furthermore, numerous mechanisms were discovered to improve efficacy of Trichoderma for desirable characteristics like better saprophytic ability, survival ability in the environment, rhizosphere competence, wider host range , tolerance to pesticides, tolerance to adverse environmental conditions, vigorous growth and long shelf life, the method used are as follows:

Protoplast Fusion

Trichoderma is known as a producer of glucanses, chitinases, cellulases and various other mycolytic enzymes. Combination of these desirable traits form different strains can give rise to superior strains. The strain improvement of Trichoderma by protoplast fusion is one of the ways. The advantage of protoplast fusion is that the possibility to obtains recombinants is higher, which also allows testing of a large number of recombinanats in a short time. Sundaram (1996) developed fusants of two isolates of *T. harzianum* (Th-1 and Th-3), among them, some showed mycological characteristics intermediate between Th-1 and Th-3. In majority of fusants, dominance of characteristics of Th-1 over Th-3 was observed. When *T. harzianum* (Th-3) was fused with *T. virens*, many fusants were developed and few of them exhibited improved biocontrol potential over parent isolates. Protoplast fusants developed by taking isolates of Trichoderma spp., as parent strains exhibited an enhanced antagonistic potential against *Fusarium oxysporum, Rhizoctonia solani, Venturia inaequalis, and Cochliobolus miyabeanus* (Lalitha kumari,, 2000).

Mutation

Mutation are employed to generate variability in populations, which give an opportunity to select the desirable type. Criteria defined for selecting a particular phenotype from the population, N- methyl-N- nitro nitrosoguanidine (NTG) has been the most widely used chemical for inducing mutations in fungal Trichoderma. By exposing the conidia of Trichoderma spp, to NTG, Ahmad and Baker (1990) generated mutants that were rhizosphere competent and superior to wild type in respect of controlling *Pythium ultimum*. These mutants were insensitive to up to 100 μg/ml of benomyl. Mukhopadhyay (1993) developed seven stable mutants of *T. virens* by exposing the cultures to 125 k rad of gamma radiation. The mutants differed from the wild type strains in phenotype, growth rate, sporulation and antagonistic potential. One of the mutants (M- 7) that produced profuse chlamydospores but no conidia was more aggressive than the wild type in antagonizing *Sclerotium rolfsii* and *Fusarium oxysporum f. sp. ciceri*. Selvakumar (2000) developed carboxin tolerant mutant *Trichoderma viride* by exposing the culture to UV – light and ethyl methane sulfonate , Triazole tolerant biotypes of *T. viride* developed by UV- irradiation showed wide variation in enzyme activity especially β-1,3-glucanase and chitinases.

Genetic Engineering

The biosynthesis of cell wall degrading enzymes like glucanases, chitinase and protease which are involved in mycoparasitism, is controlled mainly at transcriptional level and responsible genes are present as single copy genes. To overproduce these enzymes, their gene copy number has been increased by transformation (Harmon and Bjoorman, 1998). Transformants overproducing these enzymes are more efficient as biocontrol agents (Table 8.2). Biocontrol efficiency of Trichoderma has been improved by transformation with genes prbl (protease), egll (β-1, 4-glucanase) and chit 33 (chitinase). Lo *et al* ., (1998) developed transformant of *T. harzianum* strain 1295-22 by integrating β –glucuronidase (GUS) and hygromycin B (hyg B) phosphor-transferase genes, that exhibited increased biocontrol activity *R. solani* as compared with the wild type.

Commercialization of Trichoderma

Before a biological control agent can be successfully introduced into the market, a series of studies must be carried out. Concomitantly, production and formulation of an inoculums with an acceptable shelf life had to be achieved which is frequently a bottleneck. With the availability of large quantities of inoculums, field and glass house test on relevant crops are to be done to determine the reproducibility of control. In past, commercialization of Trichoderma spp. as a BCA had been hampered by the lack of a cost effective way of producing sufficient amounts of fungal material to be used in field and glass house trials. However, in recent years, many small and large entrepreneurs have entered into commercial production of Trichoderma spp. as BCA resulting in development of several products into world market. Commercialization of biopesticides is a multistep process involving a wide range of activities.

Table 8.2: Genetically Modified Strains with Biocontrol Properties Against Various Plant Pathogens

Source Organism (gene)	Transformed	Crop/Pathogenic Organism	Remarks	Reference
Trichoderma brevicompactum (tri 5-trichodiene synthase gene)	*Trichoderma brevicompactum* Tb41tri5	Aspergillus fumigates Fusarium spp.	Overexpression of tri5 gene Enhanced trichodermin activity	Tijerino *et al.*, 2011
Trichoderma harzianum (ech42 chitinase gene)	*T. virens*	*R. solani in vivo*	Improved lytic activity	Baek *et al.*, 1999
T. atroviride (prb 1 proeinase gene)	*T. atroviride* SJ3-4	Bean/*R. solani, Pythium ultimum. Botrytis cinerea*	Glucose gene insertion enhances the ISR activity in bean plants	Brunner *et al.*, 2005

Discovery

Development of bioagents begins with discovery of a useful naturally occurring microorganism. The search involves extensive screening of natural soil isolates for Trichoderma strains having the desired traits. Isolates are then screened for activity against the pathogen in laboratory assay and green house condition. Once an isolate with desirable traits is obtained. It is evaluated under field condition. Many of the promising soil isolates of Trichoderma in recent years have been obtained in the laboratories of India and abroad.

Mass Production

One of the greatest impediments to biological control by *Trichoderma* has been the paucity of methods for mass culturing and delivering the biocontrol agents. The problem in developing biopesticides, a living system, is during the process of formulation and short shelf life. The most widely used fungal antagonists, Trichoderma spp. have been grown on solid substrate like wheat straw, sorghum grains, wheat bran, coffee husk, wheat bran-saw dust, diatomaceous earth granules impregnated with molasses and so forth for their mass multiplication. Papavizas, *et al.*, (1984) produced biomass of fungal antagonists by liquid fermentation consisting of molasses and brewer's yeast. Montealegre, *et al.*, (1993) proposed liquid fermentation method consisting of molasses, wheat bran and yeast on large scale production of *T. harzianum*. Since *Trichoderma* sporulates relatively poorly in liquid media and sporulates well on various solid substrates, Solid substrate fermentation (SSF) process was preferred over the other due to some inherent advantages under Indian conditions. These include utilization of large number of agro wastes as substrate for the en masse production of Trichoderma, use of a wide variety of matrices, low capital investment, low energy expenditure, less expensive down stream processing, less water usage and lower waste water output, potential higher volumetric productivity, high reproducibility, lesser fermentation space and easier control of contamination. (Singh 2006).Fermented biomass of *Trichoderma* consisted mainly of chlamydospores and conidia with some amount of mycelia fragments. Air dried mats were grounded and mixed with a commercially available carrier. The formulation thus developed contained 10^8 to10^9 propagules/g.

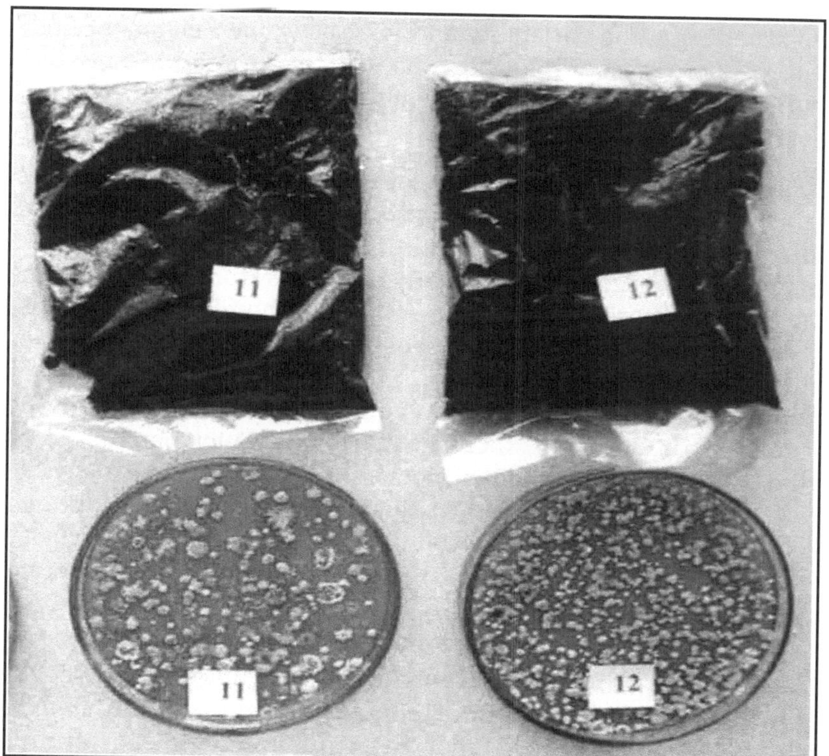

***Trichoderma* Formuation and CFU on 0 Day**

Formulation

Developing a safe, easy to use, cost effective formulation that will keep the micro organism alive is one of the most important steps in developing a biological product. Formulation is the blending of active ingredients such as fungal spores with inert carriers such as diluents and surfactants in order to improve the physical characteristics. A final formulation must have a long shelf life, at room temperature, be east to handle, insensitive to abuse and must be stable over a rage of -5 to 35°C. Failure ot meet these grid standards, however, should not stop the commercialization bioagents. What is needed urgently is the development of drying techniques, which allow retention of maximum number of viable propagules in dried product. At PDPC, Bangalore, three carrier materials namely talc, kaolin anf bentonite were tested for their effect on shelf life of *T. harzianum*. Kaolin, and talc were identified as best carriers of *T. harzianum*. (Prasad and Rangshwaran., 2000). Combination of *Trichoderma harzianum* and plant growth promotory rhizobacteria *Pseudomonas fluorescens had* greater disease suppression and enhanced consistency against the pathogens viz., *Rhizoctonia solani, Sclerotium rolfsii* and *Macrophomina phaseolina* responsible for root and stem rot disease of Soybean. Application of more than one antagonists of diverse origin is suggested as a reliable means of reducing the variability and increasing the reliability of biological control. (Mishra *et a.*, 2011) So consortium of Trichoderma with other biocontrol agents also need to be developed.

Shelf Life

One of the major impediments to commercialization of a biopesticidal preparation is the loss of viability of the biocontrol agents over time. A talc based preparation of *T. virens* conidia retained 82% viability at 5°C in refrigerator after 6 months while at room temperature (25-30°C) same level of viability was observed only upto 3 months. Shelf life was same, when *T. virens* treated chickpea or soybean seeds were stored at room temperature. Viability was better for CMC based formulations (Tewari , 1996). Conidia of Trichoderma in pyrophyllite survived better than fermentor biomass propagules alone at -5°C to 30°C. The most suitable temperature to prolong shelf life of conidia and fermentor biomasss propagules in pyrophyllite were -5 to 5°C. (Mukherjee, 1991).Seed coating with biocntrol agents has emerged as a feasible way of delivering the antagonist, i.e supplying the coated seed to the farmers directly by the seed companies/agencies. Mukherjee (1991) quantitatively assessed the viability of *T. virens* on coated chickpea seeds when the seeds were stored at low temperature (5°C) and at room temperature (15-35°C), 88% of propagules remained viable for up to 4 months.

Chlaymydospres based formulations of Trichoderma sp. exhibited longer shelf life (80% viability for 9 months) than conidia based formulations (80% viability for 4 months) at room temperature. A preparation of *T. virnes* (mainly in the form of chlaymydosproes was from peat moss czapeks broth culture) stored at 25°C for six months without loss of viability.

Green House and Field Testing

Testing of Trichoderma begins in growth chambers or green chambers. Although green house testing provide a useful preliminary screening for selecting Trichoderma for further testing , it is very difficult to mimic true farming conditions. Therefore, well designed field trials are necessary to establish the efficacy of any bioproduct. Once promising results are obtained they are tested under field conditions. It is important that field tests ultimately be conducted at several locations to prove efficacy under varying climatic conditions.

Market Potential

Presently, Trichoderma spp. based products are considered as relatively novel type of BCAs. In comparison to *B. thringiensis* biopesticides, their market size is quite small (Bt shares about 97% of overall pesticides), they fall in remaining 3% bracket, which also comprises viral and nematode based biopesticides. However, a general consensus is that Trichoderma spp. based BCAs share about 60 % of all fungal based BCAs and an increasing number of Trichoderma spp. based BCAs products are registered regularly. Moreever, field application/trials through out the world is being accepted and many biopesticide companies are endorsing these products on regular basis. The innate qualities (e.g., simultaneous biocontrol and growth promotion) of Trichoderma spp. based BCAs are driving factors for their steadily cumulating success.

Constraints in Commercialization of Trichoderma spp. BCAs

Despite all the acquired understanding about antagonistic action and growth promotion of the Trichoderma spp., there are nevertheless some hurdles to their wide spread success:

1. Raw material like, glucose, sucrose, corn steep liquor, wheat bran, soya meal, fish meal, used in culture media for production of the fungi are very costly.
2. Low efficacy
3. Low spore yield
4. Difficultie in quantification of BCA activity.
5. Most of the Trichoderma based BCAs are unregistered and are being marketed simply as osil enhancers , probably due to lack of well defined modes of action of these fungi and their underdeveloped bioassay methods.
6. Furthermore, the registration of Trichoderma spp. based BCAs as fungicides anf growth promoters is time consuming , expensive and frequently without well defined protocols.

Trichoderma Formulations

Important commercial formulations are available in India and Abroad(Table 8.3). These formulations contain 3 × 106 cfu per 1 g of carrier material. Talc is used as carrier for making powder formulation.

Table 8.3: Some Commercial Products of Trichoderma spp. Available in India and Abroad

Species/strain of Trichoderma	Product	Agency/Company
Trichoderma viride	Ecofit	Hoechest and Schering Agro. Evo. Ltd., Mumbai, India
Trichoderma viride	Funginil	Crop Helath Bioproduct Research Centre, Gaziabad (UP) India.
Trichoderma viride	Trichogourd	Anu Biotech international Ltd. Bangalore, India
Trichoderma viride	Defense SF	Wockhardt Life Science Ltd., Mumbai India
Trichoderma viride	Tricho-X	Excel Industries Ltd., Mumbai,India
Trichoderma viride	Biogourd	Krishi Rasayan Export Pvt. Ltd., Solan (HP), India
Trichoderma viride	Biocon	Tocklai Experimental Station Tea Research Association, Jorhat (Assam), India
Trichoderma viride	Bip T	Poland
Trichoderma harzianum	Pant biocontrol agent-1	Deptt. of Plant Pathology, GB pant University of Agriculture &Technology, Panatnagar, Uttarakhand
Trichoderma harzianum T-22	Top shield, Root shield	Bioworks , Geneva (Switzerland) & New York (USA)
Trichoderma harzianum T-22	T-22 and T-22 B	TGT Inc., New York USA
Trichoderma harzianum	F-Stop	Eastern Kodak Company TGT Inc. New York
Trichoderma harzianum	T-35	Makhteshim- Agan Chemical , Israel
Trichoderma harzianum	Harzian 10 and 20	Natural Plant Protection , Noguerres, France
Trichoderma harzianum strain T-39	Trichodex	Makhteshim- Agan Chemical, Israel
Trichoderma viride+ Trichoderma harzianum	Bioderma	Biotech international Ltd., new Delhi, India
Trichoderma viride+ Trichoderma harzianum	Ecoderma	Morgo Biocontrol Pvt. Ltd., Bangalore, India
Trichoderma harzianum + Trichoderma viride	Trichodowel, Trichoject, Trichopel	Agrimm, Technologies Ltd., New Zealand
Trichoderma harzianum+ T. polysporum	Binap- T&W	Bio Innovation AB, Toreboda, Sweden
Trichoderma virens	Gilogard and Soil guard	Greece- Sierre Company, Maryland

Uses

Used in Damping off caused by *Pythium* sp. *Phytophthora* sp., Root rot caused by *Pellicularis filamentosa*, Seedling blight caused by *Pythium*, Collar rot caused by *Pellicularia rolfsii*, Dry rot caused by *Macrophomina phaseoli*, Charcoal rot caused by *Macrophomina phaseoli*, Loose smut caused by Ustilago segetum, Karnal bunt diseases, Black scurf caused by *Rhizoctonia solani*, Foot rots of Pepper and betel vine and Capsule rot of several crops. Effective against silver leaf on plum, peach & nectarine, Dutch elm disease on elm's honey fungus (*Armillaria mellea*) on a range of tree species, Botrytis caused by *Botrytis cinerea*, Effective against rots on a wide range of crops, caused by *fusarium*, *Rhizoctonia*, and *pythium*, and sclerotium forming pathogens such as *Sclerotinia* & *Sclerotium*

Recommended For

Trichoderma is most useful for all types of Plants and Vegetables such as cauliflower, cotton, tobacco, soybean, sugarcane, sugarbeet, eggplant, red gram, Bengal gram, banana, tomato, chillies, potato, citrus, onion, groundnut, peas, sunflower, brinjal, coffee, tea, ginger, turmeric, pepper, betel vine, cardamom etc.

Precautions:

- Don't use chemical fungicide after application of Trichoderma for 4-5 days.
- Don't use *trichoderma* in dry soil. Moisture is a essential factor for its growth and survivability.
- Don't put the treated seeds in direct sun rays.
- Don't keep the treated FYM for longer duration.

Compatibility:

- Trichoderma is compatible with Organic manure Trichoderma is compatible with biofertilizers like *Rhizobium,Azospirillum,BacillusSubtilis* and *Phosphobacteria*.
- *Trichoderma* can be applied to seeds treated with metalaxyl or thiram but not mercurials. It can be mixed with chemical fungicides as tank mix.

Need of Future:

- Highly effective strains of Trichoderma spp. should be obtained or produced which contains several genes encoding for the products inhibitory to the plant pathogens.
- The gene/genes conferring biocontrol like activities in the Trichoderma spp. should be cloned in the crop plants that may become basis for "nature organic" crop protection and production.

- The strains of Trichoderma used for biocontrol purpose should be such that compete, proliferate, colonize and can protect the roots for the life of the crop plants from a wide range of pathogens.
- Inexpensive production and formulations of Trichoderma should be popularized.
- Base materials used for the development of formulations must ensure high viability and long lasting storage capacity.
- Delivery system adopted should ensure good growth of bioagents and high field performance.
- Public sector should also come forward to support the agencies engaged in this field.
- Intellectual property right regarding the production and development of new strains and formulations of Trichoderma always be protected.

REFERENCES

Ahmad, J.S and Baker (1990) Implications of Rhizosphere Competence of Trichoderma Harzianum. Can. J. Microbiology, 34: 229.

Ahmed, A.S., Sanchez, C.P. & Candela, M.E.(2000) Evaluation of Induction of Systemic Resistance in Pepper Plants (Capsicum annuum) to Phytopthora Capsici using Trichoderma Harzianum and its Relation with Capsidiol Accumulation. Eur. J. Plant Pathol. 106, 817-824.

Benhamou, N. and I. Chet, 1997. Cellular and Molecular Mechanisms Involved in the Interaction Between Trichoderma Harzianum and Pythium Ultimum. Applied Environ. Microbiol., 63: 2095-2099.

Bochner BR, Gadzinski P, and Panomitros E.(2001) Phenotype Microarrays for High-throughput Phenotypic Testing and Assay of Gene Function. Genome Res.11: 1246-1255.

Brunner, K. (2003) The Nag1 N-acetylglucosaminidase of Trichoderma Atroviride is Essential for Chitinase Induction by Chitin and of Major Relevance to Biocontrol. Curr. Genet. 43, 289-295 (2003).

Brunner K, Omann M, Pucher ME, Delic M, Lehner SM, Domnanich P, Kratochwill K, Druzhinina I, Denk D, Zeilinger S. *Trichoderma* G (2008) Protein-coupled Receptors: Functional Characterisation of a cAMP Receptor-like Protein from *Trichoderma atroviride*. Curr Genet. 54: 283-299.

Brunner K, Zeilinger S, Ciliento R, Woo S.L, Lorito M, Kubicek C.P. and Mach R.L. (2005) Improvement of the Fungal Biocontrol Agent Trichoderma Atroviride to Enhance Both Antagonism and Induction of Plant Systemic Disease Resistance. Applied and Environmental Microbiology, 71: 3959-3965.

Chaverri P and Samuels GJ. (2003) *Hypocrea/Trichoderma* (Ascomycota, Hypocreales, Hypocreaceae): Species with Green Ascospores. Stud Mycol. 48: 1-116.

Chet, I., Harman, G.E. & Baker, R (1981). Trichoderma Hamatum: Its Hyphal Interactions with Rhizoctonia Solani and Pythium spp. Microb. Ecol. 7, 29-38.

Chet I, Inbar J and Hadar I (1997) Fungal Antagonists and Mycoparasites. In: Wicklow DT, Söderström B (eds) The Mycota IV: Environmental and Microbial Relationships. Springer-Verlag, Berlin, pp. 165-184 13.

Cumagun, C.J.R. and Ilag, L.L. (1997a). Parasitism of Sclerotial Bodies of Rhizoctonia solani Kuehn by Trichoderma harzianum Rifai and Penicillium Oxalicum Currie and Thom. Phil. Phytopathol., 33: 17-26.

Cumagun, C.J.R. and Ilag, L.L. (1997b). Enhancing the Efficacy of Trichoderma Harzianum Rifai by Chitin Amendment Against Sheath Blight of Rice. Phil. Phytopathol., 33: 72-86.

Cumagun, C.J.R., Manalo, J.O., Salcedo-Bacalangco, N.A. and Ilag, L.L. 2009. Cellulose Decomposing Ability of Trichoderma in Relation to Their Saprophytic Survival. Archv. Phytopathol. Plant Prot., 42: 698-704.

Deacon, J.W. 1994. Rhizosphere Constraints Affecting Biocontrol Organisms Applied to Seeds. In: "Seed Treatment, Progress and Prospects". (Eds.): Martin, T. British Crop Protection Council. Farnham, U.K. pp. 315-326.

Dennis, C. and Webster, J. 1971. Antagonistic Properties of Species Groups of Trichoderma II. Production of Volatile Antibiotics. Trans. Brit. Mycol. Soc., 57: 41-48.

Druzhinina IS, Kopchinskiy AG, Komon M, Bissett J, Szakacs G and Kubicek CP. (2005) An Oligonucleotide Barcode for Species Identification in *Trichoderma* and *Hypocrea*. Fungal Genet Biol. 42: 813-828.

Druzhinina IS, Kubicek CP, Komon-Zelawoska M, Mulaw TV, Bissett J (2010). The Trichoderma Harzianum Demon: Complex Speciation History Resulting in Coexistence of Hypothetical Biological Species, Recent Agamospecies snr Recent sgsmospecies and Recent Numerous Relict Lineages. BMC Evol Biol 10: 94.

Druzhinina IS, Kopchinskiy AG, Kubicek CP.(2006) The First 100 *Trichoderma* Species Characterized by Molecular Data. Mycoscience.; 47: 55-64.

Friedl MA, Schmoll M, Kubicek CP, Druzhinina IS. (2008) Photostimulation of *Hypocrea atroviridis* Growth Occurs due to a Cross-talk of Carbon Metabolism, Blue Light Receptors and Response to Oxidative Stress. Microbiology. 154: 1229-124.

Garrett, S.D. 1956. Biology of Root Infecting Fungi. Cambridge University Press, Cambridge, UK. 293 pp.

Grondona I, Hermosa R, Tejada M, Gomis MD, Mateos PF, Bridge PD, Monte E, and García-Acha I (1997). Physiological and Biochemical Characterization of Trichoderma Harzianum, a Biological Control Agent Against Soilborne Fungal Plant Pathogens. Appl Environ Microbiol 63: 3189-3198.

Harman GE. (2000) Myths and Dogmas of Biocontrol. Changes in Perceptions Derived from Research on *Trichoderma harzianum T22*. Plant Dis. 84: 377-393.

Harmon, G.E. and Bjoorman, T (1998) Potential and Existing Uses of Trichoderma and Gliocladium for Plant Disease Control and Plant Growth Enhancement. In: Trichoderma and Gliocladium, Vol. II. G.E. Harman and C.K. Kubicek, (Eds), 229, London: Taylor and Francis Ltd.

Harman, G.E., Custis, D. and Shoresh, M. 2006. Plant Genomic and Environmental Factors that Affect the Abilities of Trichoderma spp. to Induce Plant Resistance and Increased Growth. In: "9th International Workshop on Trichoderma and Gliocladium". (Eds.): Mach, R. L. and Zeilinger, S. Vienna, Austria.

Jaklitsch WM. (2009) European Species of *Hypocrea*. Part I. The Green-spored Species. Stud Mycol. 63: 1-91.

Kopchinskiy A, Komon M, Kubicek CP, Druzhinina IS.(2005) TrichoBLAST: A Multilocus Database for *Trichoderma* and *Hypocrea* Identifications. Mycol Res. 109: 658-660.

Koike, N. (2001) Induction of Systemic Resistance in Cucumber Against Several Diseases by Plant Growth-promoting Fungi: Lignification and Superoxide Generation. Eur. J. Plant Pathol. 107, 523-533.

Kredics.L, Láday. M, Körmöczi. P, Manczinger. L, Rákhely. G, Vágvölgyi. C, Szekeres. A (2012) Genetic and Biochemical Diversity Among Trichoderma Isolates in Soil Samples from Winter Wheat Fields of the Great Hungarian Plain Acta Biologica Szegediensis. 56(2): 141-149

Kubicek CP, Komon-Zelazowska M, Druzhinina IS. (2008) Fungal Genus *Hypocrea/ Trichoderma*: From Barcodes to Biodiversity. J Zhejiang Univ Sci B. 9: 753-763.

Kuhls K, Lieckfeldt E, Samuels GJ, Kovacs W, Meyer W, Petrini O, Gams W, Borner T, Kubicek CP. Molecular Evidence that the Asexual Industrial Fungus *Trichoderma reesei* is a Clonal Derivative of the Ascomycete *Hypocrea jecorina*. Proc Natl Acad Sci U S A. 1996; 93: 7755-7760. [PMC free article] [PubMed]

Kullnig CM, Krupica T, Woo SL, Mach RL, Rey M, Benítez T, Lorito M and Kubicek CP.(2001) Confusion Abounds Over Identities of *Trichoderma* Biocontrol Isolates. Mycol Res. 105: 769-772.

Kumar Sanjeev (2014) Plant Disease Management: Advances and Challenges. Afri.J. Agric. Res. 9 (15): 1207-1217.

Lalithakumari D., (2000) Development of Effective Technology for Strain Improvement of Trichoderma spp. In: Proceeding of Indian Phytopathological Society; Golden Jubilee. International Conference on Integrated Plant Disease Managemnt for Sustainable Agriculture, p. 851.

Lo, C.T., Liao, T.F. & Deng, T.C.(2000) Induction of Systemic Resistance of Cucumber to Cucumber Green Mosaic Virus by the Root-colonizing Trichoderma spp. Phytopathology 90 (Suppl.).

Mishra D.S., Gupta A.K., Prajapati C.R. and Singh U.S. (2011) Combination of Fungal and Bacterial Antagonists for Management of Root and Stem Rot Disease of Soybean Pak. j. bot., 43(5): 2569-2574.

Monte E (2001) Understanding Trichoderma: Between Biotechnology and Microbial Ecology. Int Microbiol 4: 1-4 43.

Montealegre, J., Varnero, M.T. and Sepulveda, C.,(1993), A Method of Biomass Production of Trichdoerma Harzianum Strain V: Growth Evaluation , Fitopathol., 28: 99.

Mukherjee, P.K. 1991. Biological Control of Chickpea Wilt Complex. Ph.D. Thesis, G.B. Pant University of Agric. & Tech. Pantnagar, INDIA, 188 pp.

Papavizas, G.C., Dunn, Mt. Lewis, J.A., and Beagle- Ristaino, J.E., 1984, Liquid Fermentation Technology for Experimental Production of Biocontrol Fungi, Phytopathology, 74: 1171.

Prasad, R.D and Rangshwaran, R., 2000 Shelf Life and Bioefficacy of Trichoderma Harzianum Formulated in Various Carrier Materials. Plant Dis. Res., 15: 38.

Rifai MA. (1969). A Revision of the Genus *Trichoderma*. Mycol Pap. 1969; 116: 1-56.

Samuels GJ. (2006). *Trichoderma*: Systematics, the Sexual State, and Ecology. Phytopathology. 96: 195-206.

Samuels GJ, Dodd SL, Gams W, Castlebury LA and Petrini O. (2002) *Trichoderma* Species Associated with the Green Mold Epidemic of Commercially Grown *Agaricus bisporus*. Mycologia. 94: 146.

Schmoll M. (2008). The Information Highways of a Biotechnological Workhorse—Signal Transduction in *Hypocrea jecorina*. BMC Genomics. 9: 430.

Schmoll M, Franchi L, Kubicek CP. Envoy, a PAS/LOV Domain Protein of *Hypocrea jecorina* (anamorph *Trichoderma reesei*), Modulates Cellulase Gene Transcription in Response to Light. Eukaryot Cell. 2005; 4: 1998-2007. [PMC free article.

Schmoll M, Esquivel-Naranjo UE and Herrera-Estrella A (2010) *Trichoderma* in the Light of Day—Physiology and Development. Fungal Genet Biol (in press).

Seaman, A. (2003). Efficacy of OMRI-approved Products for Tomato Foliar Disease Control. New York State Integrated Pest Management Programme Publication 129, 164-167.

Singh H.B (2006) Trichoderma: A Boon for Biopesticide Industry. J Mycol Pl Pathol. 36(3) 273-383.

Seidl V, Seibel C, Kubicek CP and Schmoll M. (2009) Sexual Development in the Industrial Workhorse *Trichoderma reesei*. Proc Natl Acad Sci U S A. 106: 13909-13914.

Seidl V, Song L, Lindquist E, Gruber S, Koptchinskiy A, Zeilinger S, Schmoll M, Martinez P, Sun J, Grigoriev I, Herrera-Estrella A, Baker SE and Kubicek CP. (2009) Transcriptomic Response of the Mycoparasitic Fungus *Trichoderma atroviride* to the Presence of a Fungal Prey. BMC Genomics. 10: 567.

Selvakumar, R. 2000, Studies on Development of Trichoderma Viride Mutants and Their Effect on Ustilago Segetum Tritici, Indian Phytopath., 53: 185.

Sivasithamparam, K and Ghisalberti, E. L.(1998). in Trichoderma and Gliocladium Vol. 1 (eds Kubicek, C.P. & Harman, G.E.) 139-191.

Sundaram, R.M., (1996) Biocontrol Characterization of Trichoderma Harzianum Rifai, Isolate -1 and its Protoplast Fusion with Trichoderma Harzianum Rifai, Isolate -3, M.Sc.Thesis G.B. Pant University of Agric. And Tech. Pantnagar, p. 91.

Tjamos EC, Papavizas GC and Cook RJ (1992) Biological Control of Plant Diseases. Progress and Challenges for the Future. Plenum Press, New York. Vey A, Hoagland RE.

Tewari, A.K., (1996) Biological Control of Chickpea Wilt Complex Using Differential Formulation of Gliocladium Virens Through Seed Treatment. Ph.D Theiss, G.B. Pant University of Agric. & Tech. Pantnagar, India, 167.

Tijerino, A. Cardoza, R.E, Moraga, J, Malmierca, M.G, Vincente, F, Aleu, J, Collado, I.G, Gutirerez, S, Monte, E and Hermosa, R. (2011) Overexpression of the Trichodermine Synthase Gene tri5 Increases Trichdoermin Production and Antimicrobial Activity in Trichoderma Brevicompactum. Fungal Genetics and Biology, 48: 285-296.

Tulasne LR and Tulasne C.(1865) Selecta Fungorum Carpologia. Paris: Jussu.

Vidhyasekaran, P. 2004. Concise Encyclopedia of Plant Pathology. The Haworth Press. Binghamton, N.Y. p. 619.

Index

• • • • • •